WOMEN IN SOCIETY
A Feminist List edited by
Jo Campling

Editorial Advisory Group

Phillida Bunckle, *Victoria University, Wellington, New Zealand;*
Miriam David, *South Bank University;* Leonore Davidoff,
University of Essex; Janet Finch, *University of Lancaster;*
Jalna Hanmer, *University of Bradford;* Beverley Kingston,
University of New South Wales, Australia; Hilary Land, *University
of Bristol;* Diana Leonard, *University of London Institute of
Education;* Susan Lonsdale, *South Bank University;* Jean O'Barr,
Duke University, North Carolina, USA; Arlene Tigar McLaren,
Simon Fraser University, British Columbia, Canada; Hilary Rose,
University of Bradford; Susan Sellers, *University of St Andrews;*
Pat Thane, *Goldsmiths' College, University of London;* Clare
Ungerson, *University of Southampton.*

The last two decades have seen an explosion of publishing by,
about and for women. This list is designed to make a particular
contribution to this continuing process by commissioning and
publishing books which consolidate and advance feminist research
and debate in key areas in a form suitable for students, academics
and researchers but also accessible to a broader general readership.

As far as possible, the books adopt an international perspective,
incorporating comparative material from a range of countries where
this is illuminating. Above all, they are interdisciplinary, aiming
to put women's studies and feminist discussion firmly on the agenda
in subject-areas as disparate as law, literature, art and social policy.

WOMEN IN SOCIETY
A Feminist List edited by Jo Campling

Published

Christy Adair **Women and Dance: sylphs and sirens**

Sheila Allen and Carol Wolkowitz **Homeworking: myths and realities**

Ros Ballaster, Margaret Beetham, Elizabeth Frazer and Sandra Hebron **Women's Worlds: ideology, femininity and the woman's magazine**

Jenny Beale **Women in Ireland: voices of change**

Jennifer Breen **In Her Own Write: twentieth-century women's fiction**

Valerie Bryson **Feminist Political Theory: an introduction**

Ruth Carter and Gill Kirkup **Women in Engineering: a good place to be?**

Joan Chandler **Women without Husbands: an exploration of the margins of marriage**

Gillian Dalley **Ideologies of Caring: rethinking community and collectivism** (2nd edn)

Emily Driver and Audrey Droisen (*editors*) **Child Sexual Abuse: feminist perspectives**

Elizabeth Ettorre **Women and Substance Use**

Elizabeth Fallaize **French Women's Writing: recent fiction**

Lesley Ferris **Acting Women: images of women in theatre**

Diana Gittins **The Family in Question: changing households and familiar ideologies** (2nd edn)

Tuula Gordon **Feminist Mothers**

Tuula Gordon **Single Women: on the margins?**

Frances Gray **Women and Laughter**

Eileen Green, Diana Woodward and Sandra Hebron **Women's Leisure, What Leisure?**

Frances Heidensohn **Women and Crime** (2nd edn)

Ursula King **Women and Spirituality: voices of protest and promise** (2nd edn)

Jo Little, Linda Peake and Pat Richardson (*editors*) **Women in Cities: gender and the urban environment**

Susan Lonsdale **Women and Disability: the experience of physical disability among women**

Mavis Maclean **Surviving Divorce: women's resources after separation**

Shelley Pennington and Belinda Westover **A Hidden Workforce: homeworkers in England, 1850–1985**

Vicky Randall **Women and Politics: an international perspective** (2nd edn)

Diane Richardson **Women, Motherhood and Childrearing**

Susan Sellers **Language and Sexual Difference: feminist writing in France**

Patricia Spallone **Beyond Conception: the new politics of reproduction**

Taking Liberties Collective **Learning the Hard Way: women's oppression and men's education**

Clare Ungerson (*editor*) **Women and Social Policy: a reader**

Kitty Warnock **Land Before Honour: Palestinian women in the Occupied Territories**

Annie Woodhouse **Fantastic Women: sex, gender and transvestism**

The Family in Question

Changing households and familiar ideologies

Second Edition

Diana Gittins

palgrave
macmillan

Published by
PALGRAVE MACMILLAN
Houndmills, Basingstoke, Hampshire RG21 6XS and
175 Fifth Avenue, New York, N.Y. 10010
Companies and representatives throughout the world

PALGRAVE MACMILLAN is the global academic imprint of the
Palgrave Macmillan division of St Martin's Press LLC and of
Palgrave Macmillan Ltd.
Macmillan® is a registered trademark in the United States,
United Kingdom and other countries. Palgrave is a registered
trademark in the European Union and other countries.

ISBN-13: 978-0-333-54569-0 hardcover
ISBN-10: 0-333-54569-9 hardcover
ISBN-13: 978-0-333-54570-6 paperback
ISBN-10: 0-333-54570-2 paperback

This book is printed on paper suitable for recycling and
made from fully managed and sustained forest sources.
Logging, pulping and manufacturing processes are
expected to conform to the environmental regulations
of the country of origin.

A catalogue record for this book is available
from the British Library.

Printed and bound in Great Britain by
CPI Antony Rowe, Chippenham and Eastbourne

For my sister,
Cynthia Lloyd Bailes

Contents

Acknowledgements

I would first like to thank Frances Arnold, my editor at Macmillan, for the patience, encouragement and support she has given me throughout the preparation of this edition. I would also like to take this opportunity to thank my colleagues on the Open University Women's Studies course team who have offered all kinds of useful support and advice over the past year, especially Felicity Edholm and Linda Janes. I am particularly blessed with good friends who are an invaluable source of inspiration and support to me and I should particularly like to acknowledge my continuing thanks to Joan Busfield, Leonore Davidoff, Frankie Finn, Emily Gittins (both a friend and a daughter) and Sarah Hopkins.

Editor's introduction

In this timely book Diana Gittins aims to provide a radically new perspective on the family using recent feminist and historical research. Using a variety of sources, it questions many widely held theories and concepts of the family and challenges the idea that there is such a thing as *the* family at all.

It is argued that we need to see the family as a controversial political issue which is much misunderstood because of the failure to differentiate adequately between the ideology of the family and the reality of the variety of ways in which men and women, boys and girls, live and interact together. The ideology has to be seen as a historical creation of the urban bourgeoisie which has been a useful and central political tool since the early nineteenth century. Moreover, the gap between the ideology and the reality is arguably a key reason for what is usually perceived as a 'crisis in the family'.

The popular notion that there is a 'modern' egalitarian family type is challenged directly. Historical and contemporary evidence shows that the only real defining characteristic of families is their variability. Feminist research has brought the salience of inequality between the sexes, and between adults and children, to the centre of debates on families through the concept of patriarchy. The prevalence of patriarchal relations, past and present, makes the notion of there being an egalitarian family totally untenable.

This book aims to 'deconstruct' many popular myths surrounding the family by raising a number of questions central to the concept itself. These include: How have families changed? Why do people marry? Why do people have children? Does the State reinforce or destroy family solidarity? Why is a woman's work never done? Is the family in a state of crisis?

The idea of writing the book arose out of an increasing dissatisfaction with the inadequacy of (and prevalence of) outdated texts on the family, almost invariably influenced by functionalist theory, which students still rely on heavily. Few such books integrate recent feminist theory adequately, if at all. It was also felt that there was a real need to try to bring together findings from a variety of fields which, while all relating to families, are seldom brought together in one volume. Thus feminist writers have tended to ignore the findings of historical demographers, and vice versa; sociologists and historians tend to ignore one another's works; family historians neglect the findings of feminist historians, and so on. By drawing together material from a variety of fields and sources, Diana Gittins has provided a radically different, easily readable and up-to-date synthesis and reconsideration of families in Western society in both the past and the present.

JO CAMPLING
Editor

Introduction: questioning the family

Some argue that the family is the foundation of society, indeed of civilisation itself. Others maintain it is the source of most of our problems and unhappiness. These words began the first edition of this book and now, seven years later, they still hold. In that time, however, much has happened that has brought the political issues surounding the family more into public focus and debate than ever before.

At a press conference on 14 March 1986 Graham Webster-Gardiner said:

> The Conservative Family Campaign aims to put father back at the head of the family table. He should be the breadwinner. He should be responsible for his children's actions. He should be respected by those who teach his children. He should be upheld by social workers, doctors and others who may professionally come into contact with the children. ...

A year later, between January 1987 and March 1988, 545 complaints of suspected child sexual abuse were referred to Cleveland Council. Action was taken to protect 265 of them. At least one-third of the perpetrators were the children's biological fathers. The average age of the children was 6.9 years (Campbell, 1988, pp. 1 and 9). Since then controversy has raged about children's rights, parents' rights and the role of the state and state agencies. The issue will not lie down. Since the Cleveland crisis, more and more instances of child sexual abuse have been reported, including alleged ritual, or 'Satanic', abuse.

During the Thatcher years the family was seized upon by the New Right as both the cause of myriad social problems (delinquency, illegitimacy, drug addiction, divorce) and as the solution to those problems. Feminists, on the other hand, have long argued that the family is the major source of women's oppression in a patriarchal society. The pace of changes in families has undoubtedly accelerated in the past few years: the proportion of illegitimate births in England and Wales, for instance, has skyrocketed from 12 per cent of all births in 1980 to 27 per cent in 1989 – though 50 per cent of these children live with both parents. In Sweden, 50 per cent of all births are outside marriage (Wicks, 1990). While most people in England and Wales still marry, they are marrying later. Forty-eight per cent of women marrying in 1987 had cohabited, compared with 7 per cent in 1971. Childlessness has increased. Family size is expected to fall below 1.95 by the end of the century (*Population Trends*, HMSO, 1990).

These changing patterns have been going on in a wider socio-economic context of recession, unemployment, rising rates of home-lessness and poverty, an ever-larger proportion of married women going out to work (60 per cent in 1989 compared with 10 per cent in 1931), the spread of AIDS, and wide-reaching cuts in all public services. The 'rolling back of the State' and the free play of market forces has, in fact, made it extremely difficult to put father back at the head of the table at all. The 'family wage' has been deliberately undermined by Conservative policy. Unemployment means many men cannot provide adequately for their families even if they want to. Because of rising divorce rates, many fathers don't live with their children. More and more families are too poor to eat at a table anyway: the numbers of homeless families living in bed and breakfast has risen dramatically. What sense can be made of the family in all this? Certainly it is a fundamental political issue. But is there anything more to it than that, or is it just a worn-out ideology that few take seriously any more? What *is* the family?

Earlier theories of the family as a stable and universal institution composed of parents and children living together in relative harmony have been well and truly challenged – by radicals such as Laing (1960, 1971) and Cooper (1971) and by feminists in the 1970s and 1980s. But what does this leave? Because so many of the questions relating directly to the family concern the relations between men and women in terms of work, marriage, sexuality and reproduction, feminist research generated a whole new dimension to the analysis of the dynamics of families in society. Yet much of the literature – excellent though most of it may be – has not always tackled the question of what exactly the family is.

The central aim of this book is to examine, analyse, and reconsider the notion of the family in the light of recent research and findings. The first task is to question the assumption that there is, and has been, one single phenomenon we can call *the* family. Historical, anthropological and contemporary findings show otherwise. Second, it is necessary to ask a number of questions which are implicit in the concept of family, yet which are seldom articulated because they are assumed to be self-evident. They are not necessarily so.

The family has generally been treated by sociologists and historians as a unit and, as such, it is assumed that all individuals within it are, by and large, in a similar situation sharing similar resources and life-chances. Feminist research has shown clearly that men and women, boys and girls, do not share similar life-chances. There are inequalities *within* families just as there are inequalities *between* families. Assuming one identical family form denies important differences in terms of class, gender, ethnicity and age.

Thus it is essential to think of *families* rather than 'the family'. This alone, however, is not enough; there are other assumptions inherent in the concept of 'the family' that need to be questioned. How are power relations within families to be explained? Why do men sexually abuse their, and others', children? Why do people marry? Why do they have children? Tackling such questions requires a broad perspective – a perspective that locates them as an integral part of the socioeconomic, political and belief systems of society as a whole. Despite arguments that families have become increasingly privatised, it is essential to see families as an integral part of a wider culture that can only be understood in that context.

In doing this, however, it soon becomes evident that a wide gap exists, and has existed, between discourses about 'the family' and how individuals actually live their lives. In the past decade that gap has arguably grown even wider. Many studies have failed to differentiate between what preachers, politicians and philosophers say a family *should* be and how people in fact live and interact in social groups that are defined as families. Much of Lawrence Stone's work (1977), for instance, is really an analysis of changing family ideology rather than a study of actual patterns of family life. Demographers, on the other hand, have tended to concentrate on household structures and demographic events alone without reference to values, discourses or ideology. Yet *both* aspects need to be understood.

Linked to this is the question of what relationship exists between people's material circumstances, the ways in which they live their lives, and discourses and ideologies of how they *should* live their lives. The extent to which one determines or influences the other is a highly controversial problem which cannot be resolved here (if, indeed, anywhere). What I want to consider, however, is the ways in which a number of sometimes contradictory discourses about 'the family' are exercised in and through the media, religious institutions, the educational system and social policy generally to create an overall 'ideology of the family'.

Discourses within this ideology include prescriptions and proscriptions on gendered behaviour, ethnic relations (e.g. social disapproval of mixed marriages), age, masculinities and femininities. Overall, an amalgam of discourses combine to create a dominant representation of what a family should be like. This representation changes over time, but nonetheless is presented as something universal. For the past few decades this ideal has been of a young, married, heterosexual, white, middle-class couple with two children – a boy (older) and a girl, all of whom live together in their own house. The husband is the main breadwinner and the wife is a full-time housewife/mother who may, however, work part-time. The assumption of this ideal family's normality has influenced, and continues to influence, social policy and the ways in which laws are formulated and implemented for the population overall. Family ideology is not just something 'in the air', but influences and determines material life as well. By considering historical changes in both ideology and legislation, in conjunction with changes in material circumstances, it is the purpose of this book to gain further insights, and bring together existing findings, on the complexities of this relationship.

For example, prior to the eighteenth century it was believed all children should work from an early age, and the vast majority did so. As the new middle classes became increasingly powerful economically, they no longer needed their children's labour, and so argued that children *generally* should not work, even though in most families children's labour remained economically essential. As the middle classes gained political power, so they increasingly brought in legislation which actually forbade children to work. This created severe economic problems for working-class families, which were only partly resolved when working-class men organised unions and pressed for a 'family wage' (that is, a man's wage which is adequate to support himself, his wife and children). For those who did achieve a family wage – and they were a small minority – in turn came to believe that children should not work. Thus the original ideal changed markedly, not in some mysterious way, but to a large extent as a result of broader economic and political changes. At the same time, the ideology was used to bring about economic and political changes. Ideology is strongly enmeshed with social, economic and political forces, yet it is also logically distinct and can, at times, conflict with material forces.

Central to ideologies about 'the family' have been beliefs about gender and age relations – in fact, the two cannot really be separated. Ideals and statements about what a family should be are comprised of statements about the roles and behaviour deemed appropriate for men, women and children within families and society generally. Religious and legal formulations on sexuality, marriage and childrearing are all based on assumptions about, and definitions of, relations between men and women, parents and children. It is possible to see this as a *patriarchal* ideology. Though the concept of patriarchy is a problematic one, it can still be a useful way of understanding how definitions of age and gender relations are formulated both within families and within society generally.

Much of this book is therefore concerned with asking old questions in new ways. The answers are necessarily tentative, the main point being that these are questions upon which much more reflection and research is needed if we are to understand better the politics and dynamics of families. It is a diffuse book for this reason, deliberately not written in chronological sequence along the lines 'once upon a time the family was like this, and since then see how it's changed'. While not denying that there have been important changes, too often these become exaggerated and oversimplified in an attempt to present a clear-cut model of 'the family'. Families are *not* clear-cut, but are highly complex and often confusingly fluid social groupings.

Many writers have failed to acknowledge the salience of family ideology. Hence we are either presented with arguments that in the past families were wholly economic institutions where love was scarce and violence rife, in contrast with modern families formed through love and affection alone without any economic motives, or we are told that in the past families were solidaristic, caring institutions which have been virtually destroyed by the forces of industrialisation, as manifested in high divorce rates today.

In a way, both perspectives have an essence of truth, because families are and were so varied. Some families were solidaristic and caring and some still are. Others were, and are, characterised by tension and violence. Just as it would be ludicrous to argue that a society or an era is characterised by one type of individual, so it is just as ludicrous to argue that there can be one type of family. Families are not only complex, but are also infinitely variable and in a constant state of flux as the individuals who compose them age, die, marry, reproduce and move. A family made up of a widowed woman with two grown daughters is very different from one composed of a couple with five dependent children or one made up of sisters and brothers living and working together. Families vary by age, gender, ethnicity, class and marital status as well as by actual size of unit.

Thus there are a number of vital questions that need to be asked and answered before it is possible to join with those who ask broader questions like, 'is the family in a state of crisis?' At the same time, it is also important to ask at the end why people continue to live much of their lives in some sort of family, and whether there are, in fact, alternatives to the family as it is seen in modern society. Answers to such questions, of course, can only be tentative, and all that is argued here is that the importance of considering them in greater depth is crucial. To start with, then, it is necessary to consider the variety of families over time, seeking to disentangle where possible some of the changes that have occurred historically.

1

How have families changed?

Much effort has been spent in trying to analyse how families in western society have changed over the course of time. In seeking a model for explanation, sociologists divided families into two main types: the nuclear family, consisting of parent(s) and child(ren), and the extended family, consisting of parent(s), child(ren), and grandparent(s) or other kin. Before industrialisation, it has been argued,[1] the majority of families were of the extended type, society was relatively static and stable, geographical and social mobility were minimal. From about 1750 onwards rapid population growth, urbanisation, capitalisation, but above all else industrialisation, resulted in a change to the nuclear family, which was allegedly better suited to the 'needs' of industrial society.

Research by demographers and family historians[2] has proved most of these earlier assumptions to be false. Using parish records, legal records and other documentary sources people such as Laslett (1972), Greven (1970), and Demos (1970) have shown that prior to industrialisation most people lived in relatively small households – the average being about 4.75 persons. Most of these households – but by no means all – corresponded roughly to nuclear families. A substantial proportion of people never married at all and either lived with other kin or with other single people or, in some cases, alone.

Michael Anderson's (1971) research on mid-nineteenth century Lancashire showed how kin helped one another, particularly in times of crisis, by co-residing for periods of time. Thus many households were of an 'extended' type, much as Wilmott and Young (1962) found in Bethnal Green in the 1950s. These findings have suggested a complete reversal of the earlier theories put forth by people such as Parsons (1964) and Murdock (1949). The emphasis of these recent theories has been primarily on the structure and size of households, however, rather than on reasons for change, beliefs, or patterns of interaction between and within households.

Lawrence Stone (1977) proposed a history and theory of the development of the western family paying more attention to values, though rather less to structure. While conceding that families are always variable, he argues that there have nevertheless been three main types of family in Western Europe between 1500 and 1800. The first of these, the 'Open Lineage Family', was common from medieval times until the early sixteenth century, and was characterised by lack of privacy, extensive kin ties, but lack of close relationships between spouses or between parents and children. The second type, the 'Restricted Patriarchal Nuclear Family', prevailed in Europe from about 1530 to 1640, and was distinguished by declining loyalties to lineage, kin and community, increasing loyalties to State and Church, both of which encouraged the husband/father as the unquestionable head of the family to whom all must defer. The final type, the 'Closed Domesticated Nuclear Family', arose around 1640 and coincided with a rise of 'affective individualism' resulting in a strong notion of privacy within the home, close emotional bonds between parents and children, and a strong sense of individualism. Stone thus argues that it is possible to typify a historical period by one type of family; Shorter (1975) and Stearns (1975) make similar arguments.

Other research has shown, however, that it is highly misleading to assume the existence of only one type of family at a given point in time. Jean-Louis Flandrin (1979) demonstrated how a variety of family types existed simultaneously in different regions of France. Contemporary patterns are similarly varied: in the eastern Netherlands in 1950, 25 per cent of all farms were managed by married couples living with their parents or parents-in-law; in Bethnal Green in 1957, 21 per cent of people surveyed had married children living with them.[3] In Great Britain in 1989, on the other hand, 25 per cent of all households consisted of only one person, and 34 per cent of all households consisted of only two people, while only 25 per cent of households consisted of a married couple with one or two dependent children[4]

The more one considers data like these, whether past or present, the more striking the variety of families becomes. Much of the problem lies in the very concept of the family and the apparent determination to conceive of the family always in the singular, thereby implying that there can only ever be *one* type of family at any given point in time. There is no such thing as *the* family – only families. Moreover, it has been shown, notably by Lutz Berkner (1972) and Tamara Hareven (1982) that any one family will go through a series of different 'types' over time.

Families are but groups of individuals; individuals who age, work, die, may have children, marry or move. By definition families are constantly changing. All individuals and thus all families go through life-cycles. Babies become boys and girls, girls and boys become adolescents, who in turn become men and women (assuming they escape death), and so on. Definitions of where one age group stops and the next starts are highly varied; in medieval times childhood stopped at the age of seven (see Ariès, 1973), while in western society today children are defined as dependent until the age of 16 or 17.

Just as notions of 'the family' have been oversimplified, so too concepts of 'pre-industrial' and 'industrial' society tend to be used in a way that assumes each type to be monolithic and universal. It is also generally presumed that a definite division can be made between the two types at a certain point in time. Yet just as many allegedly characteristic features of pre-industrial society continued in some areas after industrialisation, so features supposedly typical of later society can be found in earlier times. Notwithstanding, there are certain fundamental features and differences which can be located.

One important factor dividing modern society from earlier times is that of mortality. Up until the late nineteenth century life expectancy for most people was very low; in England in the late seventeenth century it was 32 years; in Breslau, Germany, just over 27 years (Gillis, 1981, p. 11). This high mortality rate had important repercussions. First, it meant that the possibility of death was a fact permeating life from the moment of birth. Second, it meant that if parents wanted children to survive to adulthood it was necessary to bear a relatively large number, as they could assume that some would die. Indeed, it was not uncommon to give two living children the same name on the assumption that one was bound to die. Third, it meant that marriages – and families – were frequently broken and altered by death. Just as parents became used to losing children and, less often, spouse, so children were far more likely to have lost siblings and at least one parent, often both, before they grew up. The poorer a family the more prone were its members to early death.

Widowhood, like orphanhood, was a common experience for a large sector of the population. Richard Gough's *History of Myddle*, written in 1701, makes frequent references to widowhood and remarriage in a not dissimilar way to how we might talk of friends' divorces and remarriages today: 'James Nightingale . . . married first a daughter of Robert Higginsons of Tylley; second hee married a daughter of one Hussey, of Aston, near Wem, a handsome woman, who hardly escaped the censures that are usually cast upon a fair hostesse. And, thirdly, hee married a daughter of William Menlove, an innkeeper . . . Shee outlived him. Hee dyed of a dropsy, when hee was about forty years of age' (Gough, 1981, p. 99). As at this time most people did not marry until their mid-twenties, James Nightingale's three marriages probably spanned a total period of only twelve or fifteen years. Thus the common-sense notion that all families in the past were much more solidaristic and stable institutions cannot be borne out – death saw to that. Death, however, was an arbitrary breaker of marriages in a way that divorce is not. Then there was no choice, now there is.

As a result of a parent's death many children were likely to experience the other parent's remarriage and living with a stepparent, possibly also stepsiblings and half-siblings. This seems to have been particularly marked in the seventeenth century: 'What evidence there is suggests that a far higher proportion of all marriages were remarriages in the early seventeenth century than at any other time between 1550 and 1850. Perhaps as many as 30% of all those marrying in the later sixteenth century were widows and widowers, a situation that may owe much to mortality crises in this period' (Houston and Smith, 1982). The many tales of wicked stepmothers in fairy tales bear witness to this (the lack of tales of wicked step*fathers* reflects the lack of women writers at this time).

Many children experienced orphanhood; the most common practice in such cases was for a relative (generally a woman) to take care of the child. This experience remained quite common for children of the poorer classes throughout the nineteenth century and, for some, into the twentieth century. Mortality remained high for the poorest, although it declined markedly for the better-off from the nineteenth century. Although orphanhood in western society has almost disappeared, where it was once very common, living with a stepparent, half-siblings and stepsiblings in a 'hybrid family' remains a common experience for many children today as a result of divorce and remarriage.

High mortality had other effects on people's lives and families. It meant that it was relatively rare for children to know their grandparents for long if, indeed, at all. The few who did survive to become grandparents were usually cared for by kin – then, as now, generally by a daughter or daughter-in-law. The large age gap between generations as a result of the pattern of late age at marriage meant that grandparents were unlikely to live longer than a few years in such an extended family: 'even if the proportion of houses in which the senior generation lived with its active sons and daughters was as low as 5.8%, the overall proportion of widows and widowers in society was low too, and included only 6.2% of the population. If the two figures are compared it suggests that by far the largest proportion of the few widows and widowers in society did indeed live with their grown-up descendants' (Spufford, 1974). Given such high mortality, extended families could never have been widespread, but may have been a *stage* that some experienced for a short period of time.

In contemporary society, because people live much longer, a married couple or single child may have to care for a dependent parent for ten or twenty years. The number of elderly in society has multiplied dramatically; in Britain there are now 10 million people drawing old age pensions, and it is estimated that the number of very old will increase by 50 per cent in the next fifteen years.[5] Among all people aged 65 or over in Britain in 1981, less than 10 per cent were living in institutions, and the rest lived in private households. Of the latter, however, 74 per cent of men over 65 had a wife alive to care for them, while only 38 per cent of women of that age had a husband. Of those aged 75 to 84, 24 per cent of the men lived alone, while 56 per cent of the women did.[6] Women and men do not age equally nor do they receive equal treatment when old. This was also largely true in the past, when for those who did reach old age it was easier for men to remarry than it was for women. Berkner (1972, p. 404) found that in eighteenth-century Austria there were eight times as many widows as widowers under the age of

58, though much of the differential was a consequence of different patterns of age at marriage between men and women.

The prevalence of high mortality in pre-industrial societies has been used to argue that people were less loving and affectionate towards one another than they are in contemporary society. In particular, parents were allegedly less affectionate to children because of the strong possibility that they might die. This has been reinforced by evidence from sermons of the time where parents were exhorted by preachers to beat young children and break their wills, so that they could learn to be obedient, deferential and thereby save their souls. Yet this is scant evidence that parents were any less capable of love for children than they are today, only that it may have been expressed differently (Pollock, 1983). Moreover, evidence in contemporary society shows a high degree of violence within families, both towards wives and children. Violence may be even more common in families today than in the past. What has changed is the *ideology* about love and violence.

Parallel with a high mortality rate in pre-industrial society was an equally high fertility rate, which did not begin to decline markedly until the latter half of the nineteenth century. Two hundred years ago about half the population of Western Europe was under the age of 20 – this is now a quarter of the total. Thus until the late nineteenth century society was a very young society, while in the twentieth century it has become an increasingly old society. This fact alone affects family resources dramatically. The elderly frequently require much care, service and time, but are seldom able to contribute much in return. Women in particular are seen by the State, by others, and often by themselves, as morally responsible for the care of aged parents, often at the expense of their own children, marriages and jobs.

Increasing longevity makes this burden longer and harder. Many women will only just have completed caring for their own children over a period of some twenty years to find, not the prospect of a tranquil middle age before them, but the reality of a further ten or twenty years of caring for the demands of an ageing parent. After this they may well have to care for an infirm husband before they in turn need care themselves. This is a very modern type of pattern.

The amount of time spent bearing children is another dramatic change which has affected families, and women's work within them. Men and women in pre-industrial societies married quite late (if at all), at around the age of twenty-five. Once married, women tended to bear children at fairly regular intervals until they died or reached menopause. Forms of birth control were known and used, though the extent of use is hard to surmise (Himes, 1931; Wrigley, 1966; Gittins, 1982). On average the number of children a woman bore was far greater than now – although fewer survived, because of high mortality (and particularly infant mortality) rates. Caring for young dependants was thus a constant feature of family lives – especially women's lives.

In contemporary society, couples tend to have one or two children soon after marriage and then usually cease childbearing. Most women will have stopped having children by their early thirties, if not before, and thus have the prospect of perhaps a further forty years free of childbearing. In 1981, of married couples aged 30 to 44 in Britain, 36 per cent had one child, 36 per cent had two children, 18 per cent had three or more, and 10 per cent had none.[7] Although less time is now spent in bearing children, much more time is spent in *rearing* them than before, in addition to which women are more apt to have a long period of caring for elderly relatives than was the case in the past.

The task of caring for dependants, young or old, is one that has been defined as women's responsibility for a long time. Up until the end of the nineteenth century (earlier or later, depending on class situation), it was common for a daughter or daughters to take on a large proportion of these responsibilities from an early age, thus releasing the mother for wage labour or other domestic work. Since then, compulsory education has meant that the resources a daughter could offer in domestic work have been reduced. The contribution of sons has always been minimal and erratic. Greater longevity as a result of the decline in mortality is thus one great division between our society and the past, but its blessings are obviously mixed.

The majority of wealth until the nineteenth century was in land. In 1750 agriculture employed about 65 per cent of all English people, and 76 per cent of all French people (Tilly and Scott, 1978). Industries were also important, although organised generally on a small scale within households and/or guilds. The manufacture of cloth, mining and fishing have all been important industries for centuries, although to different degrees according to geographical area. Unlike modern society, it was common for one individual to engage in a variety of occupations depending on his or her age, the household situation, the season, and the local environment. One household might well contain members who engaged in various agricultural activities during the year, some who would fish or mine for part of the year, and others who engaged in spinning or weaving part-time during the day.

Apart from the very wealthy (who still had their duties to perform), everyone in medieval and early modern society was expected to work in one way or another. Economic survival for the majority depended on the participation of men, women and children from an early age in a wide range of economic activities. The type of work depended on the type of local economy, age, sex, and the needs and resources of a particular household at a given point in time.

One of the most common and widespread activities for many individuals until the eighteenth century was the manufacture of cloth. For centuries this had been the traditional preserve of women, with the help of children and occasionally men. Spinning in particular had always been women's work, hence the term 'spinster'. As an activity which can be taken up or left as needed, it was ideally suited for combination with other tasks in the farm or involving the care and demands of young children. It was also a task which children could learn from a young age. Because few could afford their own wool (and this was increasingly the case as time passed), spinning and also weaving were usually jobs carried out for others and rewarded by wages.

Cloth manufacture in many areas was capitalised as early as the late medieval period. As it was a part-time job co-existing with other occupations for that individual, the wages paid were very low. To what extent the rationale of the merchant capitalists paying low wages for spinning was influenced because it was women's work, or because it was part-time, cannot be surmised. Whatever the reason, merchant capitalists became increasingly wealthy under this system at the expense of the spinners and weavers.

Wage labour and a nascent capitalist economy were thus in existence centuries before the industrial revolution. The proportion of wage earners in England in 1523 'varied widely from an average of 22% in Leicestershire and 36% in Devon, to ... between 28% and 41% in Lincolnshire ... between a quarter and a third of the entire population in rural areas were wage labourers' (Spufford,

1974). Not all of them were weavers or spinners; some were agricultural labourers or resident servants. In medieval times and up to the seventeenth or eighteenth centuries, wages for the majority were only a part of their total resources; the rest came from subsistence agriculture or mining. Some families were wholly dependent on wages, and this was becoming increasingly the case. The assumption was that, because everyone worked, all households needed more than one wage to survive – which, indeed, they did. There was no such thing as a 'family wage'.

The division of labour in agriculture was varied, but as a rule men tended to engage more in fieldwork while women were responsible for the dairy, poultry, orchard, buying and selling at market, brewing, baking and cooking. Men were more likely to work for wages as agricultural labourers if such work was available. Harvesting was something in which the whole household – indeed virtually the whole community – engaged. Running a farm, whether small or large, necessitated more than one person, and all except the very young had work to do. The size of a farm directly affected the amount of labour needed, as well as the number of people it could support. Balancing the number of individuals in the household that could be supported and who were needed to work was a delicate operation and could make the difference between survival, starvation and relative plenty. The vagaries of death made such a balance doubly precarious.

Reproduction of children was an obvious way of increasing the potential labour, but it meant a period of years during which the labour was not yet available when considerable resources in terms of time and service were needed to care for the young. Often female relatives were brought in to take on such tasks. Another way of balancing the resources and labour required was by hiring other people to live in a household in exchange for the use of their labour, usually supplemented by some money payment. Alternatively, where farms were rented, people would move to a different size farm to suit the changing structures and composition of their families.

In most cases setting up a farm involved marriage; to marry it was first necessary that land was available, which was by no means always the case. Second, a couple (or group of persons) needed some money to buy or rent the farm, which usually came from savings accrued through working as servants in other households.

Among the wealthier sectors men usually inherited some land while women brought dowries to a marriage. It was not unusual for brothers and sisters to run farms together, often never marrying at all. The assumption that it should be women who care for young children, although not entirely universal, has been very strong in most cultures, and was certainly the case in pre-industrial Europe. This by no means meant it was always the *mother* – it was often the case that the mother's labour was more essential to tasks such as brewing. While many mothers did take primary responsibility for their children, it should be remembered that these tasks were frequently taken on by servants, daughters, other female kin, or neighbours.

Thus during the early period of a family cycle many households needed extra help. Some offered other kin board and lodging in return for labour, others hired servants. Often kin were hired as servants; the diary of Ralph Josselin, a seventeenth-century clergyman in Essex, revealed how he hired his sister as a servant (Macfarlane, 1970). Between 1574 and 1821 approximately 60 per cent of the population in England aged 15 to 24 were servants, and 46 per cent of farmers' households contained servants, though few had more than two: 'most youths in early modern England were servants; that so few are now is one of the simplest differences between our world and theirs' (Kussmaul, 1981, p. 3).

Over half of the young people in pre-industrial England would have experienced a period of living in someone else's household as a servant. It was for them an important transition in their life cycle: 'leaving home at an early age (often seven or eight), both boys and girls moved from a state of dependence to one of semidependence that would characterise their existence until the age of marriage' (Gillis, 1981, p. 8). Servants shared the same facilities as those with whom they lived; they were perceived as, and defined as, members of the family, whether or not they were kin. Many families, therefore, were 'extended', not by kin so much as by servants. Other families, where children had left to work as servants elsewhere or had died, were very small.

Entering service was largely dependent on the life-cycle of a child's parent(s), their position in relation to other siblings, and their parents' relative wealth and need for labour. One couple might have borne eight children, but if only two survived they were likely to be kept at home to work the farm. Another couple, less affected by death, might have six children between the ages of 2 and 14; unless their holding was unusually large, there would be pressure for some of the children to go and work elsewhere as servants. A daughter of 14 might be kept at home to help with the dairy and mind the young children, a son of 12 might be kept to help in the fields; children of 8 and 10 might then be sent to work elsewhere. If the same household had only sons, more would probably be sent away and a servant girl hired. Alternatively, if there were only daughters, more would be sent as servants while a servant boy would be employed. Some undoubtedly solved the problem by reconstructing the sexual division of labour and using, for instance, daughters' labour power in the fields. The size of a household, its sex and age composition, were thus apt to be very diverse.

Service was an important means by which people whose families had little property or wealth could accrue enough savings to be able eventually to set themselves up in marriage. It also regulated household size, as well as being a vital source of both geographical and social mobility for young people. The very existence of service on such a large scale disproves the notion that society was static and immobile. Pre-industrial society was both mobile and varied, and so were the families and households within it.

Customs pertaining to service varied by region and by country. In Austria and Central Europe, there seems to have been a much greater tendency than in England for servants to be related to the head of household, and even sons and daughters were referred to as servants (Mitterauer and Sieder, 1982). In areas of Eastern Europe, a household form known as the 'zadruga' was common; it was a large household relative to Western European standards (mean household size was around nine to twelve, though some contained as many as eighty or a hundred individuals). It was organised around a core of males, usually brothers, and their wives and children and sometimes other kin (Hammel, 1972). Zadrugas never employed servants, but always kin. However, the ambiguities of the terms 'servant' and 'kin' suggest that the difference lay more in social meaning ascribed to the terms. Both service and kinship were crucial ways of regulating household size and needs. Notions of age, status and work imbued the concept of servant, as well as the concepts of boys and girls.

For the better-off sectors service was less common. Boys were more likely to be sent to live elsewhere as apprentices; girls were more apt to remain at home. Apprenticeship usually involved a money payment for entry, although it was possible to gain entry through kinship claims: 'well into the eighteenth century the custom of "claiming kin" was a way families relieved themselves of the burden of surplus children. Friedrich Klöden's parents asked his uncle to take the boy in and train him in the trade. The claim of kin was accepted very grudgingly and young Friedrich became the object of abuse in the relative's household' (Gillis, 1981, p. 18). In England from 1601 orphaned children, if not taken in by kin, were bound apprentice by the parish until the age of 24. In some cases children were taken from parents who were deemed as idle or vagrant and bound apprentice, in a way not unlike current practices of fostering children from 'problem families'.

Apprentices lived and worked in their master's house, usually for a period of seven years, and were under his control, regarded as part of the family, and were paid little or nothing. Later they became journeymen for a period of years, and eventually masters themselves. Apprentices had their own elaborate organisations around the principle of brotherhood, as did other youth groups in the seventeenth and eighteenth centuries: 'horizontal bonding of young single persons was a feature not only of the schools and universities, but also of many of the professions, the army, the bureaucracy, and the clergy as well' (Gillis, 1981, p. 22). Youth groups often had elaborate initiation rites symbolising the loss of the individual's identity with his particular family and entry into the secret rites of the new brotherhood. The conflict between lateral allegiances of brotherhood and the vertical allegiance to parents and superiors generally is one that was just as prevalent in earlier times as it is in contemporary society. It is a tension that permeates families as well as society.

Originally guilds were not exclusively male preserves, but as time passed they became increasingly so. In medieval times many crafts were open to women, and some – brewing, for example – were monopolised by them. The guilds had initially been religious organisations treating men and women equally, but as they became more associated with certain trades and skills women's importance in them declined. By the seventeenth century most guilds only allowed widows to practise their husband's craft, and apprenticeship for women was virtually non-existent.

A woman had access to work, skills and knowledge in her father's house where the craft was an integral part of the household and its life, but to continue to practise she either had to remain single in her father's household or to marry a man of the same occupation. Only if her husband died could she practise her skills independently and in her own right. As capital became increasingly consolidated and wage labour grew, access to such skills became scarcer. Men were therefore more anxious to exclude any competition to their trades and thus excluded women, unless as wives or daughters, from practising. The right of widows to practise their husband's trade became increasingly challenged. As time passed unmarried women and widows found it more and more difficult to survive economically on their own.

The growth of capital and wage labour meant that fewer people had access to any land at all. Spufford estimated that in the 1660s over half the population of Cambridgeshire was landless. Continental Europe, however, continued to support a substantial peasantry for a long time. For the landed, the question of how it would be divided and who was to inherit was crucial. There are essentially two main ways of handing down property; either the whole estate is given to one individual alone (impartible inheritance) which keeps it intact, or it is divided up in one way or another between a number of people (partible inheritance). Inheritance patterns were extremely variable between classes, regions and families. As a general rule the pattern in England was that among the wealthy classes primogeniture became increasingly normative (the eldest son got the entire estate). Careful provision was usually made for the widow, the rest of the children were given education for entry into the professions if they were sons, and dowries were provided for daughters. This resulted in a concentration of capital, an expansion of the professions, and a particular importance attached to marriage for women. In families where there were financial problems (which was quite frequent), these practices meant that many daughters were not allowed – or not able – to marry at all. In other countries, notably France, the estate was more often divided equally between sons, which led to a fragmentation of wealth and lack of large sums of capital generally.

Among the less well-to-do with some amount of property, equal care was taken in trying to provide for both widow and children. Circumstances varied widely, but it seems that whenever possible fathers/husbands tried to provide for their widows and all their children and, when they could, to set up sons with some land. Often this was done before the father died. Widows were usually left a life-interest in the house, or at least part of it was designated for their use alone. If there were no sons, and it has been estimated that in early modern England about 20 per cent of families would have daughters only (Goody, 1976), then daughters would inherit the land. Otherwise they would be given a 'portion' of money as dowry. Gough's *History of Myddle* has frequent references to daughters receiving 'portions', usually of £50 or £100, and also of young men anxious to marry them so as to get access to their money.

The ability to decide who inherited what put the father in a very strong position, and yet there are numerous examples of sons who went against their father's wishes – usually in marriage – and were disinherited, and also of daughters who were similarly disendowed. For sons or daughters not established independently before their father's death, there must have been considerable strain in the household if, for instance, a son of 30 had been wanting to marry and establish his own household but had to wait for his father's death to do so. If the father's economic situation was precarious, marriage for both sons and daughters might be postponed for years, often for ever. Some obviated this problem by entering service or going away to work as apprentices. On the whole, it seems that most fathers tried to establish their children in one way or another independently by the time they were in their mid-twenties. The *ideal* of a married couple setting up an independent household at marriage was widespread in early modern society – as it remains – although economic circumstances meant that in reality it often could not be realised.

For the propertyless there was no problem about inheritance, and some have argued that such families would have been more egalitarian. As mentioned earlier, however, wages were so low that it was virtually impossible for a family to survive on only one wage. Because the wages paid to women were invariably lower than men's, the vast majority of woman needed to co-reside with another man or men as well as work themselves. The economic viability of a household depended on a very precarious balance of wage earners and dependants, and its relative prosperity or poverty depended on the ratio of wage earners to dependants. This could easily be upset by a wage-earning child wanting to leave home when there were few other wage earners and too many dependants. Pressures of all sorts undoubtedly existed to stop such situations when possible. Death, premarital pregnancy and untimely marriages were the most common ways in which the balance became upset. Pregnancy and marriage were easier to control than death, and there were a variety of controls exercised by parents to try to prevent them, especially with regard to daughters. They were not always successful, of course, but there is no doubt that power relations existed between parents and children among wage-earning families, just as they did among wealthier sectors. In the former they were based around labour power, in the latter, around land and capital.

Thus the situations of individuals and the households in which they lived were highly varied in pre-industrial society. They depended on age, sex and economic circumstances. There were sharp differences in land, wealth and skills, and the differences became more pronounced as capital became more consolidated and wage labour more widespread. The differences between men and women in terms of access to skills and wealth were also marked, and became more so. For women in particular these were accentuated by their marriage opportunities. By no means everybody married; before industrialisation some 20 per cent of the population never married at all. For many, too, marriage only lasted a short time. Remarriage was common, but more so for men – as now. Marital status and age thus demarcated people from one another, as did wealth and skills.

Death was probably the only great leveller in a society otherwise characterised by inequality and diversity. It is therefore impossible to speak of there being *one* family type during this era; families were in a constant state of change, as were the individuals within them. The most that can be said generally about families at this time is that while the core of many households was composed of a parent or parents and children, many of the children would not always be actual offspring, and most households would also at times consist of servants, or apprentices, or grandparent(s), or other kin – or, indeed, any permutation of these. Families and households were characterised above all by their marked variability and variety.

What happened to families during the Industrial Revolution? The Industrial Revolution is really a misnomer. It was not an *event* so much as an acceleration of a myriad of changes that had been going on for relatively long periods of time. Capitalism had been developing since the fourteenth century. Although technological changes had a profound effect on the socio-economic system in the eighteenth and nineteenth centuries, there had been earlier technological 'revolutions', such as the harnessing of water power in the thirteenth century. The development of mechanised factories from the late eighteenth century was for some time a very localised event, occurring primarily in Lancashire. Throughout the nineteenth century many important industries, such as boot and shoe making, were not mechanised at all, even though many of them were located in large factories. The pace of mechanisation did increase rapidly during the nineteenth century, but was again localised and uneven in its development. Similarly, although urbanisation increased dramatically in some areas, other older cities like Norwich and Exeter diminished in importance and decreased in size. Thus to ask what effect industrialisation had on 'the family' is to ignore the variability of both industrialisation and families.

Nevertheless, there were certain fundamental changes which occurred during the eighteenth and nineteenth centuries which had important effects, in various ways, on all individuals and families. There were dramatic and unprecedented changes in the population structure and in the rate of population growth. This was particularly marked in Britain, but was also a characteristic of Western Europe generally – and was thus not a characteristic of industrialisation *per se*. Between 1700 and 1800 the population of England and Wales increased from nearly 6 million to 9 million; by 1900 the population (of Great Britain) stood at 37 million. The population of France increased from 19 million in 1700 to 41 million in 1900; that of Italy from 11.5 million in 1700 to 33 million in 1900 (Wrigley, 1969, pp. 153, 185).

Of equal and parallel importance was the increasingly rapid development of capitalism and the growth of an urban bourgeoisie and an urban and rural proletariat. Consolidation of capital and the spread of wage labour were particularly marked in Britain, but also characterised most of Western Europe and America. By the eighteenth century there was no longer a peasantry in Britain, although certain areas were still dominated by subsistence farming and smallholdings, while in Western Europe the peasantry remained an important sector of society throughout the nineteenth, and into the twentieth, centuries.

Although the population had grown rapidly in previous eras, it had also been counteracted by mortality crises such as bubonic plague. After the seventeenth century, for a variety of reasons, these crises diminished and had virtually disappeared by 1800. Consequently 'by 1791 there were not only more births but more survivals each year, with the result that each generation of those entering the marriage age was slightly larger than the last' (Chambers, 1972, p. 106). There was also an increased tendency for people to marry younger, largely as a result of the growth of wage labour which meant people were no longer constrained by waiting for land or accruing savings through service before they married.

Younger marriage and fewer mortality crises resulted in, at a family level, the probability of more children surviving and thus larger families. At a societal level, it meant a larger and younger population than ever before. In Britain, as elsewhere, these trends were not uniform; rapid growth, for example, was most marked in the northern and northwestern counties before industrialisation. Mortality was much higher among the poorer sectors than among the wealthy.

More people meant more pressure on resources. Land, previously the main economic resource for the population as a whole, because increasingly concentrated in the hands of the wealthy. This was partly a result of economic factors such as inflation, which made it impossible for many small and medium-sized landholders to compete with larger landholders, and partly a result of political factors. Because the wealthy monopolised political as well as economic power, they had been able since Tudor times to enclose common lands – which were a vital resource to the poor for grazing and for fuel – by acts of parliament, and the number of enclosures in the late eighteenth and early nineteenth centuries grew dramatically. As a result more and more people became reliant on wage labour, not just to supplement their smallholdings but as their sole source of income.

The enclosure of commons affected women in particular, as it was mostly women who had used commons for grazing cattle and poultry, for collecting fuel, and for access to herbs essential for making medicines and cures.[8] Enclosure and the 'agricultural revolution' also resulted in a decline in dairy farming and a switch to arable which, again, affected women adversely, for their role in dairy farming had been important. As Ivy Pinchbeck notes:

From enclosure awards widows and unmarried women seem fairly frequently to have been tenants of cottages with common rights, and to have rented or owned small plots of land. In this way they seem to have been able to earn their own livings and in the case of widows to bring up their children. The most usual method adopted was to set up as a dairy woman, especially if it were a grazing district where there was often a difficulty in procuring small quantities of milk and butter. Here a woman with a cottage and rights of common could easily gain a living for herself by supplying the non-farming population with a regular supply of eggs, milk and butter. (1981, p. 22)

The demise of this form of livelihood as a result of enclosure meant that survival for widows or single women was more difficult than ever, particularly as the wages they could earn were only a fraction of those a man could command. Women were therefore less able to survive independently, and were becoming more dependent than ever on marriage *and* wage labour, sometimes separately, often together, as the only way to survive. The precariousness of their situation meant that a marriage broken by death or desertion could easily result in an intolerable amount of labour having to be carried out for a wage that was inadequate for physical survival, or, having to turn to kin for help, or, in the last instance, resorting to prostitution or parish relief.

While women's wages were appallingly low, wages generally were low, and economic survival for a man alone was also precarious, although not impossible. Any individual, man or woman, stood a far greater chance of economic survival by living with other wage earners, whether kin or non-kin. Where the number of individuals needed to run a smallholding had been limited, the number who could engage in wage labour was potentially infinite. When work was plentiful there was an obvious premium on having a large household with as many members as possible working. Under such circumstances there was no need to send children away as servants. Moreover, from the early eighteenth century farmers had been employing residential farm servants less and less – except in areas where labour was scarce – as it was cheaper for them to hire labourers on a weekly, daily, or even hourly, basis and thus not have to provide board and lodging during slack periods. Girls continued to be hired as servants, but for domestic duties alone, and they were no longer treated as part of the family, but lived and ate separately from the rest of the household.

The growth of wage labour thus tended to alter the age structure of many working-class households. There was a real premium on keeping as many children of working age at home as possible, and so more households were characterised by adolescent – and often older – children co-residing with parent(s) than had been the case earlier. The decline in mortality – although mortality rates varied widely – meant that more children were surviving to adolescence. Thus households were apt to be larger than in the past. This increase in both size of household and age of those within it, must have had important repercussions on power relations within families and undoubtedly added new strains and conflicts between parents and children, brothers and sisters. The decline in age at marriage also meant that there was much less of an age gap between parents and children than there had been.

When a young person's income was a vital part of the household economy there was bound to be considerable pressure from parent(s) not to marry. While not having the ability to control children's behaviour by threatening to disinherit or disendow, working-class parents could still exert considerable emotional and indirect economic pressure. A child wanting to leave home could be made to see how this action would jeopardise the lives of the rest of the household. He or she might be threatened with withdrawal of help from kin in times of hardship, which was a very serious threat. Equally, a compromise might be reached whereby parents would offer their household as a place for the young couple to live for a while (which would double the household income if the wife continued working), until perhaps a younger child was earning. Co-residence of young working-class couples with parents was quite a common phenomenon, although generally it would only last for a year or so after marriage. In a study of newlyweds in Providence, Rhode Island in 1865, Chudacoff (1978, p. 192) found that approximately 10 per cent of all newly marrieds lived at the same address as one set of parents, about one-third of them lived within walking distance of at least one parent, and between 25 per cent and 33 per cent had at least one parent living in the city, but over a mile away. This type of arrangement is still quite common in twentieth-century Europe and America, particularly among the poor and during times of recession.

One of the most crucial determinants of the relative ease or difficulty with which a young person could become independent of parents related to that child's position in the family as a whole. Older children were more likely to have to start work young, often foregoing education or training because of the high number of dependants in the household, but were then more likely to be able to become independent, or to marry, at a fairly early age when their younger siblings started earning. A younger child, on the other hand, would be more likely to spend a longer period of time at school or in apprenticeship while older ones were still co-residing and earning, but was more likely to be pressurised into postponing or foregoing independence and/or marriage when older. In particular, a younger daughter was often constrained to stay at home so that she could care for her ageing parent(s).

Household strategies depended on local work resources. In areas where more work was available for men, for instance in shipbuilding or mining, more pressure would be put on boys to live at home while girls might be sent away as domestic servants, or encouraged to marry young. Yet strategies were by no means as limited as this, and extended far beyond the immediate household. One of the most common ways of balancing a household's resources was to use links *between* households, often over considerable geographical distances and often between radically different kinds of employment.

Tamara Hareven, in her study of the Amoskeag Corporation in Manchester, New Hampshire, found extensive and strong kinship links were maintained between households over considerable space and periods of time: 'strong ties over several generations can still be maintained under conditions of kin dispersion . . . the social space of French-Canadian kin extended from Quebec to Manchester and spread over New England's industrial maps' (Hareven, 1982, p. 115). The use of kinship links as a way of balancing household resources is well illustrated in the following account: 'at times . . . family decisions ignored individual feelings to a degree that would seem callous from the vantage point of our times; Mary Dancause . . . was at age four sent by her parents back to live with relatives in Quebec when she had an eye disease. When she reached age twelve, her parents uprooted her from a loving environment in Quebec to bring her back to Manchester to take care of younger siblings' (ibid., p. 109).

Kinship ties were used to find relatives from rural Canada jobs at the Amoskeag (in much the same way Anderson (1971) described for nineteenth-century Preston). They were used at times of crisis, as agents of adaptation for those who had newly arrived; to some extent as a means of bargaining with the management at the mills, and, as a last resort in cases of industrial crisis, links were maintained with rural relatives 'by maintaining subsistence farming as a backup if the factory failed. Even when entire families moved to industrial centers, they did not completely abandon their rural base' (ibid., p. 3).

In a study of a Devon town (Gittins, 1983) during a period when the local woollen industry shifted from a protoindustrial (Medick, 1976) type of organisation to becoming mechanised, other strategies were found. Prior to 1850, the most skilled and organised sector of the woollen industry was that of woolcombing. Woolcombing as a craft had a long tradition, was still organised on a household or small workshop basis, was well paid and was entirely male-dominated. The mechanisation of woolcombing after 1850 effectively ousted men from the industry and it then prospered primarily through the employment of female labour. This, because of the low wages paid to women, made the industry highly profitable. The 'take-off' of the Industrial Revolution in the Lancashire cotton industry, of course, was also achieved largely by the extensive use of female and child labour.

The relative plenty of factory work for girls, and the relative scarcity for boys and men, put a premium on the wage labour of unmarried daughters. Many families seem to have used the labour power of their unmarried daughters as a means to promote the social and geographical mobility of sons. Families with more than one son usually put them into a variety of occupations – industrial, agricultural and artisan. This can be seen as both a strategy for family insurance and survival, and as a means by which one or two sons were able to become socially mobile at the expense of their siblings – generally their sisters.

A similar situation was found by Braun (1978) in a study of a textile area of Switzerland in the eighteenth century. He recounts the words of an old woman silk weaver to a father: ' "Only wait until your daughter grows up" the neighbour said to the father, "then you can put some money aside"... Children, especially daughters, were desired'. This type of household was not specific to a particular historical era, but to a particular type of economic organisation.

Although never an entirely secure institution, marriage in pre-industrial society had provided women with a reasonable means of economic survival involving both production and domestic work in and around the home, with a good chance of some minimal security in the event of widowhood. The growth of wage labour and the increasing separation of home from work put women more than ever before at the mercy of two increasingly unstable markets: the marriage market and the labour market. In both their position was weak, and economic survival was precarious whether a woman entered one or both.

In other areas the response to mechanisation, de-skilling and proletarianisation was different. Sometimes machine breaking was an immediate response, as in the Luddite and Captain Swing riots (Hobsbaum and Rudé, 1973). More often, men in skilled crafts or industries formed themselves into associations or unions. Their general purpose was to defend their members against further capitalist exploitation, mechanisation and wage cuts, and to protect themselves from cheap labour. Since most cheap labour was made up of women and children, the unions tended to contribute further to the already disadvantaged position of women. Until the second half of the nineteenth century, however, the majority of unions were made up of men from only the most skilled trades and crafts, and one of their main aims was to procure a 'family wage' – a single wage that was adequate to support a man and dependent wife and children on his work alone. This new emphasis on the father/husband as sole earner was a powerful factor in the development of modern notions of 'masculinity'. While the concept of a single male breadwinner had started with the rise of the middle classes in the late eighteenth century, this was the first time a sector of the working class – and a very small sector at that – did so.

As Hilary Land (1976a) points out, it is hard to know whether their argument for wanting to keep their wives and children out of the workforce was more a matter of conviction or a rationale for higher wages that they knew would appeal to middle-class ears. Whatever the rationale, the ideal of a family wage became increasingly important as an ideal of the organised trade union movement, and it was an ideal which coincided with the new middle-class ideology of women and children as dependants of the husband/father.

During the nineteenth century, however, the proportion of working-class families who could survive on the basis of the man's wage alone was very small. Nevertheless, the objective of a single male breadwinner per family was one of the most radical changes in family ideology of the modern era, and one that had dramatic effects on notions of fatherhood, masculinity, motherhood, feminity, family life and family policy, and still has. The ideal, then as now, was often very far removed from the reality, and the majority of working-class families in the nineteenth century still relied heavily on a household economy based on several wages. Working-class men and women, but women in particular, were therefore dependent on both wage labour in the labour market and a partner through the marriage market in order to survive economically. Both markets were insecure and in fact many individuals had to find extra economic support through children's or other kin's labour.

The shift from working in or around the home to working outside it for the majority of the day had important effects on the lives of most families. For many, it meant that fewer activities went on in the household; the spinning wheel and the loom ceased to be commonplace articles of furniture. The space left by the departed loom, however, was soon taken up by the extra number of people a household had to keep in order to survive. For women with children it posed a dilemma of what to do with young children. Some took them to the factories, others put them with relatives, friends or neighbours, others changed their work itself and worked from home. Anderson (1971) found that only 25 per cent of married women in his sample of Preston were listed as employed, this undoubtedly under-represents women's work, given that much of it was casual, part-time or seasonal. Nevertheless, it highlights the fact that the separation of home from work often meant that women would work in factories only at certain periods of their life-cycle or during certain times of year – in particular, when a husband left or was unemployed, died, or when children began to leave home or older daughters took charge of young children at home.

It is important to reiterate that factory work was by no means the general experience of all during the nineteenth century. Although the numbers were declining, a large proportion of the population was still engaged in agricultural work, in mining, street-selling, and an increasing number in service trades. Many women and children carried out an enormous amount of 'outwork' at home: making matchboxes, straw-plaiting, glove-making, needlework, etc. This kind of work is still very common in modern society, has the great advantage to employers of being extremely cheap and totally unorganised so that exploitation is easy and virtually undetectable. Because of this, there are no reliable figures on the precise number of people engaged in such work. Like spinning in earlier times, outwork could and can be continued at odd times when a woman also has to care for others at home.

Young children were often cared for by others in a way that might seem casual to us, but which was not necessarily any less adequate. The following extract is from an interview with a man born in the Devon textile town mentioned previously. Born in the 1880s, his father never lived with them, indeed, he had no knowledge of who his father was:

I was born up over that hop. A hop was – a court. You go in a court, well then there was two rooms over. Our mother had to rear us up there. Her worked in the mill. Before us, her worked on the mines . . . After my brother was born her come in mill then, in town – burl, what they call burling. Six o'clock mornings till six night times . . . Generally neighbours would be all around to look after us after school. Neighbours would let 'em go out and play out in a room. Course some didn't work and some did. Then my mother used to wash night times – I'd be up there with her, be ten o'clock at night. After six o'clock we would go home and have our tea, and then her be off.[9]

Childcare for the poorer sectors of the working class was very much an informal arrangement based around the women in the community, rather than being a specifically kin-related or mother-specific task, although often a high proportion of a community was kin anyway. As Ross notes:

Neighbours and indeed neighbourhoods functioned as auxiliary parents. An early twentieth century report on Lambeth working mothers showed that a large group had formal childcare arrangements with neighbours, and a still larger group with no formal plans for their children may well have relied on informal supervi-

sion by women living nearby. Another survey of London working mothers, made a few years earlier, found that half left infants with relatives, thirty percent with neighbours. Landlords, and especially landladies . . . in·exercising general superintendence over renters, kept a casual eye out for children as well as for old people living in the house. (Ross, 1983, p. 12)

In families where the mother did outwork, the result was often such acute overcrowding that many homes could only really be used for sleeping purposes, as this account from Arthur Harding, born in the Nichol area of East London in 1886, bears witness:

> Because she was a cripple, mother couldn't go out to work. Instead she used to take in work for Bryant and May's, making matchboxes. Every day she made eight gross of matchboxes, 2½d a gross, 1s.6d. a day . . . The room we lived in was very small – twelve foot by ten foot – and it was the only room we had . . . Our home was very crowded. The floor being the drying ground for the matchboxes, there was no room to move about. Everything was done in a single room . . . I used to be put in a box outside the door, or sent into the street with my sister . . . if you wanted to eat she might give you a couple of slices of bread and you'd go out and eat it on the doorstep – there was no room for you inside. (Samuel, 1981a, p. 21)

Arthur's father played little part in their family life: 'I never been out with my father in all me life. He never took me out anywhere. He was a man that lived for himself alone. We never had no contact with him whatsoever and he didn't care at all. And there was thousands like him about' (ibid., p. 39). For many families, fathers were either non-existent – having died or moved away – or largely peripheral. The assumption was always that the mother or a sister or other female relative or neighbour was ultimately responsible for children. A man's participation in fatherhood was largely voluntary. Then, as now, it was infinitely more common for a man to leave a woman with the children, whether temporarily or permanently, than it was for a woman to leave a man with the children.

Periodic and often prolonged father absence is still common today, for instance, among service families or families where the husband/father's work demands his absence for periods of time.

Arthur Harding's experience of knowing his father only superficially was, and is, a quite common experience for many children. Fatherhood is very much a social category that is subject to much variation; between different social sectors in different circumstances and at different periods of time it may be either stressed, de-emphasised, or denied altogether.

Fatherhood for the Victorian middle classes was a social category of absolute prime importance. While middle-class families were a minority in relation to the whole of society, in terms of economic and political power and influence their ideals and beliefs dominated nineteenth-century ideology and legislation. As their political power grew, so their ability to influence and direct legislation enforcing many of their ideals also increased. But no matter how many laws were made to restrict children's and women's labour, the vast difference between a professional man's earnings which could keep an entire household of dependants and servants in comfort, remained very different from most working-class households where sheer physical survival necessitated a number of inadequate and erratic wages.

The middle classes promulgated the ideal that 'a woman's place is in the home'; the élite of the working class, the unionised, met some success in gaining a family wage by using this theme to their advantage. The semi-skilled and unskilled, the ill, the widowed, separated, and mothers of illegitimate children – indeed, the majority – had to try to reconcile a very different household economy and way of life and work with this increasingly dominant ideology. The dilemma remains for many today. It is helpful, therefore, to remember how recent it is, and that it was, and is, an ideology specific historically to the rise of the middle classes.

The ideology developed between 1780 and 1850, and 'the central belief that emerged ... was that of a male breadwinner gaining a livelihood through work and maintaining his female (and child) dependants within the home ... In this view, husband and wife were the archetype, but father and child, brother and sister, uncle and niece, master and servant reproduced the relationships of clientage and dependency' (Davidoff, 1977, p. 64). It was not just a family ideology, but also a *gender* ideology, a careful and deliberate attempt to reorganise the relations between the sexes according to middle-class ways and values, and then defining the new division as 'natural', 'biological' and eternal.

Obviously the growth of capital, industry and urbanisation had dramatic effects on the development of the middle classes, particularly in terms of work patterns and family life. An abundance of cheap labour meant that more and more household, agricultural and business jobs could be done by people other than family members for very low payment. The growth in the scale of capital and capital enterprises meant business was becoming increasingly separate from family relations, although many businesses were in fact still carried out at home – often with unpaid administrative and clerical help from wives and daughters.

Nevertheless

the trend was for more and more household relationships to involve a cash nexus, whether in the form of proletarian wage earner, salaried or professional occupation, tradesman, rentier, capitalist or a mixture of these ... This shift was associated with a higher proportion of families living in towns ... The final and complete break ... was not reached in England until full extension of limited liability with the passing of the Company Acts of 1856–62, which once and for all freed business activity from any restraints imposed by kinship obligations. (Davidoff, 1976b, p. 132)

Part of this whole process was a concern with reordering, restructuring and redefining relationships of all sorts, most essentially those between classes, but equally essentially those between the sexes and between age groups, residential areas, households and families. As the middle classes became wealthier and more powerful within a fairly short time period, they also had to develop and define a particular way of life, distinctive values and ideals which they could both claim as differentiating them from the rest of society, and as a means by which they could develop a whole new way of life for all of society according to their terms and values. The lynchpin of their new philosophy was *their* definition of *the* family. The ideology of the family, as we have come to know it, was both historically specific and class specific.

Thus, after a brief consideration of families before and after industrialisation, we can reach certain conclusions. First, families were extraordinarily variable in terms of wealth, age composition, sex composition and occupation. The growth of capitalism meant more and more families became dependent on wage labour alone, and for most this meant as many family members as possible needed to work just to survive. On the other hand, it meant that the new middle classes were increasingly powerful economically, socially and politically, and their new wealth enabled them to keep wives and children within the household as dependants of a male bread-winner. This situation they then defined as both desirable and 'natural'. Family types thus varied considerably by class situation.

The decline in mortality crises and the decline in age at marriage resulted in an unprecedented population boom which swelled the ranks of wage labourers. Plentiful and cheap labour meant it was easier for the middle classes to employ help on a short-term basis; residential service and apprenticeship for young people virtually disappeared, with the important exception of female domestic servants. Many more working-class children – and sons in particular – spent their adolescence with their original families.

The increased separation of home from work created new problems for working women with young children. Many resolved this by relying more on the help of neighbours, older daughters and other female kin to care for children while they worked outside the home. This new division between 'work' and 'family' had previously been irrelevant because so much work had been centred in and around the household. There thus arose an artificial division between 'productive work' (i.e., paid work), and 'non-productive work' (i.e., unpaid domestic work). Before, milking the cow or spinning or cooking or sowing the seed had *all* been part of a general household economy with one task as important to survival as another. Now, while all were still crucial for survival, the payment for certain types of work with wages and the non-payment for housework resulted in a new status accorded to 'productive work' and a general degradation of 'non-productive work'.

Yet many families still continued to live in ways which they had before. For most, it was still necessary for several members of the household to work, and although wage labour had begun centuries before, by the nineteenth century the majority of the population had become dependent on wages alone. Certain patterns of behaviour continued as they had done for a long time, for example, pre-marital intercourse remained common among the working classes. But as the new middle classes gained political power in the 1830s, so more changes were imposed on the rest of society through

2

Is patriarchy relevant in understanding families?

Definitions and ideals of how men, women and children should behave are a central organising feature of all societies. The content of such rules, however, is highly variable between cultures and over time. It became apparent in the last chapter that in Western European society, despite extensive involvement in all spheres of work before and during the development of capitalism, women and children were not accorded the same status or economic rewards as men. In spite of a variety of changes since, inequalities based on sex and age remain. Why has this been the case, and how have they been justified?

Women and children have for centuries been defined in terms of their relationship to the kinship system. Men, although also located within the kinship system, have been defined primarily in terms of their place within the occupational system – hence the origin of many surnames such as Smith, Taylor, Sawyer, Miller, and so on.

The original meaning of 'family', in use until the eighteenth century, referred to the authority of the *paterfamilias* over all others in a household. The 'others' included servants and apprentices as well as women and children. Implicit in the concept of the western family, then, is the notion of male – and specifically, paternal – dominance over others. Thus by definition the family has been an unequal institution premised on paternal authority and power. Inherent in this definition is the notion of the husband/father as a patriarch, literally 'the father and ruler of a family or tribe'.[1] Patriarchy is thus both a gender and an age relationship, based on power, and is essential in understanding families.

Feminists have spent considerable time trying to define and

analyse patriarchy as an important means of understanding social inequalitites. Millett (1970) for instance, defined it as the universal oppression of women and younger men by older men. Mitchell, on the other hand, put more emphasis on the importance of seeing patriarchy in terms of the symbolic nature of paternal domination over both women and children. Hartmann (1979) and Eisenstein (1979) argued that capitalism and patriarchy should be examined as co-existing systems, the one influencing and affecting the other, and vice versa. The problem with this is that it leads to an artificial division between the economy and the ideology of male domination exercised within families. This is problematic because families, kinship and the relations between the sexes and between age groups are all imbued with economic, political and ideological relations and duties. As Lown (1983a) points out: 'when political relations are recognized as a pivotal organizing principle of society. . . the need to distinguish conceptually between "the economy", on the one hand, and "the family" on the other, becomes irrelevant. Power relationships between men and women cut across every aspect of social existence, and, being located historically, are subject to change.'

Patriarchy has been increasingly criticised as an ahistorical concept that does not take adequate account of differences in gender relationships between social groups, cultures and over time. Black feminists in particular have criticised it, arguing that slave fathers rarely had power over their families in slave culture and that in colonial situations 'it is equally unsatisfactory because it is unable to explain why black males have not enjoyed the benefits of white patriarchy' (H. Carby 1982). Nonetheless, there is no equivalent concept that delineates power relations between men and women and adults and children in a similar way, and for that reason I believe it is important to retain it.

The essence of patriarchy, then, can be seen as the ways in which power relations between women and men, and men and children, are defined and exercised. Power is always a 'contested concept', as Lukes (1974) and Davidoff (1979) point out. Wherever unequal relations of whatever sort exist then there are inevitably power relationships, even if these are not acknowledged as such by the actors involved. Power does not have to result in overt conflict, but can be exercised 'covertly' by withholding knowledge, decisions or affection from others and by ensuring that potentially controversial topics are simply not raised, whether at a governmental or a household level (Stacey and Price, 1981, p. 6).

Defining power is notoriously difficult. In a general sense, it is useful to see it as lying along a broad continuum ranging, on the one hand, from general acceptance by others of a person's or institution's legitimate or natural right to give orders and expect obedience and deference, to, on the other hand, the ability to use force and violence to ensure that orders or wishes are carried out. It is only when, and if, a person's or institution's authority is challenged that power relations in terms of overt force become evident.

Men for centuries were legally entitled to use violence on both wives and children; this was seen as an essential support to their patriarchal authority. Despite recent legislation to protect women and children from family violence, the agencies of the law remain highly reluctant to 'interfere' or prosecute cases of family violence or rape of wives or children. To do so is seen as an infringement of 'privacy', but is better understood as a challenge to the patriarchal authority invested in the notion of fatherhood and enshrined in the ideology of the family. Relations of power and authority between the sexes aand between adults and children permeate, and permeated, society at all levels from the simplest household to more complex social and political institutions.

A central theme running through all ideologies of gender, age groups and families in western society, and imbued in the concept of patriarchy, is the notion of dependence. The *paterfamilias* in the feudal world, the lord of the manor, was head of an economic, political, social and religious unit which was at one and the same time a form of extended household. His authority was legitimated by the sovereign whose authority came directly from God. Those over whom he ruled and who worked for him were dependent on his protection, his land, his goodwill. He was also dependent on their services and labour, and was expected to fulfil certain obligations to them, but it was not an equal relationship. He owned and controlled the land and the household. Because his power came directly from the king and from God it was both economic and ideological. Disobedience was therefore an act against the lord of the manor and the sovereign and God; it was, in effect, a defiance of the whole social order.

Everyone under the lord's tutelage was therefore dependent on him, and this relationship was seen and defended as a paternal one. Economic supremacy, political power and religious control were all defined with reference to the *father*, who was at the same time the head of a household, whose members were dependent on his superior position in all spheres.

Vassals and serfs were dependants of the lord as were wives, sons, daughters and sisters, yet the fact that all power and authority came from the male-as-father meant that wives and children were in a situation of double dependence – both on the lord and on their father/husband. That women and children were expected to work just as much as men did not reduce this fact. Work for and within the household was an inherent part of their service and duty. A serf or vassal had to serve his lord, but was himself (or in time would be) served by his wife and children or sisters. Rendering service was the corollary of dependence; a man simply by being a man could always claim service from a woman or child, even if he himself served others.

The only way in which women could escape this double dependence was through widowhood (assuming the lord allowed her to continue occupying the holding), and serving the lord directly. Work did not bring women independence from patriarchal authority, even if in some circumstances it brought them relative economic independence. Whatever the individual circumstances of a woman or family 'women, children and servants were always a separate category. They never had the same legal, educational, religious, political or property rights as men. They never had access to the equivalent "work identity" as men. They were always expected to provide services for men' (Lown, 1983a, p. 35).

These notions of servitude and dependence were bolstered by, and were an integral part of, the teachings of the Roman Catholic Church. Whereas Christ had emphasised the spiritual equality of all, and had a number of women disciples, St Paul and later theologians preached a far more misogynistic message, claiming in particular that the husband must be 'head of the wife', as Christ is head of the husband and the Church.

As both Church and State became more organised and centralised, so women were increasingly excluded from positions of power, and the duty to serve men and families was increasingly re-emphasised. Because authority was implicitly patriarchal, any chal-

lenge to patriarchy (e.g. by women becoming independent economically or seeking education) also implied a challenge to that authority. An event like the trial and execution of Joan of Arc in 1431 can
be seen as a political event as well as a religious and ideological act
by a patriarchal society that had begun 'to associate "unfeminine
behaviour" with heresy and witchcraft' (McNamara and Wemple,
1977). Whenever women have taken public political action,
whether in eighteenth-century bread riots, the French Revolution,
the suffragette campaign, or the contemporary women's movement, their actions have invariably been defined as both a threat to
the socio-political order and as 'unfeminine', 'unnatural' and
threatening to 'the family'. Inherent in all such accusations has also
been the notion of sexual aberration and 'abnormality'.

Definitions and ideals of sexuality imbue all religious systems.
Heterosexuality is only one form of sexuality among several. Some
religions have endorsed other forms of sexuality, for example,
homosexuality in ancient Greece. The Judaeo-Christian ideology,
however, has always emphasised monogamous heterosexuality as
the only acceptable form of sexuality, apart from celibacy. Unlike
other religions, Judaeo-Christianity has never defined sexuality as
pleasurable or desirable. It is either seen as sinful lust, or as an
unfortunate means to the necessary end of reproduction.

Women's sexuality, moreover, is seen as very different from
men's. The myth of the temptation of Adam by Eve created one
stereotype of women as evil, lustful and untrustworthy – in short, as
the cause of all men's sorrows. The myth of immaculate conception,
on the other hand, accords to God all credit for the miracle of
conception, and to God-as-man the chance of all redemption. Mary
is a passive, asexual figure who, having acted as a vehicle for God's
will, is therefore Good. In other words, the only way in which
women can be religiously acceptable is by denying their own
sexuality, yet passively accepting their husband's sexual 'needs' –
and by being mothers. These two visions of women remain strong
symbols in western culture and can still be seen as influencing and
informing attitudes to rape and women's sexual behaviour generally.

The growth of wage labour from the late medieval period posed a
problem for traditional religious ideology and feudal patriarchal
relations, for there was an increasing severance with existing relations of dependency and deference to authority. Instead of direct

dependence and service to the lord of the manor, the worker became dependent on the more impersonal wage. It was a new form of dependence rather than independence as such, yet it emphasised the individual at the expense of the traditional patriarchal relationship. At the same time the State was becoming more centralised with a shifting emphasis on to the importance of allegiance to the sovereign rather than to the individual lord.

Parallel with changing economic relations and political allegiances – or arguably in response to them[2] – there arose a revised religious ideology with the advent of Protestantism in the sixteenth century. Ostensibly a revolt against the perceived abuses of the Roman Catholic Church, Protestantism stressed the importance of *individual* responsibility to God rather than to temporal delegates. By so doing, Protestantism contained within it a challenge to hierarchical relations based on patriarchal definitions of authority. It thus made an implicit assumption that men, women and children were in fact (in the eyes of God) equal. If women were as good as men in God's eyes, why should they not share equal access to temporal wealth and power? Similarly, why should anybody have more than anyone else, whether man, woman or child, rich or poor?

The ways in which this dilemma was resolved – at times uneasily – were varied. The structure of authority was shifted away from clerics, holy objects and the pyramidical feudal notion of hierarchy to one which stressed the importance of paternal authority within the household, allegiance to the state and king, and direct responsibility to God. Women and children were equal in God's eyes, but only in a spiritual sense and only if they served God through serving father or husband in a temporal household. There was thus a division created between spiritual and temporal in a way that had not been distinguished before. This was the origin of the concepts of 'public' and 'private', an artificial resolution to a contradiction between individual equality and hierarchical patriarchal authority.

Women could attain salvation through good works and a devout life within the 'private' spiritual realm of the family (which implied a sanctification of the family), while men had to attain salvation through good works in the 'public' sphere as well as being a responsible *paterfamilias* guarding the spiritual welfare of his dependants. Women remained doubly dependent, because their means of salvation was only really possible through dependence on a father's or husband's authority within a family household. Celibacy and nunneries were no longer options for Protestant women, and this put an added importance on marriage for women.

Yet many women could not, or would not, live in a patriarchal household. Spinsters, widows, abandoned wives formed a substantial minority of the female population. To survive economically, most had to live with other women and/or children in similar situations. Being 'outside marriage', and thus outside patriarchal control and authority, made such women threatening in various ways: economically, socially and sexually. Fear and suspicion of women in such situations resulted eventually in the massive persecution and execution of 'witches' in sixteenth- and seventeenth-century Europe and America.

The overwhelming majority of people accused of witchcraft were women. They were most frequently single or widowed, and often old. As widows or spinsters alone they had no male head of household whom they should, or could, serve, and on whom they could be dependent. As such they were suspect in religious terms as well as being a potential source of economic liability to neighbours within the parish. Then, as now, women were paid on the assumption that they should form part of a male-headed household, and that their earnings would be simply supplementary to a man's. Thus women's wages were always lower than men's. The growing numbers of enclosures (as discussed elsewhere) meant that women's traditional access to common land, and often to a cottage, was being eroded and destroyed. Their economic situation deteriorated notably during this period.

Living outside a male-headed household also meant that such women were often perceived as sexual threats to other women's husbands and lovers (much as separated and divorced women are today). At this time women were believed to have much greater sexual needs than men, so that unattached women were seen as particularly dangerous. If a spinster or widow were to bear illegitimate children she posed a further economic threat to the parish.

Women had for a long time been healers in the community and knowledge of herbal cures was an important aspect of their daily lives, and one of the ways in which they served and helped others from the omnipresent threat of disease and death. As knowledge, however, it also constituted a basis of power and authority for them. One of the most common accusations made of alleged witches was their curative power: 'nine hundred witches were destroyed in a single year in the Würzburg area, and a thousand in and around Como ... women made up some 86% of those executed ... again and again the "crimes" included what would now be recognised as legitimate medical acts – providing contraceptive measures, performing abortions, offering drugs to ease the pains of labor' (Ehrenreich and English, 1979, p. 31). It is not surprising that this was also a time when increasing attempts were being made by men to take over medicine as an exclusively male profession. Women healers posed a threat both professionally and because they were women – for healing to be authoritative it had to be percieved as a male preserve.

Thus the persecution of witches, albeit a highly complex phenomenon, can be seen as a reaction to fears of women who, by living outside male-headed households, threatened patriarchal authority. It can also be seen as a fear of growing poverty and a need to formulate new policies to cope with the poor, as well as fears of women's sexuality and their powers as healers and controllers of the forces of life and death.[3] All these fears were expressed in religious terms, so that women were alleged to be more prone to the 'temptations of Satan' than men.

Perhaps most of all, women who lived outside a patriarchal household, wherein they could achieve spiritual equality through service and dependence, threatened the uneasy compromise on the conflict between equality before God and the need for patriarchal authority. Women without a husband or father resident challenged directly the new notion of women's 'natural' dependence, and were thus perceived – and persecuted – as 'unnatural' and 'dangerous'. As policies dealing with poverty were implemented, as men increasingly took over medicine, and as women whenever possible sought to escape the stigma and persecution of being single by marrying and remarrying, so the persecution of women as witches subsided. The last execution of a witch in England took place in Exeter in 1685. Yet the fear of women who live outside marriage, their powers, their sexuality and the economic liabilities they pose have remained to the present day, even if such fears are no longer expressed in terms of witchcraft. Derision and accusations of lesbianism are the common attacks on such women in contemporary society.

The main way in which the ideological conflict between spiritual equality and the need for authority was resolved was by elevating the status of women within the household as guardians of religion and morality, and by creating the notion of the home as a separate 'private' sphere. Puritan sects in particular preached that marriage needed to be a partnership in which great emphasis was put on the importance of raising children carefully in a well-ordered home where they learned obedience to parents and to God.

Whereas in medieval times children were regarded simply as 'little adults' and treated accordingly, childhood was increasingly coming to be seen as a special, and a problematic, time. The belief that children were born evil gave Protestant, and particularly Puritan, theologians much cause for concern, and this concern focused on the family. Like women, children were seen as dependants of a patriarch and in need of careful control and discipline. Children had to be taught to accept authority unquestioningly, and to do so it was believed that physical punishment was essential. Fear of punishment was inculcated early as a necessary means to obedience. It remains, of course, a much-used method of childrearing and testifies to the prevalence of force and violence as the logical 'back-up' to unequal relations between parents and children, as well as between men and women.

One of the central Puritan doctrines was that a family should be a 'little commonwealth' with the father at the head. The notion of the *paterfamilias* remained strong, but now focused on the family household and its father rather than on a feudal lord. Stone comments that 'a diffuse concept of patriarchy inherited from the middle ages that took the form of 'good lordship' – meaning dominance over kin and clientage – was vigorously attacked by the State as a threat to its own authority. Patriarchy was now reinforced by the State, however, in the much modified form of authoritarian dominance by the husband and father over the women and children within the nuclear family' (1977, pp. 153–4). *Ideologically* this was indeed the case, yet as mentioned before not all families were nuclear nor were they all by any means male-headed. The political power of the lord in being able to command armies and recruit soldiers, the very castle itself, had gone or were greatly weakened, but the economic and ideological authority remained heavily imbued in ideals of masculinity, fatherhood, and the family.

For a man, marriage was a crucial status passage from dependence or semi-dependence to one of independence and authority, an explicit part of which was being able to command and expect the services and deference of wife and children. A woman, however, was by definition always dependent, and thus women who through widowhood or separation not only put themselves in a frequently precarious economic situation, but were also seen as a contradiction to the very idea of womanhood. Women were becoming increasingly dependent on marriage for both economic security and social status.

A holy and spiritual woman was one who was a pious mother and wife, always serving her family to the best of her ability, obedient to both husband and God (the two could conflict, of course). She could also attain high status by fulfilling these duties to her father or brother. But there was no other way in which she could become man's spiritual equal outside a patriarchal household. She could, and was expected, to work both within the home and often outside it, but her access to various occupations was dependent on living with a husband or father. Not all women did live like this – indeed, the persecution of witches shows that many did not – but that this was the ideal preached by both Church and State. More than ever, it reinforced the exclusion of women from areas of authority and power, and was used as a rationale for their being paid less than men. It thus forced women, to a large extent, to conform at least partly to the ideal. The ideal of womanhood and 'femininity' became defined so closely with marriage and motherhood that unmarried or widowed women became increasingly perceived as *un*womanly, threatening, and peripheral.

Protestantism also emphasised the importance of the Bible and the saying and reading of prayers within families. This put literacy, and thus education, at a premium: 'but the wide gap between men and women in the sixteenth century placed the latter at a new and serious disadvantage ... the doctrine of priesthood of all believers meant in practice that the husband and father became the spiritual as well as the secular head of the household' (Stone, 1977, p. 155). The 'diffusion' of knowledge as a result of the invention of the printing press and the spread of education was not an equal one. Few of the poorest had access to education, and women – both rich and poor – had considerably less than men. Education and literacy were becoming an important divider both between economic classes and between the sexes, where once they had been the preserve of a tiny minority of the very wealthy and of religious clerics.

The problem of women's equality with men before God remained one that perplexed people until the present day. The growth of rationalism and science from the seventeenth century addressed itself in particular to this question in seeking 'scientific' explanations to justify women's perceived inferiority. One of the major problems facing all cultures is not only to understand the anatomical differences between men and women, but also the significance of biological reproduction. Explanations have been varied, some not even acknowledging paternity. In Western Europe, women had been defined as closer to nature, more mysterious, more sexual and more likely to be tempted by Satan. By virtue of this, they were in need of men's control. Seventeenth-century philosophers tried to eradicate what they saw as myth, superstition and any divine or mysterious attributes of nature or women. Descartes argued against the commonly held notion that nature was a 'living womb' of semi-divine character, and proposed that God had created an infinity of miniature males and females who only needed to grow. He therefore tried to remove 'any possibly mysterious, creative powers from females and rendered such creative powers to God the Father alone' (Easlea, 1981, p. 75).

The attempt to 'prove' women's inferiority in relation to reproduction was given an added force by the discovery by Leeuwenhoek in 1677 of spermatazoa in semen. This discovery led him to conclude 'that it is exclusively the male semen that forms the foetus, and all that woman may contribute only serves to receive the semen and feed it' (ibid., p. 75). Scientists were thus increasingly trying to prove that women did not have any special life-giving force, but that it was man, aided by God, who was the true life-force. This was, of course, a similar message to that of the immaculate conception. Early science to a large extent 'substantiated' many of the theological attempts to reconcile the conflict between equality before God and patriarchal authority. Early scientific definitions of womanhood took up existing Judaeo-Christian definitions of sexuality and femininity, in particular, the assumptions that all women were heterosexual, that women were by definition inferior to men, and that the sole purpose of sexual relations was reproduction.

As secularisation increased so too did the importance ascribed to science and 'rationality'. Science acquired more and more authority as a means of understanding society and the world generally. Its authority was, however, very much a patriarchal one, both by defining women as 'naturally' inferior, and by insisting that science was a male preserve. The crusade against myth and superstition was often expressed by scientists as a fight by men under the banner of rationality and logic against irrational, uncontrollable female forces, and they often described their work in terms of sexuality and sexual conquest. Women could indeed be equal, even superior, spiritually, but the very doctrines of science itself were defining and 'proving' that spirituality was irrelevant, or at least peripheral, to the rational and material world.

Thus spirituality was increasingly defined as the polar opposite to rationality and scientific truth. As truth itself became perceived as wholly scientific, and ultimately male-defined, women came to be seen and defined as wholly inferior to men. Their equality in spiritual matters remained, but as this no longer provided the 'ultimate truth' in the way that science could, it was therefore seen as of little consequence. Thus while science, rationality and truth came to be equated with masculinity and a somewhat revised version of patriarchal authority, so the importance ascribed to religion, as it became 'feminised', also diminished. These debates, of course, were largely limited to the wealthier classes of European society, and at the poorer levels no doubt many of the earlier beliefs and interpretations remained as strong as before.

Increasing scepticism about religion led to a veneration of science (and thus implicitly also of men) and an increasing challenge to the rationale for social and economic inequalities in the eighteenth century. Enlightenment thinkers like Voltaire methodically and rationally set about exposing the extent of social injustice and economic inequality in eighteenth-century Europe, and yet his writings are permeated with assumptions of man's superiority to woman. In *Candide*, the hero is naïve, innocent and inherently honest, good and rational. His exposure to injustice, corruption and vice leads him to be a wiser, fairer and more reasonable man. The heroine (or anti-heroine), while initially innocent, is lured into a love of sexual escapades, wealth and luxury, and sinks into an endless series of sexual misadventures, prostitution, and so on. It is only with the wise guidance of Candide that she eventually comes to accept that the only answer to life's problems is to 'cultiver notre jardin' as Candide's wife. In other words, freedom and experience make men wiser, but make women degenerate, frivolous and in need of male control. The writings of Rousseau, which had an enormous impact on the French Revolution, argued that 'man is born free, yet everywhere he is in chains', that men were essentially good, honest and rational, but were corrupted by an unjust society. Rousseau put forth radical new ideas on childrearing in *Emile*. He argued that children – or rather, boys – should not be beaten into submission, but should be allowed more freedom to explore, investigate and develop 'naturally' with loving guidance from teachers and parents. His romantic notion of education as a means of bringing out the best in children has remained influential to this day. It is worth noting, however, that his ideas for educating Emile were quite different from those he proposed for educating girls in *Sophie* – where girls should learn to be tender, loving, caring and obedient appendages as wives and mothers to the Emiles of the world. These ideas, of course, also remain influential in contemporary educational philosophy. Nevertheless, Rousseau's ideas on children marked a real watershed in notions of childhood.

Increasingly, children came to be seen as essentially good, rather than evil, and the span of childhood and dependence extended into adolescence rather than ceasing at 7 or 8. These were very much middle-class concepts inherent to their new family ideology, yet they were to have far-reaching consequences for the whole of society as legislation restricting children's labour and enforcing education was enacted during the nineteenth century. While it was still ardently believed that children needed careful control and discipline in order to learn to defer to authority, the idea of their essential goodness and innocence meant that ideals of discipline became notably less severe than in the past.

Writers and philosophers of the eighteenth century thus resurrected the problem which had faced sixteenth-century Protestants concerning the conflict between the equality of all in God's eyes versus the inequalities between classes, age groups and sexes. While there were a number of early feminist attacks on prevalent sexual inequalities, the most famous of these was Mary Wollstonecraft who wrote *A Vindication of the Rights of Women*. She spelled out the economic, political and social injustices suffered by women and, though the book was well received in France at the time, it created outrage and derision in Britain. Many women were active in the French Revolution, yet they gained remarkably little from it. The revolutionary leaders, like those of the *ancien régime*, did not want to see women or children anywhere except within a patriarchal household under male control.

The turbulence and rapid changes of the late eighteenth century brought about by the French Revolution, the American Revolution, and the Industrial Revolution caused great fear and disquiet among the ruling classes of Western Europe. Their terror of social, economic and political upheaval elicited various responses in an attempt to reimpose – or reinforce – the existing order. At the heart of these attempts was the desire to reimpose religion, morality and, above all, *authority* to combat what was seen as the polluting forces of disorder and chaos. Science and medicine were harnessed to redefine and reorder society; new divisions were imposed and old ones resurrected and strengthened. As Mary Douglas (1966, p. 4) points out in equating fear of social unrest with pollution and dirt: 'ideas about separating, purifying, demarcating and punishing transgressions have as their main function to impose system on an inherently untidy experience. It is only by exaggerating the difference between within and without, above and below, male and female, with and against, that a semblance of order is created.'

Late eighteenth- and early nineteenth-century Europe and America witnessed an efflorescence of attempts to divide, demarcate and separate – in terms of social class, gender, age, housing, education, industry – all of which were informed by concepts of separation and division, of a reimposition of order. Notions of purity and pollution, dirt and cleanliness, permeated the ever-growing number of books written on household management, childrearing and education, sexuality, and relations between classes, the sexes, and age groups. Servants were to be kept apart from the rest of the family, in contrast with earlier times when they were treated as part of the family, both because they came from a different class and because by now they were mostly female. Fears that servants might pollute or contaminate the rest of the family morally, sexually or medically increased. Children were to be kept apart from adults in separate nurseries. The division between 'public' and 'private' was given greater force than ever with the growing separation of home from work. The ideological differentiation between the public as exclusively male, dangerous and threatening, and the private as female, home-centred, pure and spiritual reinforced material separations and divisions. This new ideology was at one and the same time a redefinition of patriarchal relations between classes, the sexes, and age groups. Just as the working classes were seen as a threat to the middle classes, so it was reaffirmed that men were superior to women except, again, spiritually. Emphasising womanhood as a unique category with its own special characteristics in total contrast to those of manhood, while at the same time stressing the inherent differences between classes, posed the problem as to whether working-class women and middle-class women were in fact almost identical simply because they were women, or whether working-class men and women were the real contrast between middle-class men and women. Middle-class women were for the first time being defined as incapable of work except within the home, yet at the same time working-class women were working in mines, factories, iron foundries and farms. So were working-class children. Their labour, so much cheaper than men's, was indeed a crucial means by which the expanding middle classes were able to make substantial profits from which they could maintain their wives and children as total dependants.

The middle classes tried to resolve this paradox initially in terms of religion, morality and, above all, 'the family'. Increasing emphasis was put on the family itself as a religious and moral institution: 'the family was not only on a par with the church but also analogous in organization and function' (Ryan, 1981, p. 22). The middle classes sanctified 'the family' as something holy, essential, and monolithic. As the Puritans had done, they stressed the importance of a male authority in the household with wife and children both dependent on, and servile to, his needs and desires. The importance of a careful moral education by a morally pure mother was equally stressed. The 'gospel' of the family, as a religious and authoritative institution upon which all order depended, was preached by evangelicals in both Britain and America. Yet it was much more than a religious movement *per se*; both spiritual salvation and temporal order were increasingly defined as only possible through living in a middle-class family structure imbued with middle-class domestic ideals. The values inherent in middle-class domestic ideology were implicitly and explicitly patriarchal. These values influenced a plethora of parliamentary legislation and social policies.

The exclusion of women and young children from working underground in the mines in 1842, for instance, was not a result of concern over physical health or danger so much as a concern with moral danger. Working underground in hot, sweaty conditions, wearing little clothing and, above all, working with men, was seen as the epitome of immorality and potential pollution. Similarly, factory legislation was greatly influenced by the fear of moral danger, particularly the mixing of young unmarried girls with married women and men in close proximity.

Try as they might, however, the middle classes could not escape the fact that the vast majority of working-class children and women had to work in order to survive. Their partial resolution of this conflict between the need to work and the need for women and children as dependants within a patriarchal family was to stress the need for working-class girls to work as domestic servants within middle-class homes. This was, of course, very useful for the middle classes. Kept apart from the rest of the family as far as possible, servants could perform the menial, dirty and demeaning household tasks which might 'pollute' middle-class wives and daughters, and yet at the same time the servants could benefit from being part of a respectable, clean and well-ordered middle-class household. Middle-class wives were expected to teach them not only to be good domestic workers, but also to be moral, pure and clean – an inherent part of which was learning to know and accept their inferior position and the importance of deference, service and dependence. Domestic service was a very common experience for working-class girls; one in three of all girls aged 15–20 in 1881 were working as servants.[4]

Underlying much of the discourse on class, gender and divisions generally was a whole debate on, and attempt to classify and analyse, sexuality. Although most people think of the Victorians as prudish and exercising a total taboo on discussing sexuality, some (Foucault, 1979) have pointed out that in many ways they were obsessed by it. It was very much part of their overall concern with purity and pollution, with divisions and categories. In terms of an ideology of sexuality, the Victorian era witnessed revolutionary changes brought about primarily by scientists and doctors. For the first time women were defined as incapable of sexual excitement or passion. Sexual excitement was defined by many doctors as an exclusively male preserve and power, and because it was inherently male it was therefore totally inappropriate for women. Sexual arousal in girls or women was viewed as a devastating danger; doctors argued that girls who masturbated were in immediate danger of insanity, nymphomania (a word coined in the late eighteenth century), and homosexuality. In the mid-nineteenth century, in a few 'extreme' cases clitoridectomies were performed on middle-class girls and women to 'prevent' their inappropriate sexual propensities, particularly masturbation.

The arguments that women were, or should be, asexual, were put in scientific terms and were thus seen as both 'natural' and 'true'. This was a very real departure from earlier thinkers who had always accorded women much greater sexual desire than men. Montaigne had written in the sixteenth century that 'no normal man with a normal penis could hope to satisfy a normal woman' (Easlea, 1981, p. 78). Why did attitudes change so dramatically? Apart from the general obsession with classification, it can be seen as the logical solution to the dilemma posed by Protestantism and, indeed, by Christianity. For if women were spiritually equal, but not temporally, then there must be a sharp division between body and soul. If women reigned supreme, or at least equal, in the sphere of the soul, then it followed logically that men reigned supreme in the physical and temporal. Since sexuality was defined as by nature *physical*, it therefore followed that it was an exclusively male preserve and trait. Thus for a woman to be sexual was a denial of all womanhood and 'feminine nature'. Sexual women were regarded as pathologically ill. What had once been defined as 'sin' now became defined as 'sick'.

Yet because heterosexuality was seen as an essential need for men, and was also necessary for biological reproduction, it was women's duty to 'put up with' their husbands' sexual desires and thence be able to fulfil their real role of mother. Women had to 'receive' and tolerate men's sexual needs as part of the service they owed them. Women, as passive and asexual objects serving to receive their husbands' lust, symbolised the rigidity of the concept of patriarchal authority. A woman who refused to serve her husband sexually, no matter how repugnant the idea to her, was denying the very foundations of patriarchal authority. Viewed in this way, the rationale for the unequal treatment of women in cases of adultery, rape, incest and homosexuality – both past and present – becomes apparent. For it is in sexual relations that the essence of patriarchy – the power relations between men and women and between adults and children – becomes manifest.

Western religious and scientific ideology has stressed women as either passive (the ideal) or as lustful and sinful (the fear). Submitting to a man, or father, is part of the authority structure of patriarchal ideology. A woman who is raped is at one and the same time supposed to be passive and is immediately suspected of enticing the rapist. Refusing a man's sexual wishes – whether husband, father, or rapist – is immediately challenging his authority. If she gives in and accepts the situation to protect her life, the patriarchal assumption of Church and State agencies has been that this implies consent.

There have been severe laws to penalise rape since Anglo-Saxon times, yet prosecution has always been minimal. Close examination of the laws reveals that they have basically not been to protect the woman, but to protect her as the *property* of her father or husband. Thus prosecution for rape has been more successful if a woman was a virgin living at home or a married woman. Women outside patriarchal households – spinsters, widows, separated or divorced women – are taken less seriously, and are assumed to have 'invited' rape. Any sign of 'immoral' qualities in terms of dress, language or behaviour, have similarly tended to result in failure of a raped woman's prosecution.

Until recently a similar 'double-bind' has existed with regard to incest. Because children, like wives, were defined as a man's *property*, and because his authority in the family was backed up by Church and State, a man's sexual relations with his children (usually daughters), while not actually endorsed, were seldom challenged or penalised. Incest was not made illegal until 1908. Incest, rape, and physical violence towards wives and children are all the logical conclusion to an unequal power relationship defined in terms of male authority within the family. Violence within families is the raw end of patriarchy and patriarchal relations. The persistence of incest, violence and rape in modern society bears witness to the persistence of patriarchy, even though wives and children are no longer defined as a man's property.

Victorian doctors and scientists also imposed strict rules on men's sexuality. While men's passion was accepted as a natural need (unlike women's), it was still deemed essential that their passion should be very carefully controlled. Masturbation was regarded as a terrible evil which was bound to lead to 'feebleness of mind', insanity, epilepsy, and homosexuality. Semen was believed to be an essential source of energy, the wasting of which would lead to the ultimate downfall of boy or man. Control of male sexuality was frequently described in monetaristic terms, arguing that it was more prudent to 'save' sperm than to 'spend' it unwisely – and, of course, we now have sperm banks. Carefully saved, or invested, sperm would produce healthier and more intelligent children, while control and abstinence would provide a man with more energy to direct into business activities. Intercourse more than once a week was to be avoided at all costs. The analogies with money-making and saving suggest how the ideology of sexuality and sexual relations was informing business matters, as much as the latter were influencing ideas of sexuality. Both were aspects of a world obsessed with control, definition and division. The denial of women's sexuality can also be seen as part of the denial of her access to business and the 'public' world. Notions of gender and sexuality informed and influenced definitions of social class, just as social class influenced and defined definitions of gender and sexuality. Bound up with both was an implicit notion of patriarchy.

The new middle-class ideology of domesticity and the family did not, however, go unchallenged. In the early nineteenth century others were already trying to formulate new ways of social organisation that embraced earlier notions of the equality of all. Foremost among these was Robert Owen. The Owenite socialist movement of the 1830s and 1840s argued for a society based on real equality both between classes and between the sexes. Their goals included

the establishment of a worldwide network of Communities of Mutual Association, all institutional and ideological impediments to sexual equality would disappear, including oppressive marriage laws, privatised households, and private ownership of wealth. The nuclear family (which was held to be responsible not only for the direct subordination of women to men but also for the inculcation of 'competitive ideology') would be abolished and

replaced by communal homes and collective child-rearing ...
housework ... would be performed on a rotational basis. (Taylor,
1981b, p. 158)

Owenite socialism emphasised the importance of restructuring
the political, economic and gender systems, and thereby challenged
hierarchical patriarchal concepts of dependence and service.
Owenite women, in particular, challenged the acceptance of patriarchal authority by working-class men: 'The working men com-
plain that the masters exercise authority over them; and they
maintain their right to associate, and prescribe laws for their own
protection ... but speak of any project which will diminish the
authority of the male, or give him an equal, where once he found an
inferior, and then the spirit of Toryism awakes' (ibid., p. 159).
Women were thus explicitly demanding a change from their dual
dependence and exploitation by both the socio-economic system
and male domination within marriage and families. In so doing they
were challenging the whole social order as well as resurrecting
earlier dilemmas of the equality of all. Others, such as Charles
Fourier, Ann Lee who founded the Shakers, and John Noyes who
established the Oneida Community, similarly challenged patriarchy
and patriarchal definitions of women and the family.

As the skilled working class became increasingly organised,
women's work became more marginalised into the unskilled and
unorganised sectors. Thus Chartism, and later socialism influenced
by Marx and Engels, put most emphasis on the class struggle and
peripheralised the struggle for sexual equality. Although Marx and
Engels took note of the exploitation of women through the
'bourgeois family' system, this, they argued, was entirely a result of
property relations, the abolition of which would automatically
result in an end to bourgeois families and thus to sexual inequalities.
They ignored the importance of patriarchal relations throughout
history. Marx claimed that under communism 'man will be able to
fish in the morning, hunt in the afternoon and criticise in the
evening' (Marx and Engels, 1977). But who was to cook the fish and
meat, do the washing up and mend the socks? In attempting to claim
his theories to be scientific, Marx embraced many masculinist
notions of authority inherent in the concept of science. The political
struggle of the classes was seen as a male struggle.

The nineteenth century also witnessed a polemical controversy among biologists, anthropologists and scientists generally about the origins of male dominance, families, and whether society might have at some earlier time been ruled by women (see Coward, 1983). Darwin argued that male dominance, sexual jealousy and parental love were universal attributes of all societies, while others saw these as resulting from private property. Increasingly, however, there was a tendency to claim that both the animal and the human world were made up of 'natural' procreative units. The concept of 'nature', as well as that of evolution, came to take paramount significance. Sexuality was defined as natural and instinctive (meaning, of course, *hetero*sexuality). Marriage was seen as the crucial dividing point between 'nature' and 'culture'. The implications of this were that anything other than heterosexual relations was unnatural and pathological.

These notions were informed by the theory of the 'survival of the fittest' and also by eugenicist arguments that it was important to keep the race 'pure', strong and fit through careful breeding. These claims reinforced, and were reinforced by, the theories of sexuality discussed earlier. By emphasising the importance of careful breeding and the 'natural' aspect of male heterosexuality they also gave further credence to patriarchal authority. It was assumed that men's natural instincts and women's role as mothers of a pure race needed to occur within the 'natural procreative unit' of the family.

Nineteenth-century science thus gave the ideology of the nuclear family a scientific buttress in terms of nature and universality. It gave scientific status to the ideology which bourgeois families had been advocating as moral and religious from the late eighteenth century. Failure to comply with this model was seen as dangerous and threatening to society. Much of bourgeois family ideology was enshrined in legislation relating to marriage, sexuality and women's and children's labour, but also became an inherent part of medical ideology and practice. Women who did not conform to this model, or who challenged it, were seen as unnatural or insane. Those who dared to seek educational reform and political reform were warned of the damages education could do to their reproductive abilities, their menstrual flow, and their ability to be good mothers. Those who never married, whether through lack of opportunity or through choice, were pitied, scorned, and peripheralised.

At the end of the nineteenth century another revolution in the ideology of sexuality occurred. Sigmund Freud challenged earlier ideas of both women's and children's asexuality and the assumed 'natural' heterosexual instinct by arguing that all children, boys and girls, are initially bisexual: 'instead of masculinity and femininity assumed as irradicably different somatic and psychic states, Freud advanced a non-essentialist theory of sexuality. He insisted that the sexual behaviour of children of both sexes was indistinguishable. The infant is initially bisexual; there is no given object of the sexual drive. The child is, in fact, "polymorphously perverse", seeking all forms of sensual gratification' (Coward, 1983, p. 192). Freud thus returned to women and children their sexuality. The problem was, however, that if all children were initially bisexual, how did this become a 'heterosexual drive'?

Freud's answer was that in the early years of life the girl had to learn to change and redirect the nature and object of her sexual desires; she must first 'undergo a very radical change in the *form* of her sexuality – from active to passive, from clitoral to vaginal. Second, she must undergo a very radical change in the *object* of her desire – from mother or woman to man. This ... is the point of no return for biologism. No longer can the theory retain any notion of the essential attraction of each sex for the other, or of the essential antagonism for the same sex.'[5]

For Freud this change was essentially the change from nature to culture. Heterosexuality, the acknowledgement of paternity, exogamy and a prohibition on incest formed the basis of kinship and society. Freud thus embraced the idea of patriarchy and heterosexuality within the family as the basis of civilisation, yet his theory was revolutionary in that this claim was not based on an assumption that these were natural, but that they were inherently social. He also argued that these were universal characteristics of all families at all points in time, and assumed a patriarchal form of authority within all families. He did not account for the wide variety of forms which families and households take in other cultures, nor could the theory account for cultures in which paternity was not recognised. Basically, he assumed that the bourgeois family of nineteenth-century Europe was a universal form, and thus also implicitly assumed that patriarchal relations were universal. Nevertheless, the theory was revolutionary in the way in which it challenged earlier theories of heterosexuality and gave indirect credence to the idea that inequalities between the sexes are socially constructed and thus potentially changeable and challengeable. It also revolutionised concepts of childhood and childrearing.

The nineteenth century produced a number of theories of sexuality, male domination and 'the family'. The conflict between the concept of the equality of all men and women, and the notion that women should be dependent on and subservient to men took on new scientific, medical and political dimensions. In some ways the conflict became more open and politicised. From the middle of the nineteenth century onwards, feminists increasingly challenged many patriarchal assumptions, particularly with regards to women's and children's status as men's legal property, to divorce and the 'double standard' of men's sexuality, whereby men could indulge in adultery without being penalised while women could not. Women began to demand the right to a good education, access to the universities and professions, the right to better jobs generally, and, of course, the right to vote. Middle-class feminists tended to be more concerned with gaining educational and political equality with men, while working-class feminists were more concerned with improving women's economic situation and getting equal pay. The challenge to patriarchy was certainly there, and gained momentum during the latter half of the century, reaching a climax in the suffragette campaign. Women's resistance to patriarchy was seen as increasingly threatening by a number of men.

Fears about 'unfeminine' women, about the falling birth rate (which had begun among the middle classes in the 1860s) and about a 'threat' to the family were increasing. At the same time, socialism was gaining in strength as a political force and was also seen by those in power as highly dangerous to the *status quo*. World recession after the First World War added fuel to these fires of fear which resulted in a right-wing backlash against socialism and feminism (as in the 1980s), and took political shape in the Fascist movement during the inter-war period. Although most obvious in Nazism, all western conservative leaders were expressing concern with issues of race, reproduction and eugenics, and the fear of socialism and feminism was by no means specific to Fascism.

The Nazi movement defined itself as being in total opposition to what were seen as the decadence and immorality of feminists, Marxists and socialists. It was an extreme reaction against notions of equality and co-operation, and in contrast to these put great stress on the virtues of heroic male leaders, on war and warriors, and of a 'pure' race. Inherent and explicit in their ideology were ideals of patriarchal authority consigning women to the role of dependants, servers of men and reproducers of the Aryan race. The habit of taking psychological differences between men and women for granted reinforced assumptions about irrevocable divisions between Jew and 'Aryan'. In place of class, cultural, religious divisions, race and sex became the predominant social markers. (Koonz, 1988, p. 6) Weakness of any sort was seen as a threat to social and political order and to the race itself.

To these ends the Act for the Prevention of Hereditary Diseased Offspring in 1933 made sterilisation compulsory for all suffering from 'physical malformation, mental retardation, epilepsy, imbecility, deafness or blindness' (Easlea, 1981). Birth control clinics were closed, abortion made illegal, and while the fit were exhorted to reproduce prolifically, the unfit were sterilised. By 1939, approximately 375 000 people had been sterilised. Women were told in no uncertain terms that their place was in the home, serving their warrior men and reproducing Aryan children. This ideology of 'Kinder, Küche, Kirche', however, had only limited success because of the urgent need for women's labour in the economy as a result of the chronic labour shortage.[6]

Many of the nineteenth-century scientific and philosophical debates were used by the Nazis to justify their policies. Nietzsche and Darwin gave them particular force. The problem of the 'purity' of the race was an echo of fears of pollution, dirt and disease expressed by the Victorian middle classes when they perceived themselves threatened by political and social upheavals. Poverty, unemployment and political resistance struck terror in the hearts of the Nazi ruling classes just as they had with their forebears. The reaction in both instances was a frantic attempt to drive out disorder and pollution and to embrace hierarchical authority based on patriarchal values. The result, as we all know, was the mass murder of 11 million people selected as 'undesirable'.

Thus patriarchal values arise in, and are inculcated in, families, yet they are not specific to families. They permeate and influence society at all levels: political, economic, ideological and familial. Defined earlier in religious terms, then in scientific and medical terms, the form they have taken has been variable, but the essence lies in a concept of a social order premised on a male, but particularly paternal, authority which by definition presupposes the dependence and service of women, children and other 'inferiors'. At the root of the concept are notions of inequality, subordination and dependence.

The locus for unequal relations between men and women and adults and children is perceived as lying in 'the family'. As such, the family has become a vital and central symbol to notions of authority, inequality and deference. The symbolic importance of the family cannot be underestimated, for it goes beyond political allegiances of left or right and has arguably come to be seen as the most important institution of modern industrial society. The problem, however, is that it is seen as an institution grounded in reality rather than as a symbol-system or ideology. What orators *say* about the family is frequently very far removed from how men, women and children actually live out their lives. It is thus necessary to re-examine elements of the concept of family in more depth, trying to disentangle the ideological elements from the material and structural elements of people's living arrangements.

3

What is the family? Is it universal?

Until recently, most sociological studies of the family have been
dominated by functionalist definitions of what the family is and
what 'needs' it fulfils in society. Functionalists' theories of the
family are treated elsewhere at length (Morgan, 1975; Gittins,
1982), but it is worth examining some of their main assumptions
briefly. Generally, functionalists have argued that the family is a
universal institution which performs certain specific functions essential to society's survival. Murdock, for instance, defined the
family as a 'social group characterised by common residence,
economic co-operation, and reproduction. It includes adults of both
sexes, at least two of whom maintain a socially approved sexual
relationship, and one or more children, own or adopted, of the
sexually cohabiting adults'.[1] The four basic functions of the family,
therefore, are seen as: common residence; economic co-operation;
reproduction; sexuality. Let us examine each of these in more
detail.

Household is the term normally used to refer to co-residence.
Murdock's assumption is that it is also a defining characteristic of
'the family', and vice versa. It is generally assumed that a married
couple, or parent and child(ren) will form a household, and that
family implies and presupposes 'household'. Yet this is by no means
always so. Margaret Mead (1971) showed how Samoan children
chose the household where they wanted to reside, and often
changed their residence again later. Sibling households – or fré-
rèches – were common in parts of Europe, and are a dominant form
of household among the Ashanti (Bender, 1979, p. 494).

There are numerous examples in contemporary society of

families who do not form households, or only form households for periods of time. Families where the husband is in the armed services, is a travelling salesman or travels frequently abroad may only have the husband/father resident for short periods of time. Families where partners have jobs some distance away from one another may maintain a second household where one of them lives during the week. Children who are sent to boarding school may spend little more than a third of the year residing with their parent(s).

Gutman (1976) found that it was common among black slave families in the USA for a husband and wife to live on different plantations and see one another for a few hours once or twice a week. Soliende de Gonzalez found this type of household very common in Black Carib society: 'there are groupings which I have called "dispersed families" in which the father, although absent for long periods of time, retains ultimate authority over a household for which he provides the only support, and where affective bonds continue to be important between him and his wife and children' (1965, p. 1544). Obviously people can consider themselves 'family' without actually co-residing, and can also co-reside without considering themselves to be 'family'.

On the other hand, households might be characterised by a shared set of activities such as sleeping, food preparation, eating, sexual relations, and caring for those who cannot care for themselves. Some have argued that household can be defined to some extent in terms of a range of domestic activities. 'Sharing the same pot' has traditionally been the boundary drawn by census enumerators for demarcating one household from another. Yet these activities need not necessarily, and often do not, occur within one household. Some members of a household may eat there all the time, while others only part of the time. Similarly, as mentioned before, some members may not always sleep in the household for a majority of the time. They may well consider themselves notwithstanding to be a family. Conversely, prisoners eat and sleep under the same roof, but do not consider themselves to be a family.

There is no hard and fast rule, much less a definition in universal terms, that can be applied to household in terms of domestic activities. Whether in modern industrial society or in Africa or Asia 'there is no basis for assuming that such activities as sleeping, eating, child-rearing and sexual relations must form a complex and must always occur under one roof' (Smith, 1978, p. 339). Household is thus in some ways just as nebulous a term as family, although it lacks the ideological implications that 'family' carries.

Murdock further posits 'economic co-operation' as a defining characteristic of all families. This is a very broad term and can encompass a wide range of activities from cooking to spinning to resources in terms of people and skills. Economic co-operation is something which can, and does, occur throughout all levels of society and is not specific to the family. Economic co-operation frequently occurs *between* households as well as between individuals within households. Undoubtedly households do entail an economic relationship in various ways; in particular, they entail the distribution, production and allocation of resources. Resources include food, drink, material goods, but also service, care, skills, time and space. The notion of 'co-operation', moreover, implies an equal distribution of resources, yet this is seldom so. Allocating food, space, time and tasks necessitates some kind of a division of labour; different tasks need doing every day and may vary by week and by season. The number of people living together will be finite but also changeable – not just in terms of numbers, but also in terms of age, sex, marital status, physical capacity.

All resources are finite and some may be extremely scarce; some form of allocation therefore has to occur, and this presupposes power relationships. Food, work, and space are rarely distributed equally between co-residing individuals, just as they differ between households and social sectors. Most frequently, the allocation of resources and division of labour is based on differences according to sex and age. Rather than using Murdock's definition of 'economic co-operation', it is thus more useful to understand families in terms of the ways in which gender and age define, and are defined by, the division of labour within, and beyond, households. These divisions also presuppose power relationships and inequality – in effect, patriarchy – rather than co-operation and equality.

Power relationships define and inform concepts of sexuality, Murdock's third defining category. His definition of sexuality is *hetero*sexuality, although this is only one of various forms of sexuality. Presumably this is because the final – and perhaps most important – 'function' of families as seen by such theorists is reproduction, which necessitates heterosexual relations, at least at times. Sexuality is not something specific to families; rather, the assumption is that heterosexuality *should* be a defining characteristic of families. It also, according to Murdock, presupposes a 'socially approved relationship' between two adults.

Social recognition of mating and of parenthood is obviously intimately bound up with social definitions and customs of marriage. It is often assumed that, in spite of a variety of marriage customs and laws, marriage as a binding relationhip between a man and a woman is universal. Yet it has been estimated that only 10 per cent of all marriages in the world are actually monogamous; polyandry and polygyny are common in many societies, just as serial monogamy is becoming increasingly common in our own. Marriage is not always a heterosexual relationship; among the Nuer, older women marry younger women. The Nuer also practise a custom known as 'ghost marriages', whereby when an unmarried or childless man dies, a relation of his then marries a woman 'to his name' and the resulting children of this union are regarded as the dead man's children and bear his name (see Edholm, 1982, p. 172).

Marriage customs are not only variable between cultures and over time, but also vary between social classes. Moreover, Jessie Bernard (1973) has shown that the meanings which men and women attribute to the same marriage differ quite markedly. Undoubtedly marriage involves some form of status passage and public avowal of recognising other(s) as of particular importance in one way or another, yet it does not occur universally between two people, nor between two people of the opposite sex, nor is it always viewed as linked to reproduction. Marriage, in the way in which we think of it, is therefore not universal.

Similarly, definitions of sexuality with regard to incest have not been universal or unchanging. In medieval Europe it was considered incestuous to have sexual relations with anyone less than a seventh cousin, and marriage between cousins was proscribed. Now it is possible to marry first cousins. In Egypt during the Pharaonic and Ptolemaic period sibling marriages were permitted, and, in some cases, father–daughter marriages. This was seen as a way of preserving the purity of royalty and was not endorsed for the whole of society – although it was permitted for everyone after the Roman conquest of Egypt.

Incestuous marriages were also permitted among royal families in Hawaii and Peru. The Mormons of Utah allowed incest (and polygamy) as a means of ensuring marriage within their church; this was not banned until 1892 (Renvoize, 1982, p. 32). Obviously these examples are more related to marriage customs and inheritance or descent problems, but serve to illustrate that even an incest taboo cannot be taken as a universal defining characteristic of families: 'who could Adam's sons marry except their sisters?' (ibid., p. 32). Nevertheless, the almost universal existence of some form of incest taboo is a useful illustration of the fact that all societies do, in a myriad of ways, have some form of social organisation of sexuality, mating and reproduction.

Murdock's definition does not take adequate account of the diversity of ways in which co-residence, economic relations, sexuality and reproduction can be organised. Various theorists have made amendments and refinements to Murdock's definition of the family, but all tend to make similar errors. In particular, they translate contemporary western (and usually middle-class) ideas and ideals of what a family should be into what they assume it is everywhere.

Far more precise attempts at definition and analysis have been made by anthropologists who prefer the term kinship to that of family. A feminist anthropologist recently defined kinship as 'the ties which exist between individuals who are seen as related both through birth (descent) and through mating (marriage). It is thus primarily concerned with the ways in which mating is socially organised and regulated, the ways in which parentage is assigned, attributed and recognised, descent is traced, relatives are classified, rights are transferred across generations and groups are formed' (Edholm, 1982, p. 166). This definition of kinship is a vast improvement on functionalist definitions of family because, first, it stresses the fact that kinship is a social construction, and, second, it emphasises the variability of kinship depending on how it is defined. The social nature of kinship has been stressed by many others elsewhere,[2] and yet there remains a strong common-sense belief that kinship is in fact a quite straightforward biological relationship. It is not.

We assume that because we (think we) know who our parents are and how they made us that kinship is therefore a biological fact. Consider, however, stories we have all heard about children who were brought up by parent(s) for perhaps twenty years, who all along believed their parents were their biological parents, but then discovered that they had in fact been adopted. Such people often suffer severe 'identity crises' because they no longer know 'who they are' or who their parents are. Their suffering is caused by the way in which we define kinship in our society, namely, in strictly biological terms, differentiating clearly between a 'biological' and a 'social' parent. The biological parent is always seen by our society as the 'real' parent with whom a child should have the strongest ties and bonds. Knowledge of parenthood through families is the central way in which individuals are 'located' socially and economically in western society. This, however, is a culturally and historically specific way of defining parenthood and kinship. Other cultures and groups in modern society believe that the person who rears a child is by definition the real parent, regardless of who was involved in the actual reproduction process.

In many poor families in Western Europe and America well into this century it was not uncommon for children to be raised by a grandparent, other kin, or friend, and such children often thought of those who raised them as their parents, even though acknowledging that they also had biological parents who were different. R. T. Smith found such practices common in Guyana and Jamaica, and reports how 'close and imperishable bonds are formed through the act of "raising" children, irrespective of genetic ties ... What is erroneously termed "fictive kinship" is a widespread phenomenon ... while a father may be defined minimally as the person whose genetic material mingled with that of the mother in the formation of the child during one act of sexual intercourse the father "role" varies a good deal in any but the most homogeneous societies' (1978, p. 353).

Others have shown the ways in which kinship is a social construction, and how those who are not biologically related to one another come to define themselves as kin: 'Liebow, Stack, Ladner and others describe fictive kinship, by which friends are turned into family. Since family is supposed to be more reliable than friendship, "going for brothers", "for sisters", "for cousins", increases the commitment of a relationship, and makes people ideally more responsible for one another. Fictive kinship is a serious relationship' (Rapp, 1980, p. 292). It is possible to argue that this is how all kinship began and becomes constructed. Kinship, whether we choose to label it as 'biological', 'social' or 'fictive' is a way of identifying others as in some way special from the rest, people to whom the individual or collectivity feel responsible in certain ways. It is a method of demarcating obligations and responsibility between individuals and groups.

It is thus essential to get away from the idea that kinship is a synonym for 'blood' relations – *even though it may often be expressed in those terms* – and to think of it as a social construction which is highly variable and flexible. Some anthropologists recently have argued that kinship is no more and no less than a system of meanings and symbols and that it is 'absolutely distinct from a biological system or a system of biological reproduction. Animals reproduce, mate, and undoubtedly form attachments to each other, but they do not have kinship systems' (Smith, 1978, p. 351). Indeed, just as Marx argued that it is labour that distinguishes people from animals, it could equally be argued that it is kinship systems that do just that.

This is not to say that many kinship relations do not have some sort of biological base – many do – but the fact that not all of them do, and that the type of base is highly variable, means that it cannot be assumed that there is some universal biological base to kinship. There is not. As Edholm (1982, p. 168) argues: 'notions of blood ties, of biological connection, which to us seem relatively unequivocal, are highly variable. Some societies of which we have anthropological record recognize only the role of the father or of the mother in conception and procreation . . . Only one parent is a "relation", the other is not. In the Trobriand Islands . . . it is believed that intercourse is not the cause of conception, semen is not seen as essential for conception . . . (but) from the entry of a spirit child into the womb . . . it is the repeated intercourse of the same partner which "moulds" the child.'

Because fatherhood is always potentially unknown, and always potentially contestable, it is therefore also always a social category. Motherhood, on the other hand, is always known. Yet apart from carrying and giving birth to a child, the biological base of motherhood stops there. The rest is socially constructed, although it may be – and often is – attributed to biology or 'maternal instinct'. Whether or not women breastfeed their children has been historically and culturally variable. Baby bottles are no modern invention, but were used in ancient Egypt and in other cultures since. Historians have noted the number of babies given to 'wet nurses' in earlier times in Europe as a sign of lack of love and care for infants on the part of mothers. But we can never really know the emotions felt by people hundreds of years ago or their motivations for their practices. The most we can do is to note that their customs were different. To use our own ideology of motherhood and love and apply it universally to all cultures is a highly ethnocentric and narrow way of trying to understand other societies.

Notions of motherhood and 'good mothering' are highly variable:

in Tahiti young women often have one or two children before
they are considered, or consider themselves to be, ready for an
approved and stable relationship. It is considered perfectly acceptable for the children of this young woman to be given to her
parents or other close kin for adoption ... The girl can decide
what her relationship to the children will be, but there is no sense
in which she is forced into 'motherhood' because of having had a
baby. (Edholm, 1982, p. 170)

Who cares for children and rears them is also variable, although in
most cases it is women who do so rather than men. Often those
women who rear children may well claim some kinship tie to the
biological mother – for example, grandmother or aunt, but this tie
may simply be created as a result of rearing another woman's child.
Motherhood, therefore, if taken to mean both bearing and rearing
children, is not universal and is not a biological 'fact'.

Nor can it be argued that there is such a thing as maternal
'instinct', although it is commonly believed to exist. Women are
capable of conceiving children today from the age of 13 or 14, and
can continue to bear children approximately every two years until
they are 45 or 50. This could mean producing around eighteen or
nineteen children (although fecundity declines as women age), and
this, of course, seldom occurs. Few women in western society marry
before they are 18 or 19, and few women in contemporary society
have more than two or three children. Contraceptives control
conception, not instincts, and unless it were argued that women are
forced to use contraceptives,[3] there is little scope to argue for such a
thing as maternal instinct.

Consider further that women who conceive babies now when
they are *not* married are not hailed as true followers of their natural
instinct, but are considered as 'immoral', 'loose', 'whores', and so
on. As Antonis (1981, p. 59) notes: 'maternal instinct is ascribed to
married women only.' That women can conceive and bear children
is a universal phenomenon; that they do so by instinct is a fallacy. So
is the notion that they always raise them. From the moment of birth
motherhood is a social construction.

Sociological and historical studies of the family have tended to
pay most attention to the vertical relationships between parents and
children. Less attention is paid to the lateral relationships between

siblings. Yet in other cultures, and in Western Europe in earlier times, the sibling tie has often formed the basis of households and may be seen as more important than that between parent and child. Among the poorer sectors of western society until quite recently it was common for the eldest daughter to take responsibility for supervising and caring for younger siblings from quite an early age, thereby freeing her mother to engage in waged or domestic work. This remains common in many contemporary societies. In Morocco, for instance, girls 'from the age of about four onwards look after younger siblings, fetch and carry, clean and run errands. The tasks themselves are arranged in a hierarchy of importance and attributed to women and girls according to their authority within the household ... Boys tend to be freed from domestic tasks and spend their time in groups of peers who play marbles or trap birds' (Maher, 1981, pp. 73–4).

The content and importance of sibling ties varies, and this is partly a result of different interpretations of reproduction. In societies where the role of the male is seen as peripheral or unimportant – or even non-existent – in reproduction, then his children by another woman are not seen as having any relation to those of the first mother, or vice versa if the mother's role is seen as unimportant. The salience of sibling ties also depends on the organisation of kinship generally. The relative neglect of studying sibling ties as an important aspect of – or even basis of – kinship betrays our own assumptions about the primacy of parenthood in families and, particularly, the assumption that reproduction is the 'essence' of kinship, with the mother and child forming the universal core of kinship. As Yanagisako (1977, pp. 197–8) points out in writing about Goodenough: 'while he is undoubtedly right that in every human society mothers and children can be found, to view their *relationship* as the universal nucleus of the family is to attribute to it a social and cultural significance that is lacking in some cases.'

Implicit in definitions of kinship is a way of perceiving the social organisation of reproduction and mating, at the centre of which therefore is an organisation of relations between the sexes. The organisation of, and differentiation between, male and female takes many different forms, but all societies do have a social construction of the sexes into gender. Gender is an inherent part of the manner in which all societies are organised and is also a crucial part of the different ways in which kinship has been constructed and defined. The social, economic and political organisation of societies has been initially at least based on kinship – and thus also on gender. Understanding society means understanding the ways in which a society organised kinship and gender, and how these influence one another. Gender and kinship are universally present – as are mothers and children – but the content of them, and the meanings ascribed to them, is highly variable.

The most basic divisions of labour within any society, as pointed out by Durkheim (1933) and others, are based on age and sex. While age as a category can eventually be achieved, sex is ascribed, permanent, and immutable. The biological differences between men and women are such that only women can conceive and lactate; only men can impregnate. In spite of these obvious differences, none of them is great enough to be adequate grounds for allocating one kind of work to women and another to men. Indeed, cross-culturally and historically there are very few jobs that can be claimed to be specifically and universally performed by either men or women. Women have ploughed and mined and still do; men have laundered, gathered fruit and minded children. Hunting and warfare have almost always been male activities, while care of the young and sick has usually been a female activity. But allocation of tasks is also strongly based on age, so it is important to remember that it may be *young* men who hunt and *old* men or women who care for children; old women may be responsible for cooking, while both young men and women may work in the fields or mines.

Age is an important factor to consider in trying to understand the organisation of kinship and households. Nobody remains the same age – contrary to contemporary images in the media of the 'happy family' where the couple is permanently 30 and the children forever 8 and 6. As individuals age, so the composition and structure of the unit in which they live change. Consider the ways in which the household composition and resources of a couple change as , first, aged 20, they marry and both work; second, aged 25, they have had two children and the wife has left the labour market for a few years to rear the children until they attend school; third, at 30, one partner leaves or dies and one parent is left with total care of the children; fourth, at 35, one or both may remarry someone who perhaps has three children from an earlier marriage, or may take in an elderly parent to care for, and so on. The number of wage earners and dependants changes over a household's cycle, just as it changes for the individuals within the household.

Thinking in terms of 'the' family leads to a static vision of how people actually live and age together and what effects this process has on others within the household in which they live. Moreover, the environment and conditions in which any household is situated are always changing, and these changes can and often do have important repercussions on individuals and households. As Tamara Hareven (1982) points out, it is important when analysing families to differentiate between individual time, family time, and historical time. Thus in considering the structure and meaning of 'family' in any society it is important to understand how definitions of dependency and individual time vary and change, how patterns of interaction between individuals and households change, and how historical developments affect all of these.

The notion of there being such a thing as 'the family' is thus highly controversial and full of ambiguities and contradictions. Childbearing, childrearing, the construction of gender, allocation of resources, mating and marriage, sexuality and ageing all loosely fit into our idea of family, and yet we have seen how all of them are variable over time, between cultures and between social sectors. The claim that 'the family' is universal has been especially problematic because of the failure by most to differentiate between how small groups of people live and work together, and what the ideology of appropriate behaviour for men, women and children within families has been.

Imbued in western patriarchal ideology, as discussed previously, are a number of important and culturally specific beliefs about sexuality, reproduction, parenting and the power relationships between age groups and between the sexes. The sum total of these beliefs make up a strong *symbol-system which is labelled as the family.* Now while it can be argued that all societies have beliefs and rules on mating, sexuality, gender and age relations, the content of rules is culturally and historically specific and variable, and in no way universal. Thus to claim that patriarchy is universal is as meaningless as claiming that the family is universal.

If defining families is so difficult, how do we try to understand how and why people live, work and form relationships together in our own society? First, we need to acknowledge that while what we may think of as families are not universal, there are still trends and patterns specific to our culture which, by careful analysis, we can understand more fully. Second, we can accept that while there can be no perfect definition, it is still possible to discover certain defining characteristics which can help us to understand changing patterns of behaviour and beliefs. Finally, and most important, we can 'deconstruct' assumptions usually made about families by questioning what exactly they mean. Before doing this, however, it is useful to attempt some definition of what is meant by 'family' in western society.

Problematic though it may be, it is necessary to retain the notion of co-residence, because most people have lived, and do live, with others for much of their lives. Thus 'household' is useful as a defining characteristic, while bearing in mind that it does not necessarily imply sexual or intimate relationships, and that, moreover, relationships *between* households are a crucial aspect of social interaction. 'Household' should not be interpreted as a homogeneous and undivided unit. Virtually all households will have their own division of labour, generally based on ideals and beliefs, as well as the structure, of age and sex. There will always tend to be power relationships within households, because they will almost invariably be composed of different age and sex groups and thus different individuals will have differential access to various resources.

Because the essence of any society is interaction, a society will always be composed of a myriad of relationships between people, from the most casual to the most intimate. Relationships are formed between people of the same sex, the opposite sex, the same age group, different age groups, the same and different classes, and so on. Some of these relationships will be sexual – and sexual relations can occur in any type of relationship. Some relationships will be affectionate and loving, others will be violent or hostile. They may be made up of very brief encounters or may extend over the best part of a person's life-cycle. Thus while relationships are extremely varied in the ways in which they are formed, their nature and duration, *ideologically* western society has given highest status to long-term relationships between men and women, and between parents and children. Ideologically, such relationships are supposed to be loving and caring, though in reality many are not. They are presented as 'natural', but as we have seen, they are not. These ideals have become reified and sanctified in the notion of 'family', virtually to the exclusion of all other long-term or intimate relationships.

Ideals of family relationships have become enshrined in our legal, social, religious and economic systems which, in turn, reinforce the ideology and penalise or ostracise those who transgress it. Thus there are very real pressures on people to behave in certain ways, to lead their lives according to acceptable norms and patterns. Patriarchal ideology is embedded in our socio-economic and political institutions, indeed, in the very language we use, and as such encourages, cajoles and pressurises people to follow certain paths. Most of these are presented and defined in terms of 'the family', and the family is in turn seen as the bulwark of our culture. The pressures of patriarchal ideology are acted out – and reacted against – in our inter-personal relationships, in marriage and non-marriage, in love and hate, having children and not having children. In short, much of our social behaviour occurs in, and is judged on the basis of, the ideology of 'the family'.

Relationships are universal, so is some form of co-residence, of intimacy, sexuality and emotional bonds. But the *forms* these can take are infinitely variable and can be changed and challenged as well as embraced. By analysing the ways in which culture has prescribed certain, and proscribed other, forms of behaviour, it should be possible to begin to see the historical and cultural specificity of what is really meant when reference is made to 'the family'.

4

Why do people marry?

The proportion of people who were married by the age of fifty in Britain fell from 96 per cent in 1971 to 83 per cent in 1987. Nearly 40 per cent of marriages now end in divorce. In 1989 36 per cent of all marriages were remarriages for a least one partner. Thus while an increasing number of people never marry and some may experience married life for only a short period of time, marriage is still a very popular institution. If, however, you ask people *why* they marry, their responses tend to be very vague, to the effect that 'it just happened', or 'we were in love, or 'everybody does'. Considering the serious vows that are taken in marriage, and the difficulties and pain of getting out of marriage, it seems puzzling that people lack more concrete reasons than the ones usually given. Arguably this is a result of historical developments and social forces which have made it very difficult for people not to marry. Despite contemporary ideals that marriage is a totally free choice between two individuals who happen to fall in love, there are other very real pressures now, as in the past, which act to make people think that they should marry.

The most powerful force – and yet that most inimical to our ideology of romance – is economic. Sociologists and historians freely admit that in the past, particularly before industrialisation, marriage was an economic transaction. Their antipathy to the idea that it might still be just that has led to theories of 'sexual revolutions',[1] 'modernisation',[2] and the growth of 'companionate' or 'symmetrical'[3] families created from marriages based on love and sexual attraction between two wholly free individuals. This is not to question that the notion of love is important and crucial to ideologies of marriage, but it can also be argued that it was equally

73

important in the past, just as now there are other ingredients to marriage besides love.

Engels (1972) argued that marriage and 'the family' were a historical result of the development of private property and the need for legitimate heirs. Without private property, he maintained, there was – in the distant past – no need for marriage and, in the future, if property were abolished, there would again be no need for marriage. While property transactions have been an important aspect of many marriages, this argument tells us little as to why those without property chose – and choose – to marry. Engels was right to draw attention to the economic aspect of marriage, but his definition of 'economic' as solely relating to property was too narrow.

Economic resources, as we have seen, also encompass factors such as time, space, service, sexuality and, of course, labour. Different groups and different individuals have different economic needs, so that while marriage may for the wealthy be a very important property or political negotiation, for others it may be necessary because of services, skills, labour or household space. Moreover, as Jessie Bernard (1973) has shown, the needs and expectations that men bring to marriage can be very different from those of women. A woman may want to get married because she cannot support herself by her income alone, or because she no longer wants to live with her parents, while a man may seek marriage for reasons of service or sexual fulfilment or status.

For the wealthy, marriage has long been an important way of enlarging and consolidating property and wealth, as well as a crucial means of political alliance. Daughters of the wealthy were given dowries by their parent(s) when they married; this was both a useful way by which parents could try and control marriages to their own advantage, and was also a valuable incentive for men to marry and thereby increase their wealth.

The cost of educating sons, purchasing or dividing property for them, and endowing daughters could result in considerable expense and fragmentation of wealth. The timing of marriages was therefore very important and depended to a great extent on parents' economic situation. The pattern of late marriages in Western Europe and the consolidation of wealth were inextricably linked. Unless a child was willing – and able – to embark on marriage without parental consent and property, he or she had to wait until their parents were willing to permit, and finance, marriage. For many this meant foregoing marriage altogether.

While propertied parents were thus in a very strong position to control and influence the selection and timing of a child's marriage, the Church insisted that marriage should be an agreement between the man and the woman, and tried to discourage arranged marriages: 'From the late 12th century until the Council of Trent it was unambiguously the case that at the heart of every marriage lay an act of consent; and that consent *de praesenti* in the presence of witnesses . . . made a marriage which could not be dissolved, even if no religious ceremony, and no consummation, had taken place' (Brooke, 1981, p. 27). The Church believed parental consent was highly desirable, but also insisted that the consent of the couple was of prime importance.

The Pastons, a prosperous fifteenth-century landowing family in Norfolk, tried to arrange shrewd marriages for their children. They wanted one daughter, Elizabeth, aged about 20, to marry a well-to-do widower of 50. She, however, refused her consent, and her mother related how, having locked up Elizabeth 'she has since Easter for the most part been beaten once in the week or twice, sometimes twice in one day, and her head broken in two or three places' (Bennett, 1979, p. 30). Although Elizabeth did eventually agree, the marriage never took place and her family spent the next ten years trying to arrange a suitable alternative marriage. Parents could cajole, persuade, beat and threaten children, but the children did retain the final choice, and there is certainly evidence to show that attraction and affection between a man and woman were important aspects of their consent to marry, even if it meant relinquishing wealth.

This option was easier for men than it was for women. A disinherited son could still try to accrue wealth through his own work, and might eventually be able to achieve reasonable prosperity. A woman without a dowry was a serious financial liability for a husband, and she had no means available of accruing wealth. A daughter who did not want to marry, or did not want to marry someone her parents chose for her, might enter a nunnery (before the Reformation) or might feign, or even induce, illness as a means of resisting an unwanted choice of partner, but to engage in paid work on her own was virtually impossible among the propertied classes. Women were therefore more dependent on marriage and on parental control than were men. The notions of patriarchy were such, particularly for the wealthy, that women were seen as by definition dependants – dependent on living and working in either a husband's or a father's household. Then, as now, women were brought up to see marriage as their main aim in life. It was their duty to work and serve their husbands, their children and other members of the household. Marriage for men, on the other hand, was an important step in achieving independence and authority. They could expect service and deference from both wife and children, and in turn had the responsibility of providing for their welfare.

When a woman married, all her personal property (leasehold land and chattels) became her husband's to do with as he chose. Her real property (freehold land) came under his control, although he could not sell it without her consent. If he were to die intestate 'his personal property was divided according to statutory provisions under which his widow never received more than half, the remainder going to his children, or other near relatives, or if he had none, to the Crown' (Holcombe, 1977, p. 5). A wife could not make a will, as '"by marriage, the husband and wife are one person in law": that is, the very being or legal existence of the woman is suspended during the marriage, or at least is incorporated and consolidated into that of the husband under whose wing, protection, and cover, she performs everything.'[4]

Marriage for propertied men was thus a means of increasing their wealth through their wife's dowry, as well as thereby gaining full independence and authority. Marriage for the daughter of a propertied father was quite different. She might or might not improve her standard of living, depending on the assets of her husband. She remained dependent, but her allegiance switched from father to husband. She did, however, gain in social status from being a daughter to being a wife, and this generally gave her more authority within the home. This authority was enhanced when she began to produce children. She might also take on, or learn, new kinds of work within her husband's home, but she remained a dependant – economically, socially and politically. She, her children, and all her property, literally *belonged* to her husband.

The laws on married women's property were not reformed until the late nineteenth century, following pressure from middle-class feminist organisations and liberal reformers. A series of acts were passed between 1870 and 1882. The Married Women's Property Act of 1882 bestowed upon every married woman an equitable marriage settlement, thereby carrying out the principles of the Judicature Act that the common law amd equity must be fused . . . A married woman after the Act came into effect . . . was to have as her separate property all property from whatever source which she owned at the time of marriage and which she acquired after marriage . . . Women could enter into contract and sue and be sued with respect to their separate property, and could dispose of this property fully. (Holcombe, 1977, pp. 24–5)

One reason why these laws were more acceptable by this time was that a number of economic changes had made a wife's property less important in marriage. The growth of life insurance, the decline of family businesses, and the growth of joint stock companies all contributed to making a wife's property less essential to a husband's financial success than in the past. These changes, of course, only affected the propertied. Nor did they go far in eroding a wife's position of dependence – it was not until very recent times that any allowance was made for the unpaid services and labour a wife performs within the household.

Labour has always been a very important aspect of marriage, although it is one which has tended to be ignored in legal, religious – and, indeed, sociological – definitions of marriage. Diana Leonard (1980, p. 5) argues that we need to see marriage 'as a particular form of labour relationship between men and women, whereby a woman pledges for life (with limited rights to quit) her labour, sexuality, and reproductive capacity, and receives protection, up-keep, and certain rights to children'. A husband who fails to provide adequately for his dependants is seen as failing to keep a contract in the same way as a wife who fails to take adequate care of husband, home and children. Caring for husband, children and home is implicitly seen as the job a woman undertakes – albeit unpaid – by marrying, and her failure to carry out these duties can be grounds for divorce or for losing her children. Choosing a husband, there-fore, is equivalent to choosing an employer 'from whom it is very difficult to separate, in a "job" whose organizational embrace is near total' (ibid., p. 6).

This is as much the case now as it was in the past. Young girls are, from a very early age, socialised and encouraged to see their future, their career, as lying in marriage. Boys, on the other hand, are socialised to see their future as lying in paid work in the 'outside world' – marriage is something to contemplate only when they have secured a job and are in a position to support dependants. Because of early and continuous socialisation of boys and girls to accept these different careers, or roles, marriage – especially for women – is regarded as both 'natural' and essential. Essential it certainly is for most women, given the very low rates of pay they have been able to earn relative to men. The rationale for this, of course, is that because their main career lies in marriage, paid work is less important and deserves less remuneration.

Thus the economic basis of marriage is just as important now as it was in the past:

> In many societies women are physically forced into marriage, should their socialization to accept it fail; but in Western Europe for the last few hundred years the final constraint has generally been financial. Most women have not inherited land or businesses etc. and those who work for wages have earned approximately half what men earned in comparable occupations. Consequently ... they have needed to marry a man from the same background as themselves if they were (or are) to live at the same standard as they enjoyed in their father's house. (Leonard, 1980, p. 5)

Marriage offers women their one main chance of social mobility. A woman who works as a secretary has almost no chance of improving her socio-economic position in her work career – as does a man in most white collar jobs – but she does have (or is encouraged to think she has) the chance of social mobility by making an advantageous marriage with a man who is 'on the way up', if not the boss himself. These ideas are very much encouraged by the media, and often given as reasons by employers for not promoting women in their jobs. Equally, of course, marriage can result in downward mobility for women. A man's mobility is less affected by marriage, except if he is able to acquire extra capital, or uses a wife's earning capacity to support him while he studies for further degrees or qualifications. Women continue, therefore, to be economically dependent on both a marriage market and a labour market. In both they are disadvantaged economically. Men are only dependent on a labour market.

Thinking of marriage as important economically in terms of labour as well as property clarifies why the majority of people in both the past and present have chosen to marry – whether or not they owned property. Women's marriage rates, and the age at which they marry, tend therefore to be particularly dependent on the employment opportunities for them where they live. Where women's employment opportunities are poor and scarce (such as in mining or shipbuilding areas), women tend to marry much younger than where employment is relatively plentiful and/or well paid.

In pre-industrial societies there was little scarcity of work for women to do, both within and outside the household. Their work was crucial both to parents and to potential husbands, but they could also live and work in other households as servants, thereby gaining slightly more independence as well as a chance to earn and save. Arguably, therefore, there was generally less need and pressure to marry young. As MacFarlane (1970, p. 94) notes in talking about the family life of Ralph Josselin in the seventeenth century: 'The system of farming out children, which permitted them a moderate freedom without forcing them to resort to marriage, allowed them to marry late . . . there seems to have been no particular urge to marry.' The age at marriage for men and women was consequently high (others have seen this as reflecting a scarcity of land alone), and the proportion who never married at all was much higher than now, varying around 20 per cent of the total population.

In areas where wage labour was prevalent, the age at marriage was considerably lower and a far greater proportion of the population married at some point. Some have seen this as reflecting a greater freedom from parental control and less reliance on land availability, parallel with a 'discovery' of love and sex (Shorter, 1975). It is probable that the decline in residential farm service and the increasing reliance on children's wage-earning meant that more children lived at home longer than before. This would mean a very careful balancing of household resources in terms of space and labour power. As younger children were able to enter the labour market, as more babies arrived, so the household would become increasingly cramped and it was easier, even desirable, for older children to leave, marry and set up their own household.

Much would depend on a particular household's age structure and sex composition. If a family had only daughters – earning half of what sons could have earned – then there would be pressure for them *not* to marry. If there were a large number of sons and thus greater household earning capacity, older sons and daughters could, and indeed might be encouraged, to marry early. Similarly, if a husband was in a fairly secure occupation that paid reasonably well, there would be less need for the wife to engage in wage labour and it would be easier for children to leave. A widow heading a household, on the other hand, would be in a far more tenuous position, and would need all the wages she could get from her children as well as from herself simply in order to survive.

Marriage does not, and did not, result automatically in the establishment of a new and separate household, although that has been the ideal for a long time. While setting up a new household was common among the propertied when they married, the less well-off sectors had much less rigid patterns. Frequently a son or daughter would marry and reside with his or her parents for a considerable length of time. Moreover, the definition of household itself was very fluid, and although a child and spouse might be living in a separate dwelling, this was often nearby – often a part of the parent's household – and interaction, help and service between households was frequently very great indeed. As Chaytor (1980, p. 48) re-marks: 'Households, while technically separate units of production, reproduction and consumption, were not fixed or isolated structures; the boundaries between them and the hierarchies within them were continuously broken and rearranged as marriages and deaths moved people between households, re-defining their status and relationship between them.' Property, cash, services, labour, indeed people, were exchanged regularly between households, and in such a system the whole meaning ascribed to marriage may well have been quite different from that which we use today.

A strong network system between households was not, however, a peculiar characteristic of the distant past. Rather, it needs to be seen as an important economic means of survival used by people in precarious situations regardless of time and place. Carol Stack's study of a poor black area in a midwestern city in the USA ('The Flats') in the late 1960s reveals this clearly. Stack 'found extensive networks of kin and friends supporting, reinforcing each other – devising schemes for self-help, strategies for survival in a community of severe economic deprivation . . . Their social and economic lives were so entwined that not to repay on an exchange meant that someone else's child would not eat' (1974, p. 28). Time and again she found that 'responsibility for providing food, care, clothing and shelter and for socializing children within domestic networks may be spread over several households' (ibid., p. 90).

The combined factors of extreme economic insecurity and the social welfare's system of cutting relief if a husband were co-resident resulted in a tension between kin and marriage, and resulted in very insecure sexual and marital relations. If a man were earning, Stack relates how his kin 'may become very jealous and compete for any money he earns, and discourage him from sharing his resources with his girl friends and their children. The incompatibility between the bonds that men and women, girlfriends and boyfriends feel towards one another and the obligations they accept toward their kin also encourage short-lived sexual relations' (ibid., p. 113). Consequently marriage is seen by kin as a risk to both the woman and her children and as a threat to the kin group.

Ellen Ross found similar networks in nineteenth-century London, where the poorer the street the greater the number of female-headed households there were. She also found contradictory pulls between the demands of marriage and those of kinship ties. Marriage, moreover, 'was not viewed as creating a new unit; the fissure between wife and children on the one hand, and husband on the other was an accepted part of cockney marriage arrangements well into the twentieth century' (1983, p. 7). Thus it is important to see marriage as only one of many means of economic survival for the poorest sectors, a means which was frequently far less secure and dependable than the network ties between kin and neighbours within a local community. It is also important to view the variety of reasons for, and types of, marriage as co-existing over time, varying more according to economic situation of a household or social sector, than in terms of an historical era. Lawrence Stone argues that extensive kin networks as a vital means of support died out in the early modern period; while this was largely true for the well-to-do, it was obviously not the case for the poorer sectors, and is still not.

For a long time, marriage has been encouraged by both Church and State. The reasons for this have been primarily economic, although often veiled in moral terms. The Church, and after the Reformation, the State in Britain, have been the prime institutions responsible for the relief of poverty. The disadvantageous position of women in the labour market has meant that bearing an illegitimate child or children made the most meagre subsistence almost impossible. Women with illegitimate children have been potentially one of the main claimants on parish or State relief. Rather than questioning women's disadvantaged economic situation, Church and State have used the patriarchal assumption that women must be dependent on a man to inform harsh policies on illegitimacy since Elizabethan times.

The problem was defined clearly in terms of the State's or parish's reluctance to support unmarried mothers financially. The Elizabethan laws were designed to force women into naming the father and – until the nineteenth century – forcing men into marrying women who alleged to be bearing their children. Through marriage the parish was thus able to abrogate any financial responsibility by assuming the wife and children to be dependent on the male. Marriage has thus been an important means for delineating responsibility for dependants: 'the Church (gradually from the third or fourth century) and the State (especially from the eighteenth century) were concerned with establishing a public marriage ceremony so that they could recognise and penalize promiscuity and/or the dereliction of marital, parental or kin duties' (Leonard, 1980, p. 10).

Prior to the eighteenth century marriage law was in many ways quite lax. The Church's insistence on the importance of freedom of consent between partners meant that for many – but especially the propertyless where questions of inheritance were irrelevant – sexual intercourse followed by eventual cohabitation was regarded as marriage. Such marriages could equally be easily broken up, and often were. 'Broomstick weddings', common in Wales and in parts of the USA, simply required that a couple jump over a broomstick leaning against a door to constitute marriage. Jumping over a broomstick backwards out of the door was regarded as valid dissolution of the marriage. Marriages could therefore be made and broken relatively easily, but proof of them could prove a headache for parish officials.

Socio-economic changes from the sixteenth century which resulted in increasing poverty and also vagrancy of people in search of work meant that parishes were concerned more than ever with delineating financial responsibilities. Increasing pressures were therefore put on couples to marry. Eventually these pressures culminated in Lord Hardwicke's Act of 1753 which required sol-eminisation of marriage in the Church of England. Although the

Act was ostensibly to curb 'clandestine marriages' whereby lovers –
particularly of the propertied classes – solemnized marriage without
parental consent, it also had repercussions for the rest of society.
First of all it made common law marriages, which had been prevalent among the poor for centuries, no longer valid or binding.
Although it did not result in a great rush of church marriages, it is no
coincidence that rates of illegitimacy from this time began to rise
dramatically. People were not changing their habits and customs so
markedly as some have claimed,[5] but the officials who registered
births were having to define illegitimacy more narrowly than before. This was not the *only* reason for the rise in illegitimacy, but it
was certainly an important factor.

The Poor Law Bastardy Act of 1832 was another attempt to
tighten up marriage regulations with regard to illegitimacy and the
State's omnipresent desire to cut expenditure on poor relief. The
Commissioners concluded that bastardy would never decline until a
bastard was 'what Providence appears to have ordained that it
should be, a burden on its mother, and, where she cannot maintain
it, on her parents' (Henriques, 1967, p. 109). One of the most
misogynistic pieces of legislation ever, much of it was eventually
amended or revoked. It nonetheless provides a good example of
how patriarchal attitudes to women, childbearing and marriage,
informed by economic 'rationalisation', were becoming more severe. Women were no longer encouraged to name the father, but
were wholly condemned for their 'immorality'. Men were seldom
penalised at all. Marriage thus became more important for women
as a means of survival, while it arguably became less so for men.

Marriage was not only an important means of acquiring property
for the wealthy, but also was a crucial means for the State of
avoiding expense on the relief of poverty. It was, therefore, widely
encouraged. Yet in other societies when, and if, marriage was not
seen as economically important it was not encouraged, or was even
discouraged. In slave plantations of the southern USA before the
Civil War, slave owners actively encouraged women slaves to
reproduce as often as possible (thereby increasing their owner's
wealth), but slave marriages were not seen as important or even
desirable. It was often more in the economic interests of the owner
to sell spouses and also children. Gutman (1976, p. 148) quotes one
Susan Hamilton, a slave in Charleston: '"one mornin' a couple
married an' de next mornin' de boss sell de wife. De gal ma got out

in de street an' cursed de white woman fur all she could find." The mother ended up in the Charleston workhouse, and Hamilton remembered her saying, "Dat damn pale-faced bastard sell my daughter who jus' married las' night."'

The economic nature of marriage seems to have been fairly widely acknowledged by people in the past. In contemporary society, however, this important aspect of it tends to be played down or denied (although couples will often make jokes about how their tax position will improve when they get married, and are thus not *un*aware of this aspect). Notions of love, romance, sexual attraction and companionship are given much greater emphasis in modern society than they were in the past. Love and romance, of course, are nothing new. The ancient Greeks eulogised – and practised – homosexual love and romance between men and boys. In medieval times courtly love was given great importance, except that by definition it was *not* based on marriage. What has changed is the development of the ideal that all love – except parental love – should be heterosexual, and that its logical and rightful locus is within marriage.

Ideals of love and companionship were only one element of marriage in earlier times, often weighted carefully against more practical considerations. The rise of the bourgeoisie in the eighteenth century brought with it added emphasis on love and romance, buttressed by an explosion of romantic novels and poetry. The majority of these, however, did not extoll love unless it occurred between 'suitable' partners, that is, of the same class. The structure of middle-class family life was organised so that daughters had very little social contact with men at all, unless they were considered acceptable. Most middle-class girls until the late nineteenth century never went to school, but were taught at home by a governess or their mother. Male visitors to the home were primarily the father's business associates, male cousins or brothers' friends from school, university or work. What public occassions she did attend would be carefully monitored, and she would be scrupulously chaperoned. While a middle-class woman might thus think of men and marriage in romantic terms, her possible marriage was essentially an arranged one because her field of choice was so carefully regulated.

An important consequence of this was that cousin marriage and marriage with father's or brothers' business associates was very common among the middle classes. This enhanced a consolidation of capital within kinship networks, and indeed often *created* kinship ties between business associates. In the late eighteenth and early nineteenth centuries Davidoff and Hall (1982, p. 12) show how 'relationships which started out as kin, for example, a sister's husband, became economic when the brother-in-law became a partner, while sisters often married men who were already their brother's partners . . . this particular form of "lateral" marriage was characteristic of this period when productive capacity was outstripping its institutional forms.' The practice largely died out in the late nineteenth century, partly as a result of economic changes and partly as a result of the decline of family size, which curtailed the available pool of siblings and cousins.

While marriage has been essential for women both for economic security and as a means of achieving status, patriarchal ideology about women's 'passivity' has meant women have been in the difficult position of supposedly being passive with regards to 'getting' a man. The man was – and is – supposed to take all the initiative in courtship; a dominant parent, therefore, can fairly easily keep a daughter 'off' the marriage market. The lower down the social scale a woman, the more difficult such control is for her parent(s), particularly if she works outside the home and interacts with men at the workplace.

If a working-class parent wanted or needed a daughter to stay at home unmarried, a common tactic was to release other siblings into wage labour outside the home while training one daughter in an occupation such as needlework which was performed at home. Often, too, they seem to have inculcated in girls the belief that they were too 'weak' or ill to marry – although it was not felt they were too weak or ill to care for their ageing parents and the household. Many daughters – especially the youngest – were thus kept at home, out of both the labour and marriage markets, more or less forced to spend their time caring for their parent(s) and taking charge of the home. Sometimes an unmarried daughter would live like this until she was 40 or 50. Unless her parent(s) had been relatively prosperous and left her some property, she would then have to live and work with and for other kin, or try to survive by her wages alone. Some had to resort to parish relief. A few married at a relatively late age.

Marriage is not just an economic relationship or a labour contract influenced by sexual attraction and ideas of love and romance. It can also be seen as an important status passage for both men and women. It confers adult status. For a man it also implies independence and responsibility for others, while for a woman it means a new form of dependence and responsibility for a household. It represents an important change from being so-and-so's child, a semidependent, to becoming someone else's spouse. This change in status has undoubtedly been an important reason why both men and women want to marry.

Cohabitation is increasing in modern society: between 1981 and 1987 the proportion of single women cohabiting rose from 8 per cent to 17 per cent (*Social Trends*, 1991). Nevertheless, becoming part of a *couple*, whether married or not, remains an important goal. Although being single has come to be seen as having a certain status and attraction, it is a very short-lived status (but especially for women) associated with late adolescence and the early twenties. It has become associated with ideals of enjoying oneself, being 'glamorous', and having few, or no, responsibilities. But by the age of 25 or so the 'glamour' rapidly fades as more and more members of a peer group marry, set up house and become more couple-oriented and child-oriented. Those still single increasingly perceive living at home as constraining and boring, while those in bedsitters or flats may yearn for greater space and more company and comfort. Many will no doubt be tired of having sexual relations on the sofa or in the car.[6]

An important reason for people – but especially women – waiting to marry or cohabit is, and has been, the desire to escape from parent(s), and frequently from a difficult or violent parental home. In Rubin's (1976, p. 34) study of white working class families in the USA, one 35-year-old woman relates her reasons for marrying thus:

> We didn't get along with each other; my brothers and I used to fight something terrible. And we didn't get along with my stepfather. He drank a lot, too ...and then ...he used to make passes at me, and I couldn't stand it. I hated him, and I hated my mother because she didn't do anything about it ...Finally, we all just took off. My older brother joined the service; and I and my younger brother kept running away. Each time I'd run away, they'd catch me and put me back in juvenile hall again ...All I could think of was getting out of that house. As soon as I turned eighteen, I just up and got married.

I just had to get away from them all – my family, parole officer, all of them; and that was the only way I could.

The older people get, but particularly women, the more difficult it becomes for them *not* to marry. To remain single after 24 or 25 (or 35 or 40 for a man) increasingly becomes perceived as being 'on the shelf', 'odd', possibly homosexual, and increasingly peripheral to social life generally. These age bars on marriage have become more rigid over time: 'in the nineteenth century it took fifteen or more years for 80% of the men who ever wed to marry and roughly twelve or thirteen years for the same proportion of women to enter wedlock ...(now) the central 80% of the 1925–34 birth cohort of male ever-marriers managed the transition in 8.6 years and the females did so even more rapidly' (Modell and Furstenburg, 1978, p. 126).

A married couple is expected to have their own household, immaculately furnished and decorated, as well as being madly in love and enjoying a full and exciting sex life together. Twentieth-century marriage has increasingly been perceived as a co-operative enterprise, with each supporting the other emotionally, each sharing their pleasures and activities, not the least of which is having children.

Such an ideal, of course, seldom matches reality. Mortgages may be scarce, flats too expensive to rent; many couples will live, for a while at least, with a parent or parents. Co-residence with parents in the USA, for example, has been more common after the Second World War than it was in 1880 (ibid., p. 132). By the time a couple does set up their own household they may have a baby, and find that this is incompatible with the ideal of an immaculate 'ideal home'. The wife may have left work with the birth of a baby and thus their income will be substantially reduced. Broken nights can wreak havoc with romance and a satisfying sex life. A wife may soon resent having to baby-sit while the husband goes out in the evenings with his mates; he may resent what he perceives as her increasingly slovenly habits, and so on. In short, the contemporary ideal of marriage with which couples are presented is, for most, so unreal that it is small wonder so many marriages end in divorce. Moreover, an ideal of equality within marriage is impossible to realise in a society where men and women have such different access to both resources and life-chances.

In England and Wales in 1961 32 000 divorces were granted; in 1971 (the year when the Divorce Reform Act came into force) there were 111 000; by 1981 this figure had reached 170 000.[7]

People are divorcing earlier than before; 11 per cent of divorces occurred within the first four years of marriage in 1961, while by 1981 this was almost 20 per cent. The median duration of marriage in 1980 was 10.1 years; for couples with children this was 11.2 years, and for those with no children it was 7.8 years.[8] Divorce, of course, has become legally easier in the past few decades. It has not, however, become any easier emotionally, economically or socially, although men's and women's experience of divorce – like marriage – differs.

Until very recently divorce was a luxury that only the well-to-do could afford. The 1857 Matrimonial Causes Act established a new Divorce Court and changed the procedure for getting a divorce. But 'in a husband's petition, simple adultery sufficed; a wife was required to prove not only adultery but the additional aggravation of desertion, cruelty, incest, rape, sodomy or bestiality' (McGregor, 1957, p. 18). In 1878, Lord Penzance's Matrimonial Causes Act made it possible for the poor to get legal separation, but divorce was still inaccessible financially for the majority of the population. Separation was common – whether legal or not – and this put separated working-class women in a very tenuous economic position, as it was very difficult (and still is) to get any maintenance. The recent reform of divorce law and the ability of the poor to get legal aid is one of the prime reasons for the increase in the divorce rate; *de facto* divorce, by becoming *de jure* divorce has simply meant that the phenomenon, common enough in the past, is now recorded in statistics where it was not previously.

The notion of a woman's dependence is retained after divorce; a wife who does not work and is given custody of children will have to be maintained by her ex-husband until, and if, she remarries. The amount he pays can be substantial and this can diminish his income considerably. On the other hand, it will also mean a decrease in the wife's standard of living, given that she only receives part of his income. Yet the middle-class husband, relatively free of family commitments, can spend much more time in building his career and thereby increasing his income; the working-class husband may be freer to work overtime. Both working-class and middle-class divorcees, however, remain totally dependent on the maintenance awarded, which is seldom changed over time. Moreover, few husbands actually fulfil their maintenance requirements. The fact that the majority of women are awarded custody of their children, although undoubtedly desired by most, is a means whereby her dependence and need to serve others is retained, while the husband's independence increases.

The divorced woman, tied to caring for her children in reduced economic circumstances, will usually experience a marked curtailment of social activities and change in social status (see Hart, 1976). Her freedom to engage in the social activities which she may have enjoyed before and during marriage is seriously hampered by child-care commitments and economic constraints. Most of her friends from her married days will be couples; no longer part of a couple herself she may well be totally excluded from couple-dominated social activities. Divorced women are often regarded as 'dangerous' to other women's husbands, and this increases their social isolation. Her possibilities of meeting another potential husband are limited to other women's husbands or divorced or widowed men (the latter likely to be much older). The emphasis which modern society puts on youth and youthful appearance for women puts divorced women at a further disadvantage. Having responsibility for another man's children also makes divorced women less attractive to many men. The fact that many do remarry is evidence, perhaps not so much of a love of marriage as an institution but of the severe social and economic situation in which divorced women are placed. Re-entry to social life depends very much on re-entry to marriage.

Divorced men, on the other hand, do not encounter the same problems. Less likely to have child-care commitments, except at weekends or holidays, they are relatively foot-loose and fancy-free. If anything, social values render somewhat older men more attractive to the opposite sex. The divorced man of 40 or 45 is generally seen as a 'good catch' for a woman of 25 or so. A woman of 40, however, who marries or is involved with a man of 25 is seen as a 'cradle-snatcher'. Divorced men do not seem to be regarded as dangerous in the way that divorced women are. Their 'pool' of potential new wives is large, particularly because of their access to younger single women. Young single women who are earning may also be very attractive to a divorced man by offering him the chance to regain his previous economic situation in forming a two-income household.

It is not surprising, therefore, that after divorce far more men remarry than women. In 1961 it was estimated that 184 000 divorced women did *not* remarry, while only 101 000 men did not. In 1981 some 584 000 men did not remarry, while 783 000 women did not.[9] Divorced women are severely disadvantaged in the market for remarriages, and, much more than men, have to 'take what they can get', if, indeed, anything at all. Many, of course, may never want to remarry, but particularly for those with dependent children, life is arguably more difficult if they do not. On the other hand, there may be consolation for them in the fact that some 40 per cent of all remarriages also end in divorce.

Remarriages where one or both of the partners has children result in a relatively complex form of family structure. The wife may have two children who spend the week at home and visit their father at weekends or once a month. The husband may have children who spend weekends and holidays with them. The new couple may in time have one or two children of their own. At times, therefore, the household will include people from different families, all with somewhat different allegiances and upbringings, all with different expectations and problems. Such families were by no means uncommon in earlier times, except that they were more frequently broken up and brought together by death rather than divorce. Moreover, the strong contemporary ideology of happy nuclear families is so much more marked than in the past that it may well make these 'hybrid families' more easily dissatisfied with the tensions and conflicts of different allegiances. The lack of match between ideal and reality is thus likely to be even more pronounced than in first marriages; the chance of divorce thus greater. Further remarriage, particularly for men, can bring *two* families from the past into a new marriage.

Unfortunately, the development of ideals of romance and romantic love in contemporary society has been so strongly all-pervasive that few people are fully aware of the bitter pill beneath the sugar coating in marriage. Virtually everybody wants to have caring and loving relationships with others; family ideology preaches that this is only possible and only acceptable through a heterosexual marriage, while of course it is possible to have caring and loving relationships outside marriage and/or with people of the same sex. Undoubtedly this imbalance between ideal and reality contributes markedly to so much disillusionment, suffering and divorce. Contemporary ideology of the family presents marriage as an equal partnership between a man and a woman who love each other. In reality, the social, political and economic structures of modern industrial society are such that only in the rarest of cases can marriage ever be equal. It is founded on a patriarchal ideology with concepts of men's and women's duties and responsibilities which are by definition the basis of an unequal relationship.

5

Why do people have children?

Just as patriarchal ideology in western society has prescribed and proscribed appropriate behaviour for marriage, so it has done the same for reproduction. Bearing children – and bearing them with much pain – was God's alleged curse on Eve for her sins. Mary, by being a passive and obedient recipient for God's will, was able, through immaculate conception and motherhood, to play a minor part in the redemption of humanity through bearing and mothering Christ. Sexuality has always been an evil in the Judaeo-Christian symbol-system, albeit a necessary one. Its inherent evil can be tempered, first, by being heterosexual, second, by restricting sexual relations to marriage, and third, by limiting sexual relations exclusively for the purpose of procreation. Heterosexuality, marriage, and having children are thus all part of the western patriarchal parcel of rules for appropriate sexual relations and behaviour between men and women. Indulging in one without accepting the rest of the 'parcel' has been, and still is, widely condemned.

The rules are not, however, strictly identical for men and women, as we have seen. The secularisation of patriarchy, in particular, accorded men different 'needs' and 'natural instincts' in scientific and biological terms. Certainly men's and women's relations to reproduction are different, albeit interdependent. Biologically, a man's relationship to reproduction is, literally, momentary, while a woman's relationship extends over a period of nine months. Childbirth, moreover, is a dangerous occurrence biologically for women, while impregnation is in no way dangerous for men.

As mentioned earlier, there are societies where the relationship between heterosexual intercourse and paternity is not acknowledged; maternity always is in all societies. Nourishment of an infant is provided biologically by the mother, although not all mothers have always chosen, or been able, to breastfeed their babies. Men, of course, have no such capacity. But a man can physically force intercourse, through rape, and thus possibly impregnate the victim. A woman cannot force a man to impregnate her. The basic biological relations of men and women to reproduction are different, and this is reflected in patriarchal rules on sexuality and reproduction.

Ideas of what being a mother and what mothering means are variable and changeable. We are so influenced by our own popular image and ideal of a mother as a married woman co-resident with a working husband who, between them, produce their own 2.4 children whom she raises to adulthood, that it is hard to imagine any other type of mother or mothering relationship. Yet, as should by now be clear, biological mothers are by no means always social mothers. Fatherhood for many has been simply unknown or irrelevant. Many men and women choose not to have children.

It could be argued that for most women, past and present, because their economic survival was contingent on marriage, having children was, and is, a price they have had to pay for that economic security. The idea that children must invariably follow marriage has been deliberately fostered by the Church for centuries. Equally, many women may have regarded (and regard) marriage and heterosexuality as a price to pay for having children. Men may have regarded children and marriage as a necessary corollary to the provision of regular sexual relations.

Sociologists and historians have long argued that children in earlier times were essential economically to parents, although they claim that in modern society this is no longer so. Undoubtedly children have been useful economically; children have often started contributing to the household economy from the age of 3 or 4. In the poorest sectors of modern society – and especially in Third World countries – a child's contribution to the household can still be crucial. The unpaid domestic labour of girls in many households today, and much more so in the past, has been important economically. Yet the price of producing children was also a high one in earlier times; childbirth frequently resulted in the mother's death, and often that of the child, and this could cause acute economic crisis for the household. High mortality constantly threatened a household's labour supply.

A sixteenth-century couple seeking to maximise their economic situation in the most rational way might well have done better by not having children, but by employing live-in servants or kin as their additional labour supply. Many did do just this, although the typical arrangement was for siblings rather than a childless couple to live and work together. If times were bad, servants could be dismissed; small children could not. If a servant died, another could soon be hired – not so with a child. Small infants took a mother's valuable time away from production for some time, death in childbirth could remove it completely. Thus while acknowledging that children did – and do – have an economic use in households, they were not the most reliable labour supply, and could often be a major liability. It is unlikely that people in earlier times had children solely for economic reasons.

Engels argued that the main reason why people wanted children was as heirs to their property, and hence in societies where private property prevails, the need for marriage and ensured legitimacy of offspring. This problem, however, was almost entirely a *male* one, as men were the property-holders (except for widows). Control of property undoubtedly gave many men a great deal of power within their households and over their children:

> During the middle ages control over landed property through entail meant that the head of the family was no more than a life tenant ... In the late fifteenth century, the lawyers found a way to break entails without too much difficulty . . . This greatly strengthened the ability of the current head of the family to dispose of his property as he chose, although it also greatly weakened his capacity to prevent his heir from doing the same thing ... (this) meant an increase in his capacity to punish or reward his children or siblings. Thus it meant the further subordination of the children, including the heir, to the father, and of younger sons and daughters to their eldest brother if he inherited the estate before they married. (Stone, 1977, p. 156)

The more property a man held, the more important producing an heir was for him. Among the nobility and the monarchy, of course, it was also a crucial political issue, witness Henry VIII's six marriages and break with the Roman Catholic Church in his desperate attempt to have a male heir. The less property there was, the less important were these issues. Yet those with no property at all still had children.

Interpreting inheritance as solely relating to property is too narrow a way of considering the question. Children have been an important source of labour power. Men and women may wish to bequeath other aspects of themselves to their children – skills, knowledge, values, traditions, beliefs – 'our stamp upon the world has been, traditionally, our stamp upon our children' (Dowrick and Grundberg, 1980, p. 7). Consider the typical behaviour of friends and relatives when they first see a new baby: remarks abound about how it 'has your hair', 'has her father's mouth', or 'looks just like Aunt Ada'. Producing children, by producing something from oneself, is arguably a way of achieving immortality, of keeping oneself and/or one's family alive. As Melba Wilson says: 'I wanted to leave something of myself behind' (ibid., p. 112). With increasing secularisation over time, and a decline in a belief in life after death, this may well have become an increasingly important reason for men and women to want children. It is perhaps even more important for women, given their inferior access to creative and fulfilling jobs outside the household.

Having children also brings status. For women, raised from the earliest age to perceive womanhood as equivalent to motherhood, bearing a child brings a dramatic change in status. It is, more than marriage even, the principal way in which a woman becomes socially recognised as being a 'real' woman, a woman who has fulfilled her 'true' destiny and role in life. Sara Maitland recalls how she 'was miraculously restored to my mother's love, and approval. I was having a baby: for her that meant I was a good girl and a good woman. Having, in her view, been neither since I was fifteen, I basked in this new state of affairs' (ibid., p. 83). For a man, no equivalent status passage takes place when his wife or lover has a child. The primary status passage for men is when they enter the workforce and thus become defined as 'real' men in terms of the work they do. The work women do in the labour force does not define them in this way at all; when they work, it is as potential wives and mothers or, if they already have children, their paid work is perceived as secondary to their role as mother/wife.

Thus while a man may add to his sexual status to a limited extent by 'proving' his virility in begetting a child, for a woman childbirth has been virtually the only means available to her of showing the world she is a 'real' woman. A man retains his full status if he is childless; a woman never achieves full status unless she has children. This perception of motherhood as a woman's only way of achieving social status is as powerful a force today as it was in the past, it is a bedrock of patriarchal ideology. For many women having a child may be seen as the only way in which they can obtain a permanent and loving relationship with another person. The notion that 'blood is thicker than water' is still a very strong part of family ideology. Such a notion, however, can be seen as largely fallacious:

> It is a myth perpetually reinforced by the assumption that only family and children provide us with purpose and place, bestow upon us honour, respect, love and comfort. We are taught very early that blood relations, and only blood relations, can be a perpetual, unfluctuating source of affection, can be the foolproof guarantee that we will not be forgotten. This myth, and many others surrounding the traditional family, often make it both frightening and painful for women to think of themselves as remaining childless. (Ibid., p. 18)

This idea has arguably become more important since the Reformation and subsequent denigration of celibacy as a highly valued way of life.

Having children creates new power relationships – between mother and child, between father and child, and between mother and father as well as between siblings. Well into the nineteenth century children were by law defined as the father's property, as, of course, were wives. With few exceptions, the father could do what he liked with his children. He might send them away to work at 6 or 7, could sell them as child prostitutes or chimney sweeps, might have incestuous relationships with them, and was always entitled to beat them. The mother could stop none of these, for she too was in a similarly subordinate position. If a couple divorced (which was only an option at this time for the wealthy), the father had automatic right to all his children. The first change to this came in the 1839 Custody of Infants Act, which 'allowed a mother to have the physical custody of her children up to the age of seven years, provided that she had not committed adultery, and it permitted her access to her minor children at the discretion of the courts' (Brophy and Smart, 1981, p. 4). Subsequent legislation gave increasing rights to the mother for custody and access to her children, although these were accorded in terms of the child's welfare rather than the mother's right *per se*.

A mother's power over her children has not been one enshrined in the legal system. Yet because women mother and generally take the majority of the burden of day-to-day socialisation and care, they do have enormous potential for influencing their children's behaviour, attitudes and education. The degree of power and control a mother has over her children varies by the presence or absence of the father, his class position, the sex of the children. Among middle-class families, where the father was the centre of family life, the mother's power was carefully scrutinised and controlled by him, and much of it was eroded by servants caring for young children. Middle-class Victorian boys were usually sent away to the all-male milieu of boarding school between the ages of 8 and 12 and were thus effectively removed from the mother's influence and control. Girls, on the other hand, remained at home, often never attending school at all, and were under their mother's tutelage and supervision until (and if) they married. Both mother and daughter, however, were also ultimately under the control of the father/husband.

Among the working classes, on the other hand, women tended to have much greater power and influence over the socialisation of both boys and girls. Sisters, aunts and neighbours could often be as important as the mother herself – being mothered was often a quite diffuse experience for working-class children in contrast with the specificity and intensity of their middle-class counterparts. Among the poorest sectors of the working class in particular, a father often had little or nothing to do with his children, witness Arthur Harding's comments:

> When I was young I didn't see much of father. He wasn't home much and when he was at home you tried to keep out of his way. He only lived for himself ... I had no respect for my father – no feeling at all ... By the time I was nine or ten he had become a confirmed of the casual poor ... A few years later we threw him out of the house and he went to live with a sister ... young or older the mother was the top Johnny in the family. What she said was law. All the money you earned went to her and she would share it out. (Samuel, 1981a, pp. 28, 30, 61)

When he was 14, and able to earn wages, his father suddenly showed an interest in him. Perhaps economic reasons for having children are more typically male reasons.

In modern industrial society, of course, the majority of fathers are still absent from home for much of the day (assuming that they are present in the first place, which many are not), and thus only see their children for very short periods of time. Whatever the class situation of a particular family-household, marriage and childrearing has undoubtedly given women a form of power and control which would otherwise not have been available to them. For those who would have had to live their lives as total, or semi-, dependants in a parent's or sibling's household, or eked out the meagrest of subsistence livings on poor wages, the appeal of being in control – at least relatively – of one's own household and children must have been, and be, great.

One reason frequently given for why people want children, especially in the past, is as a means and source of security in old age. Some have argued that the institution of welfare benefits and pensions has been a direct factor in the decline of family size[1] – people no longer needed children, or as many children, as 'insurance'. As discussed earlier, it was quite common for one child – most often the youngest daughter – to be expected to care for her ageing parent(s). To this end many daughters were kept under stricter control than their older siblings and were often not encouraged or allowed to go out to work and to see themselves as too weak, shy or unattractive to consider marriage. While oral evidence suggests that this was a very common pattern among the working classes, it was also quite common among the middle classes.

No doubt many parents in the past did have real fears about old age – in particular, the absolute dread of having to go into the workhouse. But it could also be argued that many wanted – and want – a child to care for them in old age, rather than simply providing them with economic support. Now that modern industrial societies all have some form of pension scheme and none have workhouses, the elderly still live in fear of being put into old people's homes or hospitals (which are often converted workhouses anyway). The majority of the elderly, unable to care for themselves, are cared for by daughters, as in the past. People may want children, and particularly daughters, as a general form of security for old age, as a defence against institutionalisation, a source of love and emotional support, and as a bastion against loneliness. Irene Klepfisz, who chose not to have children, expresses some of these fears: 'I am afraid I too will end up alone, disconnected, relating to no one, having no one to care for, being in turn forgotten, unwanted and insignificant, my life a waste. In the grip of this terror, I can only anticipate a lonely, painful old age, an uncomforted death' (in Dowrick and Grundberg, 1980, p. 12).

These feelings are timeless, and although individuals now may have somewhat less worry about economic provision than in the past, they are also much more likely to live far longer than their earlier counterparts, and the spectre of loneliness, isolation and death without care and comfort may be even stronger now than in the past. Because women live longer than men, these fears may be particularly acute for them; most men can assume that their wives will care for them in old age. Yet children die, marry, migrate, emigrate, and often quarrel with parents, and the assumption that having children automatically guarantees economic, emotional and loving security in old age is a dubious one, as it always has been.

Certainly the love which young children give their parents must be attractive to both men and women. The totally unqualified love of a small dependent child is unlike any other relationship in adult life; it is most similar to the usually unqualified love remembered from one's own childhood. Yet because women are more directly involved with a baby from the moment of conception, they experience a much more direct closeness and intimacy than do fathers. The bonding that often results from the act of birth and subsequent suckling is an intense experience that only a woman can know, and can often be a very sensual experience. Some mothers, of course, have very negative and painful experiences of childbirth and some cannot, or do not want to, breastfeed. Even when the experience is negative, however, it is always intense and close, and this aspect of having children is one denied to men. Men's love for their children has to develop in other, less physical ways. Jealousy of the new child and the mother's love for it is common.

So far it has been assumed that having children involves choice. Many would argue that until fairly recently there was little choice. Those who married inevitably had children as a result of intercourse and, so it is argued, the ability to control reproduction is a recent phenomenon. Certainly women of a hundred or two hundred years ago bore more children on average than they do today. Yet it cannot be assumed that this was simply a manifestation of total ignorance of means of birth control. Although it can never be known for certain the extent to which birth control was practised in earlier societies, there is evidence that methods of birth control – pessaries, primitive sheaths, herbal abortifacients, coitus interruptus, coitus reservatus, abortion, abstinence and infanticide – were known at least as far back as ancient Egypt (Himes, 1931). Delayed marriage has also been a form of birth control, especially as the older a woman is the less fecund she becomes.

Research carried out by Wrigley in Colyton, Devon, between the sixteenth and nineteenth centuries shows marked variation in fertility patterns: 'only 18% of women marrying under thirty between 1647 and 1719 and living right through the fertile period had families of six children or more . . . compared with 55% in 1560–1629, 48% in 1720–69, and 60% in 1770–1837. Very large families, on the other hand, were rare at any time in Colyton, the largest during the full three centuries being only thirteen' (Wrigley, 1969, p. 97). Research in other societies shows similar variations in family size and fertility in earlier times. Nancy Osterud and John Fulton, for example, studying Sturbridge, Massachusetts for the period 1730–1850, found 'the most immediately striking feature of the fertility of the completed families over time is the substantial decline in the mean number of children ever born over the 120-year period, a decline of 3.5 children from a high of 8.8 for the 1730–59 marriage cohort to a low of 5.3 for the 1820–39 cohort' (1978, p. 483).

The reasons for variations in fertility and family size are as complex as are individual reasons for wanting or not wanting children. Economic changes – times of scarcity or plenty, shifts to wage labour, patterns of male and female migration – all had important effects on marriage rates and fertility. No doubt political instability and dramatic ideological changes – the Civil War in Britain, the French Revolution, the Evangelical Movement in the USA, the Russian Revolution – also affected people's marriage patterns and reasons for controlling, or not controlling, family size. Mortality, too, was a crucial determinant of completed family size and the number of children a woman bore. As mortality declined, gradually at first from the eighteenth century, so the fear of losing children must also have declined slowly. But mortality has generally been class-specific, and highest among the poorest – who have also been those who have continued to have large numbers of children longest.

That some form of birth control has always existed does not mean that many were not ignorant, or relatively ignorant, of its existence. Many beliefs about birth control were fallacious, for example the belief that if a woman sat up or urinated directly after intercourse she would not conceive. Most women in earlier times breastfed their babies for one or two years after birth, and lactation does act as a mild preventive against conception. Knowledge of herbal abortifacients – some more reliable than others – was also fairly widespread. The most reliable means available before the middle of the nineteenth century were coitus interruptus, coitus reservatus, abortion and infanticide. The vulcanisation of rubber brought increasingly reliable and less dangerous means – sheaths and diaphragms – although evidence suggests that these were only used – and could only be afforded – by a very small sector of the population, overwhelmingly from among the middle classes, until well into the twentieth century.

It is usually agreed that the most common form of birth control practised until this century, and which is still common in contemporary society, was coitus interruptus which is, of course, a male method and gives the man quite literally the power to decide whether or not to have children. Abortion, which has also been widely practised, is primarily a female method of birth control (albeit a far more dangerous method), which can be carried out without a husband even knowing (see Gittins, 1982; Himes, 1931). Many abortionists before the twentieth century were also midwives, but there were in addition a number of local women known to other women in the neighbourhood who would perform abortions: 'abortion was the working woman's form of contraception. It provided her with control of her own body. It did not require the regular, business-like, sober assistance of her spouse ... Putting off the decision to a time closer to birth gave her a better idea if an additional child could or could not be supported' (McLaren, 1977, p. 4).

Because men and women often have very different reasons for wanting, or not wanting, children it is obviously very important as to which partner has knowledge and access to birth control. It is quite possible for one partner to force his or her preferences on the other by witholding information and taking responsibility without mutual discussion. Power relationships like this permeate marital situations and can obviously have dramatic repercussions on the nature and structure of a household and its individuals.

Population and birth control became national political issues at the end of the eighteenth century. The general turbulence and concern thrown up as a result of rapid economic change, urbanisation, the French Revolution, growing consciousness and polarisation of classes all coincided with, indeed stimulated, increasing concern about 'the family', 'morality', sexuality, and population as a national resource. Reproduction became seen increasingly as an important political issue because it had direct repercussions on the labour supply, the armed services, the relative size of social classes, financial responsibility for dependants, and the relative dependence or independence of women. Overall concerns about class relations and patriarchal authority were all enmeshed in such debates.

In the early nineteenth century 'repeated reports were made of factory women seeking to induce miscarriages ... The recourse to abortion or infanticide (the two often confused in the public's mind) was presented by middle-class observers as the most damning evidence of the immoral influence of factory life on women' (ibid., p. 1). Laws on abortion were made stricter. Until 1803 abortion had been a common law offence, but was then made a statutory one; further laws in 1828, 1837 and 1861 culminated in it being made a crime for a woman to abort herself, whereas previously only the abortionist was penalised. Abortion, of course, could be extremely dangerous to the woman, but what seemed to concern middle-class opponents most was the 'immorality' it posed, not least of which seems to have been the fear that it enabled women to control their own bodies and reproductive patterns. Contemporary controversies about abortion are still imbued with this fear, and bear witness to the persistence of patriarchy.

At the same time as many middle-class reformers were outraged at the working-class practice of abortion, middle-class fears about a 'proliferation' of the working class were also widespread, as epitomised in the writings of Malthus (1966). More radical middle-class reformers, such as Place, Carlile and Knowlton, tried to disseminate information to working-class women on safer means of birth control than abortion; they were frequently met with fierce opposition from more conservative middle-class reformers. Yet the middle classes themselves were increasingly limiting the size of their families, particularly in the second half of the nineteenth century. Significantly, they achieved this overwhelmingly by male means of birth control – coitus interruptus. Banks (1954) argues that the decline of family size among the middle classes was primarily a means of maintaining their standard of living and class position during a time when education was becoming increasingly important, competitive and expensive.

Working-class family size continued to be relatively large until the twentieth century, although there were marked variations. Textile workers, in particular, had been manifesting quite low rates of fertility throughout the nineteenth century. To some extent, large families were still economically very important for many of the working class. Partly it was a result of much younger age at marriage among the working classes, and, for some, relative ignorance of reliable methods of birth control. But although mortality generally was decreasing, it remained quite high among the working classes and this, too, must have affected the number of children a woman bore. To middle class eyes, often ignorant of the economics of working-class households, it seemed a threatening prospect of the country being 'overrun' by the lower classes who, they feared, might at any moment rise up in revolution against the established social, political, economic, and patriarchal order. These very real fears played a large part in early protective legislation, the pressure for a state education system, and the gradual acceptance of trade union demands for a family wage. Increasingly 'the family' (i.e. along middle-class lines and ideals) became seen as the antidote to 'irresponsible' breeding and political unrest.

Because reproduction is always a social concern, birth control is always – sometimes implicitly and sometimes explicitly – a political issue. Governments concerned about labour supply, political and social unrest, the size and quality of their military forces, have tried in various ways to enforce population policies. The very liberal laws passed immediately after the Russian Revolution relating to marriage, abortion and birth control were soon rescinded in the face of a declining birth rate and the prospect of a shrinking labour force and military (see Schlesinger, 1949). France, where fertility declined much earlier than in the rest of Western Europe, has tried consistently to stimulate a higher birth rate through tax benefits and 'bonuses' for large families – without much success. Population concerns frequently act as a convenient disguise for what are essentially serious economic problems. The spread of AIDS, of course, has brought contraceptive issues to the fore with health concerns.

The USA, particularly during the 1960s, invested vast sums of money in birth control and sterilisation programmes in the Third World, rather than choosing to see most of the severe problems there as a result of their economic systems and, in particular, their economic dependence on, and exploitation by, the USA itself. Following medical concern about the safety of the pill, the drugs industry focused their marketing on Third World countries where health regulations were less stringent, or non-existent. Few deliberate population policies or birth control campaigns have met with much success. To a large extent this is because birth control *per se* has seldom been the issue or problem for people. The real issue is whether – and why – people want, or do not want, children. For those determined not to have children there have always been some means available.

In both past and present, there have always been some people who do not want any children at all. During the past few centuries, however, pressure on people – and particularly women – to see marriage and children as the only way of achieving status, power and security have arguably increased. The demise of religious retreats, of apprenticeship and residential service have all contributed to making it more difficult for single women to survive alone. Increasing stereotyping and stigmatisation of homosexuality has made it more difficult for single people to live in same-sex households. The reasons why some people do not want to marry and do not want children are as varied as for those who do. Economically, people may not want the total responsibility which having children entails. Women who wish to remain independent, to devote most of their time to a career, are still faced with the dilemma that achieving these goals is extremely difficult if they have children. Some do not want heterosexual relationships. Others may simply dislike babies and children.

A common reason for not wanting children, or for only wanting one or two, is having had to mother one's own siblings. Eldest daughters of large families often feel very strongly about this:

I am the oldest of nine kids. For eighteen years, my mother kept up a biennial tradition of having babies, spending a year or two with each, and then leaving us with her mother for the remaining time to adulthood ... As the oldest, I had to help out with my brothers and sisters. From about twelve onwards it fell to me to take charge of things like making sure their hair was combed, the beds made and jobs around the house done ... By the time I reached my late teens, I had had enough of being 'mother'. (Dowrick and Grundberg, 1980, p.106)

Youngest daughters who were responsible for 'mothering' parents in old age may have felt similarly. Whether or not a woman actually has children of her own, she is nevertheless expected to 'mother' others as part of being a woman. Patriarchy imbues womanhood with the omnipresent notions of selfless service and caring for others in a way that has never been expected of men. The very word 'fathering', unlike 'mothering', suggests begetting only, or at the most a somewhat nebulous social and financial role in respect of a man's biological children – certainly not in relation to anyone else. But women as daughters, aunts, sisters, nieces, granddaughters, as well as wives, regardless of their age or marital status, have been expected – and usually expect – to mother others, kin and non-kin alike.

Secretaries are expected to make their bosses cups of coffee, order their taxis, arrange their social occasions, buy presents for their wives and children, and generally 'care' for them as well as work for them. Teachers of the youngest age groups in primary schools are almost invariably women. Women police officers are generally given tasks which involve caring for others – soothing distressed women or lost children, giving talks on road safety at schools. In cases of family accident or illness it is always a female relative who is called upon to care for the dependant/infirm. If none is available, state agencies tend to do all they can to take over such responsibility largely or wholly from a male relative. Whether or not a woman has children of her own, she is always expected to mother. This may, on the one hand, make some women feel that as this is what society demands of them, they might as well have their own children to mother, or, on the other hand, it may make others so disenchanted with this expectation that they choose to curtail these demands by not having their own children. These dilemmas do not face men at all.

While patriarchy defines motherhood as a woman's 'natural destiny', it is ironic that natural destiny seldom applies to women who have children out of wedlock. This alone bears testimony to the inherently social essence of motherhood. In some societies illegitimacy carries little or no stigma: 'The situation is quite different in certain African societies where the physical genitor is of very little importance and where illegitimacy in the European sense is practically impossible since the child is always welcome and always belongs to somebody' (Macfarlane, 1980, pp. 74–5). Nor does illegitimacy always carry stigma in western societies; among the poorer sectors of the working class it does not seem to have been regarded by them as a problem – although it is by the authorities. Stack (1974, p. 47) relates how in the USA in the 1960s 'black women in The Flats feel few if any restrictions about childbearing. Unmarried black women, young and old, are eligible to bear children . . . A girl who gives birth as a teen-ager frequently does not raise and nurture her firstborn child. While she may share the same room and household with her baby, her mother, her mother's sister, or her older sister will care for the child and become the child's "mama"'.

As discussed earlier, the main reason for the stigmatisation of illegitimacy in Western Europe has been economic. Neither parish nor State has ever wanted to be financially responsible for children without social fathers, and hence the harsh treatment of unmarried mothers. The patriarchal notion of the father as the head of the household and responsible for dependants, makes it a woman's responsibility to ensure that she 'has' a man before she bears children. But sexual intercourse before marriage was common in the past, just as it is in contemporary society. Frequently this is seen as an inherent part of courtship, often with the understanding that it would eventually lead to marriage. Yet in both the past and the present couples frequently have to postpone marriage because of adverse economic circumstances. In contemporary society this is probably even more true, given the strong ideological equation of marriage with starting an independent household.

Having sexual relations before marriage obviously entails some risk of pregnancy. A man's unexpected death, his having to leave the area to find work elsewhere, unemployment, disillusionment with the partner, or dishonesty, can all bring an abrupt end to a marriage promise, and can leave a woman with the prospect of bearing an illegitimate child. Cissie Fairchilds (1978) argues that the rise of illegitimacy from the late eighteenth century was primarily a result of such 'frustrated' marriages, rather than some 'sexual revolution', as Shorter and Stearns have argued. Undoubtedly some illegitimate births were the results of other factors – rape, brief sexual encounters involving no promise to marry, liaisons between masters and servants (Gillis, 1981), but evidence suggests that these were usually the minority. Arguably, agreeing to sexual intercourse as a condition to future marriage has been one way in which women 'bargain' for the expected economic security of marriage. But it is a bargain that also involves a gamble. Adverse economic circumstances and increasingly misogynistic laws on illegitimacy in the nineteenth century made it an increasingly dangerous tactic. Having an illegitimate child could leave a woman impoverished, stigmatised, and not infrequently forced to abandon the child or resort to prostitution or the workhouse.

Although there were marked variations between areas, illegitimacy on average declined between the middle of the nineteenth and the middle of the twentieth centuries. This may partly reflect an increasing reluctance of women to take the risk of illegitimacy in bargaining for marriage; it probably also reflects somewhat greater economic security for a greater proportion of the population and a wider use of birth control by those having intercourse before marriage. Recently, however, illegitimacy rates in Britain have risen dramatically from 5 per cent of all live births in 1960 to 27 per cent of all live births in 1989. Nearly half of these, however, are jointly registered by mother and father, which suggests that while formal marriage is declining in popularity, cohabitation has become increasingly popular. It may reflect an increase in 'frustrated' marriages as a result of recession, as in the past. It undoubtedly reflects a sharp decrease in the stigmatisation and penalisation of illegitimacy itself. Because of the rapid increase in divorce rates, concern has focused more on the problem of 'single parents' – a category that includes both the once-married and the never-married. Their economic circumstances are often as adverse as those of unmarried mothers of the past, but stigmatisation in terms of marital status has declined.

So far the discussion has focused on having or not having children; little mention has been made of children as boys and girls. There is plenty of evidence from both the past and the present that men and women do care a great deal about the sex of their children, and this may be particularly influential in the size of the family they eventually have. In most societies men in particular have preferred sons to daughters: 'the fathers have of course demanded sons; as heirs, field-hands, cannon-fodder, feeders of machinery, images and extensions of themselves; their immortality. In societies systematically practising female infanticide, women might understandably wish for boys rather than face the prospect of nine months of pregnancy whose outcome would be treated as a waste product. Yet, under the realities of organized male territoriality and aggression, when women produce sons, they are literally working for the army' (Rich, 1977).

Among those groups for whom property has been crucial, sons have been desired as heirs to both property and 'name', while daughters, needing dower to be married off, have been regarded as less desirable. This, at any rate, is what men in these situations were likely to have wanted. Women may well have been more anxious for a daughter or daughters as a source of domestic help and emotional support. Both men and women, however, may have wanted at least one daughter as a potential 'carer' for them in old age. This was more likely to have been the case among the poorer sectors of society who were unable to pay for servants, nurses or companions to care for them in old age.

Where women's work has been economically crucial to household survival, where there has been a dearth of work available for men, daughters seem to have been more highly desired than sons. In protoindustrial societies and areas, or places like the textile town where proletarianisation resulted in feminisation of the labour force, daughters were more valuable economically than sons. Sons were more likely to have to move away in search of work and were less likely to send any earnings home. Patriarchal values demanded that, if possible, a son should acquire skills and training through apprenticeship or education, which could be very costly for a poor family. The relative preference for sons or daughters thus probably varies somewhat according to class, local economic circumstances and to the age and sex structure of the existing household. Overriding these, however, the higher status of, and value placed on, men in a patriarchal society means that sons always tend to be more desired than daughters.

From the earliest age babies are treated differently according to their sex. Although in pre-industrial society all babies were initially put in swaddling, their dress afterwards varied significantly: 'there was also a widespread belief that unless restrained the infant might tear off its ears, scratch out its eyes or break its legs ... once removed from the swaddling bandages, the boys were left free, but the girls were encased in bodices and corsets reinforced with iron and whalebone to ensure that their bodies were moulded to the prevailing adult fashion' (Stone, 1977, p. 162). Concepts of childhood and ideas about childrearing have varied considerably over time (see Ariès, 1973; Gillis, 1981). The change in the eighteenth century from seeing children as inherently evil to viewing them as basically pure and inocent meant that treatment of children was consequently generally less harsh than in the past. The notion of childhood purity was accorded particularly to girls, but also to grown women, among the middle classes. Equating childhood purity and innocence with womanhood, however, posed certain problems: 'the ideal of feminine purity is implicitly asexual; how, then, could it be reconciled with the active sexuality that would inevitably be included in the duties of wife and mother? (It was) resolved by focusing on the femininity of the daughter ... Much more successfully than her mother, a young girl could represent the quintessential angel in the house' (Gorham, 1982 p. 7).

Unlike earlier traditions, and influenced by the idea that all children were pure and asexual, the Victorians did not treat young boys and girls very differently; both were dressed as girls for several years; both were encouraged to get plenty of exercise. Girls, however, were inculcated from an early age with the ideals of self-sacrifice and service, while boys were brought up to think of themselves as more independent. The spatially confined structure of middle-class families, the legal position of children as the father's property, and the general tenets of patriarchal ideology, made girls particularly vulnerable incest victims of fathers and brothers. Yet in contemporary society, where incest is illegal and children no longer are the property of the father, incest remains a common experience. The problems of reporting, prosecuting and thereby acquiring reliable figures are immense, yet estimates from the USA suggest that anything from 5 to 30 per cent of the entire population has experienced incest (Forward and Buck, 1981, p. 20), and that 'among the reported victims of incest girls outnumber boys by seven to one' (ibid., p. 3). Incest is probably the most illustrative example of patriarchy, in that it constitutes both oppression by age and by sex, and, because of the father's authority as father it is a power relationship premised ultimately on threat of force, yet seldom having to resort to violence *because* of that authority.

Treatment of middle-class Victorian boys and girls changed dramatically at puberty. They were to be kept quite separate; girls were to cease any vigorous physical exercise, take more rest, dress in a more restricted way, often cease all educational activities, and even practising the piano was deemed to be too strenuous when a girl was menstruating. Boys, on the other hand, entered the all-male world of work or public school, increased their physical and intellectual activities, and were encouraged more than ever to be active and independent.

In contemporary society boys and girls are still treated differently from the time of birth. Infant boys tend to be played with more aggressively than girls, who tend to receive more passive 'cuddling', particularly from fathers: 'it seems, from both psychoanalytic clinical reports and from social psychological research, that fathers generally sex-type their children more consciously than mothers along traditional gender-role lines, and that they do encourage feminine heterosexual behaviour in their young daughters' (Chodorow, 1978, p. 118). Even when there is no father resident in a household, children are exposed at an early age to gender types through books, toys, the media, the education system. Kin, friends and neighbours will tend to treat boys and girls differently, even if the mother does not. The overriding importance of a child's sex is betrayed by the fact that almost invariably the first question asked after a baby is born, by parents and by others, is whether it is a boy or a girl. Enquiries about the mother's and baby's health come later. This immediate concern about a baby's sex betrays a vital concern as to how the baby will be treated, where it belongs in society; sex remains the primary way in which individuals are categorised and treated by others from the moment of birth.

In seeking to understand why men and women want, or do not want, children, and why they want boys or girls, it is necessary to consider a number of complex factors. We cannot assume that wanting children is natural, nor that it is necessarily a result of, or a reason for, marriage, nor, indeed, a necessary result of sexual intercourse. Having children has certainly become intimately linked in cultural values to the idea of forming and of being a family, to the extent that married couples without children are persistently asked by kin and friends 'when are you going to start a family?', as though only by having children can one claim to be part of a family. Patriarchal values, notions of inheritance of both property and self, economic and political motives, a desire for status, a desire for love, fears of loneliness, a desire to be seen as 'normal' – all these influence individuals' wishes about having children.

The fact that the majority of people in contemporary society have very few children, or none at all, means that for those who do have one or two children more is expected of them. More, too, is 'invested' in them in terms of education, aspirations, emotional demands and fears. Where once in large families different children might fulfil different needs and expectations of their parent(s) – for example, one or two might be heirs or chief economic providers, one might be the 'carer', one might provide a parent with a particularly close emotional bond, another might take the bulk of domestic responsibility, now more of these demands are put on to one or two children alone. One child may be heir, carer and emotional buttress. Because of the persistence of patriarchal values, and the relative decline of direct economic utility of children, more of these demands and 'needs' are apt to be put on daughters or daughters-in-law. More is expected from daughters in family terms (not in terms of achievement of independence) throughout their lives. This may well be one reason why many women try to break free of these often heavy emotional and caring demands put on them by parents, and seek what they perceive to be independence by starting their *own* families – and thus perpetuating the same cycle of problems and demands.

6

Why is a woman's work never done?

The farmer who works from sun to sun has a more straightforward relationship to the economy than his wife or daughters. He has one clear-cut job, while they often have two. In contemporary society the word 'work' has come to be virtually synonymous with *paid* work, yet much of the work that goes on in society is unpaid. Childcare, cleaning, shopping, cooking, laundry, care of the infirm and elderly, house maintenance, are all tasks necessitating plenty of time and effort, and therefore constitute work. They are not, however, acknowledged as such by most members of society, even by those who carry out the tasks. A full-time housewife, when asked if she works, will often reply in the negative, despite the fact that she may well be performing housework for twelve or fifteen hours a day. Yet the full-time housewife is not necessarily a typical woman; many women now, as in the past, work in the household doing unpaid work as well as working for wages.

There has been a great deal of controversy about the relation of domestic labour to the capitalist economy. Marxists in particular have tried to find ways in which they can explain housework within an overall Marxist theoretical framework. Wally Seccombe argued that while housework in a capitalist economy has no direct relation to capital and produces no surplus value as such, it none the less creates value through creating, and servicing, labour power – i.e. male wage earners and future wage earners. This 'serviced' labour power is subsequently exchanged on the labour market in return for wages. Domestic labour thus contributes indirectly through the reproduction of labour power to surplus value (Coulson *et al.*, 1980).

112

The immediate products of housework, however, are use values rather than exchange values; the services and products of housework are usually for consumption by individuals within the household. Seccombe's theory does not explain women's *dual* relationship to the economy – the fact that so many work both as wage labourers and perform domestic labour. The model also supposes that everybody lives in a nuclear family-type household, which as we have seen is not the case. It is also assumed that housework and childcare are always private, unpaid tasks which never enter the market-place. This, too, can be challenged. Moreover, the nature and content of housework has changed over time, and varies between different strata of society.

In medieval times, and for many well into the modern period, production and consumption were inextricably linked. Women raised children, cooked and washed then, as now, for no payment. But they also baked, brewed, kept poultry, made various artefacts, produced dairy products, spun, and wove. All of these tasks were essential to the household's survival. If there was any surplus it might be sold in the market, but on the whole it was produced for the use and consumption of all individuals within the household. The work men did in the fields, in crafts, fishing, and so on, was also largely for immediate consumption. Women worked in the fields and crafts as well, although men almost never took on the jobs of childcare or cooking. If a wife died, a daughter or sister would take these over, or the man would try to remarry as quickly as possible. If the man died or was absent, it was common for the woman to take over his jobs, often with the help of any children who were co-resident. The sexual division of labour varied between areas, and indeed between households, but it was certainly there, and its most persistent aspect has been women's – though not necessarily the wife's – responsibility for childcare and food preparation.

Peasant women did not have the same property or legal rights as peasant men. Economically, though, their work was essential. Not all of them were housewives; the size of households was larger than now and might at various times contain unmarried or widowed sisters, daughters, as well as male and female servants. The relative size of the household and its resources – labour power, land, age structure of its inhabitants – largely determined who did what. An elder daughter or sister might tend to the cooking and small children while the other women divided their time between the dairy, brewing, mining or working in the fields. Some went to live and work in other households. Housework, as we think of it, was minimal, except for food preparation. Housing was usually crude and cramped; furniture was sparse. Standards of cleanliness were extremely low by our standards; earth floors needed no cleaning, the whole household might sleep in one or two beds or, indeed, in straw on the floor. There might only be one or two rooms in the whole household; woollen clothing was seldom or never cleaned; eating utensils were minimal, and by the age of 2 or 3, children mixed in with the general household and farm activities and needed little supervision.

Everyone who could was involved in production in one way or another. What was produced generally constituted use value for immediate consumption. Yet it also produced exchange value through payments – in labour and kind – to the lord for use of the land and for his protection. Peasant women were, as Catherine Hall states, 'free to be exploited in an equal way with men' (1980, p. 46).

Although not crucial politically, as it was for the aristocracy, marriage was an important economic transaction for the peasantry. The skills and dower which a woman would bring to the household were essential; similarly, the man's greater rights over land were vital. Yet not all households contained a married couple. Often brothers and sisters would live together and run a household and landholding together. Many men and women never married at all during this period; there were ways of surviving economically without marrying, although living alone was almost impossible. Remaining celibate in medieval times was, of course, regarded as a virtue, and not as a sign of some pathological personality disorder, as in present times.

The lives led by the aristocracy were obviously very different from those of the peasantry. Given the prime importance of land to the feudal economy, aristocratic wives and women almost never had direct ownership or control of it. Women were crucial as a means of making political alliances and accruing wealth through marriage, but marriage was largely a negotiation between two sets of parents. Feudal manors, unlike most peasant households, were largely male-dominated institutions. The lord and his wife and children were a small, albeit important, group among a large retinue of male vassals, pages, courtiers, advisers and soldiers. Most of these men would be single; if they were married, their wives usually lived outside the manor. The lady of the manor had important supervisory roles in the running of the estate, education of children, and so on, but she was usually excluded from the political and economic world outside the manor.

War was an exclusively male phenomenon, although the wife might well be responsible for running the estate during her husband's absence. The Paston Letters show how, while the men frequently travelled to London and abroad, women seldom left their immediate environs. Aristocratic women often engaged in spinning and weaving as well as supervision, but their main value was as part of a marriage contract and the political and economic alliances which that could enable. Many of the notions inherent in patriarchal ideology as explicit in Judaeo-Christian theology were consolidated by the household relations of the feudal aristocracy.

The gradual growth of wage labour from the fifteenth century did not change household routine and the work most people did very dramatically. Landholdings were increasingly paid for in cash rather than kind; surplus from farming or cloth production was increasingly sold in the market in exchange for cash. Yet the patterns of work and the division of labour remained much the same; work was done in and around the household, as it had been, with men, women and children all involved in various aspects of production. Households produced both use value and exchange value. Gradually, however, the consolidation of land and the increase of enclosures made more and more households reliant on wage labour alone.

Where this was the case – and it varied quite considerably by region – then such households had to survive though an increased reliance on the production of exchange value, and more and more household products were exchanged for cash. Severance from the land in turn made wage labourers dependent on purchasing goods in the market which had once been produced in the household. This stimulated capitalist enterprise in producing goods for the market. From the seventeenth century in particular there was a notable expansion, a professionalisation and centralisation of the production of goods and services once performed by women in the household.

The low level of wages meant that it was essential for all able adults and children within a household to engage in wage labour. This, of course, included women. Increasingly the work they could do for wages was specialised; the entire household might be involved in spinning and weaving, or in agricultural work. But this meant that the time that could be spent in other tasks such as brewing or making candles, and so on, was drastically reduced. The capitalist take-over of production of such commodities at once increased the wealth of capitalist entrepreneurs and made wage labourers more than ever reliant on their own labour power to survive. Food preparation and childcare, however, remained household tasks that were not usually paid. Because they had for so long been defined as women's work, it was women who continued to do them, thereby reducing the hours they could spend in working for wages.

In some cases, these tasks were taken on by others in exchange for cash or services: a grandmother or unmarried sister might be offered board and lodging in exchange for taking on housework. Neighbours often shared housework and childcare between households. This practice has been prevalent in poor communities for centuries, and can still be found in the twentieth century. Bakers would cook people's dinners for a small fee, witness this account from a man who grew up in a Devon textile town at the end of the last century: 'dinnertimes – wasn't no time then. You'd take your dinners up the bakehouse. They'd cook 'em, see. Then you'd call in when you were coming home and – take 'em home. Pay a penny. Penny for cooking the dinner.'[1]

Housework did – and does – have a market value. In modern society, many women pay childminders to look after their young children while they are at work. 'Takeaway' meals often form the basis of much of a household's diet during the working week. More affluent working women pay other (less affluent) women to clean their homes and do their laundry. Less affluent women will often make arrangements with a mother or neighbour nearby to perform the same tasks for *them*. While much housework does not pass through the market, it can do so, and often does. Arguably the market through which housework passes is an informal, predominantly female, market. It is also one that operates between households as well as between individuals. Because household tasks have been defined ideologically as women's work, and as part of a woman's duty to the marriage contract, they have not been acknowledged as having exchange value or having a 'real' place in the organised world of work.

Housework is a sphere of work so deeply imbued with patriarchal notions of womanhood, wifehood and dependence that few seem able to realise that such work does – and did – have an exchange value. The rich employ nannies to care for their children, cooks and maids to do their housework – this is an exchange, and involves a cash transaction. When men, of whatever class, are left without a women to do these tasks for them, they quickly employ a housekeeper (if they can afford one), or demand the help of a sister, daughter or mother to 'do' for them. Women without a husband, whether or not they have children, whether or not they do wage work, are never seen as needing such help or services. For, as women, they are by definition responsible for such jobs themselves, whatever their circumstances.

Patriarchy thus flourished before capitalism developed, but it continued to thrive as capitalism grew. In some ways, capitalism reinforced and increased some of the central tenets of patriarchy. With the growth of wage labour and the consolidation of capital, workers increasingly lost control over their work process, its pacing, quality and quantity. The more dependent a household became on wages alone, the more dependent it also became on the terms set by the capitalists buying their labour and products. To combat these forces, workers tried to organise themselves and their crafts against what they saw as unfair exploitation.

Although most occupations were based on the household and household labour, male heads of household had been defined for a long time as having greater status, and more legal rights, than women. Consequently when workers did try to organise themselves, organisation was generally of, and by, men. Guilds, associations, and later, unions, were predominantly – often exclusively – male organisations. Wives and daughters had always been invaluable assistants in the work process, but were seen as just that – assistants. This assumption became an integral part of the wage system: assistants, who were – or should be – also dependants, were paid less. This was an asset to capitalists, of course, but it also posed a threat to male workers. Their wives' and daughters' cheap labour threatened to undermine their own skills and ability to command a high wage.

The old system of apprenticeship, leading to the status of journeyman and then master craftsman, was from the seventeenth century further eroded and threatened by the growth of capitalism. As Alice Clark puts it:

> Under family industry the wife of every master craftsman became free of his gild and could share his work. But as the crafts became capitalised many journeymen never qualified as masters, remaining in the outer courts of companies all their lives, and actually forming separate organisations to protect their interests against their masters and to secure a privileged position for themselves by restricting the number of apprentices. As the journeymen worked on their masters' premises it naturally followed that their wives were not associated with them in their work, and that apprenticeship became the only entrance to their trade. (Clark, 1968, p. 10)

When and where this happened women were no longer able to acquire valuable skills and practise them in a family workshop. If they had to work – as most did – they were increasingly forced to work in unskilled occupations that required no training.

The occurrence of these changes was by no means uniform. In some occupations, and in some areas, it began as early as the sixteenth century, while in others it did not take place until the latter half of the nineteenth century, or even later. Even now, some small businesses and workshops are run within a household using family labour, for example, small grocery shops and Chinese restaurants. When such changes did occur, men organised to protect their positions and their skills; generally this meant trying to exclude women and children – cheap labour – from their craft. Their attempts were not always successful, partly because many occupations still relied heavily on family labour. Ivy Pinchbeck (1981, p. 276) relates how this happened in the file-cutting industry in which women had been working since the eighteenth century:

> In 1847 renewed attempts were made to exclude the 200 women and girls then in the trade. The file-smith's society drew up rules which limited the right to work to widows and orphans, and imposed a fine of £3 on any member who allowed his wife or daughter to work, or assisted any woman with tools. It proved impossible to enforce these new regulations, however, possibly

because three-quarters of the women at work were the wives or daughters of file-smiths, and a compromise was therefore arrived at, by which women were restricted to certain classes of work definitely given over to them.

Craftsmen, then, tried to combat the forces of capitalism and the threats of cheap labour and de-skilling by either forbidding women to work in their crafts or by relegating women to certain jobs within the craft – which were thereby defined as less skilled.[2]

Working women sometimes did try to organise their own associations and unions. When the Combination Acts forbidding unions were in force between 1799 and 1824, men and women frequently organised 'Friendly Societies', which were partly primitive insurance agencies and partly a kind of informal union. In the USA, women who worked in the early New England textile towns created their own labour associations, although 'like Bagley's Lowell Female Reform Association, these attempts were generally local or regional in scale; they seldom lasted long' (Baxandall, 1976, p. 259). Women's organisations were severely weakened by shortage of funds – a result of low wages – by male hostility, and by most women's lack of time for organisation as a result of domestic commitments. Nevertheless, on some occasions women did strike, as in 1832 when 1500 women card-setters in Peep Green, Yorkshire, came out on strike for equal pay with men (Mackie and Pattullo, 1977, p. 163).

In 1874 Emma Paterson organised the Women's Protective and Provident League, which later became the Women's Trade Union League. Male unions were at this time pressing for a 'family wage', which by its very definition presupposed women should not work in the labour force. Working women thus frequently met with hostility from working-class men. In 1877 the TUC declared that 'it was the duty of men and husbands to bring about a condition of things when their wives should be in their proper sphere at home instead of being dragged into competition of livelihood with the great and strong men of the world' (ibid., p. 163). The virtual exclusion of women from the unions during most of the nineteenth century reinforced inequality between men and women within the working class.

At the end of the nineteenth century, however, Britain witnessed a new wave of unionisation along industrial – rather than craft – lines, which was in fact instigated by the famous Matchgirls' Strike of 1889. These new unions recruited women on equal terms with men; during the four years of the First World War, female membership of unions in Britain trebled (ibid., p. 163). In the USA, on the other hand, industrial unions did not get off the ground until the 1930s, and although they increased women's membership, both women's trade union participation and the American labour movement generally remained weak and divided.

Given the ways in which patriarchal ideology influenced men's attitudes to women's work, notably their insistence that it was worth less than their own, it was by no means purely coincidental that the first industries to become mechanised and proletarianised were ones dominated by women, primarily textiles. The less a capitalist could pay his workers, of course, the more profits he could make. Women and children, long paid less than men, thus provided an ideal source of profit. By establishing mills in rural areas, capitalists were able to obviate the guild restrictions on apprenticeship and cheap labour which operated in the cities. They thereby weakened, and eventually destroyed, the power of the guilds. The first industrial proletariat in both Britain and the USA was overwhelmingly female. As Kessler-Harris (1982, p. 23) notes in writing about the early mills in the USA: 'Incipient manufacturers quickly discovered the advantages of employing children and women, preferably those who had no ties to the land and whose labour could be purchased at a minimal cost … Widows, potentially the most dependent labor population, proved particularly desirable.'

Lack of opportunities and of social mobility for women was one of the ways in which boys and men were able to achieve mobility for themselves. It was assumed that a woman's main chance of maintaining, or improving, her standard of living was through making a good marriage. This assumption to a large extent still remains with us, and is one of the principal reasons employers give for not offering women better chances of promotion and mobility. It is also a common assumption made by parents for giving sons better educational opportunities and more encouragement in furthering a career. If a woman does not marry, if she has to work to support an unemployed husband or dependent children, if she is separated, widowed or divorced, she is still, with few exceptions, obliged to work in the most insecure, least organised and worst paid sectors of the economy. In addition, she will be responsible for carrying out unpaid domestic labour within the home.

The demands of domestic labour are – and were – variable. In mining areas heavy work was involved in bathing male miners at home after work (which meant carrying and heating large quantities of water, usually from some distance), and in laundry, on top of a heavy burden of childcare, food preparation and domestic cleaning. Family size also affects the amount of domestic labour necessary. While large families could be useful in providing a greater wage-earning potential as well as a pool of domestic labour, they also created more work in terms of food preparation, laundry and childcare. In many nineteenth-century working-class families daughters worked full-time in the household from around the age of 8, thereby releasing their mother for wage work or, depending on household structure and circumstances, alleviating her domestic labour. If there were several daughters close in age, one would typically be kept at home while the others entered the labour force. When a younger daughter reached the age of 8 or so, the older one would then enter the labour force. A daughter with many brothers might be kept at home permanently – sometimes doing part-time work such as dressmaking at home – while her brothers entered the labour market and she helped with, or took over, domestic responsibilities.

To a large extent, the better off a family was, the more housework became necessary: 'even more than the equation of femininity with cleanliness was, of course, the equation of cleanliness with class position, part of the parcel of behaviour and attitudes bundled together in that imprecise but vital concept *respectability*' (Davidoff, 1976b). Families both past and present largely define their standard of living, status, and class position both to themselves and to the outside world through the type of accommodation they have, its degree of cleanliness and maintenance. Household members are similarly presented and judged by their personal appearance, the state of their clothing and personal cleanliness. The larger a house, the more furniture, the better presented its inhabitants, then the more housework is created. As always this was, and is, defined as exclusively women's work; higher status and class position thus increase women's unpaid domestic work, while it may also reduce their need to engage in paid work.

As the middle classes grew in wealth and power, so their houses became more elaborate, larger, better furnished, and more carefully segregated by age, sex, and class. Nurseries were far removed from the centre of the house; servants had separate quarters and sometimes separate entrances and staircases; boys and girls, men and women, all had separate sleeping quarters. When skilled working-class men were able to achieve a family wage, they took great pride and accrued great status by keeping their wives and children at home as their dependants. They sought more 'respectable' neighbourhoods in which to live, and attributed great importance to more spacious accommodation maintained in pristine order by their wives. Having an immaculately furnished and polished parlour – even though seldom used – was a great symbol of respectability. So, too, was a piano, even if nobody in the household could actually play it. Among the poorest sectors, status and respectability were defined by whether or not a house had curtains, whether the doorstep was cleaned every day, and whether or not children wore shoes. Thus the ways in which different sectors defined themselves in terms of class, status and respectability were intimately linked to their households – the ways in which they lived in, and maintained, them.

Increasing affluence therefore has direct implications for the amount and kind of housework performed. The twentieth-century revolution in household gadgets – themselves status symbols – have been presented as devices to lighten the burden of housework. Arguably many have actually increased it. Cleaning floors, a task supposedly liberated by the vacuum cleaner, has for more and more become a daily or twice daily task rather then a weekly one. The consumer industry, bolstered by the blossoming advertising industry, realised early in this century the economic potential of the home market for consumer goods, and both have consequently fostered the idea and the ideal of the permanently immaculate home and the need to buy more and more gadgets to keep it that way.

The irony is that as more people have become influenced by these pressures and by their desire to improve their standard of living, so it has become increasingly necessary for most households to have more than one wage-earner. If the wife works as well as the husband, so the dream of a new car, dishwasher or tumble drier comes that much closer to realisation. The result, however, is that the wage-earning wife has much less time available in which to keep the house permanently pristine. Torn between the demands of a job and those of a housewife/mother, the promise that a new gadget will lighten housework becomes inderstandably attractive. To be able to obtain it means continuing with the double burden of paid work and domestic work. This situation is generally advantageous to the capitalist economy; on the one hand, it stimulates the consumer industry, while, on the other hand, it provides a large pool of cheap labour – women who are prepared to do almost any work, full-time or part-time. Their lack of available time, moreover, severely curtails their ability to organise themselves to press for better conditions and pay.

Many women are, of course, either the *only* earners in a household, or have to work to supplement a husband's poor and/or erratic earnings. The dishwasher for such families remains a permanent dream and never a reality. Women in this type of situation in fact constitute a large part of the labour force. Hilary Land (1976a, p. 119) notes that in 1971 nearly 2 million women under retirement age were the chief economic supporters in their households, while 'in 1970 the DHSS estimated that the number of poor two-parent families in which the father was in full-time work . . . would have nearly *trebled* if the father's earnings had not been supplemented by the mother's'. Women in these situations have, generally speaking, the worst jobs in the labour market and the heaviest burdens of housework.

It is ironic that the new middle classes of the nineteenth century who so fervently preached the gospel of domestic bliss, the sanctity of the family, the woman's place as in the home, and the importance of cleanliness, hygiene and careful childrearing, were able to place so much of the burden of their own domestic work on to the shoulders of working-class servants. Middle-class 'angels of the house' whose very essence of womanhood lay in their role as custodian of the family and home, by 'nature' private and maternal, seldom questioned the ethics of relegating actual domestic drudgery to others. Their work – depending on the relative affluence of their husbands – was seen primarily as one of supervision of the household, children and servants.

More affluent middle-class women thus had a good deal of spare time to spend in calling on friends and kin – although this was by no means entirely 'non-work'; much of the rationale for such visits was to establish useful business contacts for husbands and possibly advantageous marriages for children. Many also engaged in a variety of philanthropic, religious, and educational activities. These were not 'private' pastimes, but they were unpaid and voluntary. Thus, although they were often very important indirectly in terms of business and marriage alliances, they were not perceived or defined as *work*.

Many middle-class women were able in this way to establish important networks, and often organised themselves into pressure groups. Their campaigns were varied, from protective legislation for working-class factory women and girls and improved religious education and facilities, to more controversial areas such as birth control, suffrage, better educational opportunities for women. Their ability to engage in such activities was at the expense of those for whom they seldom campaigned – their women servants. The capital which enabled the middle classes to reach a higher standard of living was thus a result of the exploitation of working-class men, women and children in the labour market, while the maintenance of that standard of living within their homes was achieved through similar exploitation of working-class girls and women who worked as their servants.

The spread of mass literacy and compulsory education from the end of the nineteenth century, the expanding clerical sector and the growth of the light industries during and after the inter-war period, has meant that fewer and fewer working-class girls have elected to, or have had to, work as domestic servants. The proportion of residential servants declined dramatically this century, but especially after the Second World War. For some middle-class women this has meant a severe cutback in their time available for leisure or political activities, particularly as they themselves have been increasingly drawn into the double burden which their working-class sisters had known much longer.

Nevertheless, as educational and occupational opportunities have been greater for middle-class than for working-class women, as husbands' earnings have been much higher, so the middle classes have still been able to buy more service, leisure and convenience than the working classes. Many employ domestic help on a daily basis; they are able to afford far more domestic gadgets; sending children to boarding schools relieves much domestic drudgery. Nor is it coincidental that middle-class pressure for more 'help' from husbands in the house and with children has increased notably with the disappearance of the ready availability of domestic servants.

Despite marked class differences, however, women generally tend to participate in leisure activities less than men. More men are active in unions and clubs; more men are actively involved in sport than women, and more attend pubs regularly. Much of this is due to the double burden which both working-class and middle-class women increasingly experience. Some is due to a persistent social stigma against women going out alone, particularly to pubs or clubs. For couples with children, going out together involves finding and paying for a babysitter; many seem to 'economise' by the wife staying at home while the husband goes out. Much of it is a result of a lack of any tradition of women's leisure activities outside the home – with the notable exception of bingo. For a long time those activities which have been defined as providing 'leisure' for women have been largely home-based: sewing, embroidery, knitting – all arguably more related to work than leisure – playing the piano, reading, writing, watching television – though many women seem to feel justified in watching television only if they are simultaneously darning or knitting. Men feel no such constraints.

Yet in Victorian times it was quite common for working-class women to attend pubs, and many were heavy drinkers. In late nineteenth-century London 'in poor neighbourhoods there was a considerable women's pub culture . . . Women of all ages went into pubs, bringing babies and children with them until the 1908 Childrens Act restricted the entry of children . . . some pubs were frequented exclusively by women. On Mondays, a slow day in the weekly rhythm of London laundry work, laundresses gathered in the pubs' (Ross, 1983, pp. 10–11). Middle-class Victorian morality earmarked drink as one important area for defining respectability – drunkenness, particularly for women, was severely condemned. It was acceptable, however, to drink in moderate quantities within the home – it was women drinking in public that the Victorians found so offensive. Recently it has become more acceptable for women to drink in pubs – if they are accompanied by a man, or at least are with a group of other women rather than alone, and providing that they never drink in excess. There are numerous instances of publicans who have refused to serve a woman a pint of beer, insisting that women can only drink half-pints.

The idea that households should be 'private' and inhabited only by blood relations gained increasing strength during the course of the nineteenth century as a result of middle-class domestic ideology. The dramatic growth of wage labour and concomitant decline of living and working in other households as a common experience of youth (except for working-class girls) was reinforced by state policies on male responsibility for wife and children, illegitimacy laws and, later, housing policies. Nevertheless, the private, well-kept home inhabited by a nuclear family alone remained unattainable for many working-class families. Working-class households continued to need more than one wage-earner. Unemployment and underemployment meant many women continued to be reliant on neighbourhood networks for exchange of services and goods. Networks frequently also involved kinship: 'neighbourhood relationships in many London districts overlapped with kinship . . . At the time of her death in 1902, a Mrs. Spooner had 34 grandchildren and 42 great-grandchildren on the street' (ibid., p. 9).

Women took common responsibility for neighbourhood children, often acted as moneylenders, and helped one another in sickness and confinements. It was also common for wage-earners within a household to pay not only for room and board, but also for any extra services: 'working sons paid their younger siblings to polish their shoes and perform other small tasks for them. A Hoxton man even arranged to pay his wife for serving him lunches at home when he suddenly transferred to a new job nearby' (ibid., p. 12).

Housework and childcare were not, and are not, necessarily always private unpaid jobs outside the market economy. On the contrary, for the poor such sharing of work and resources between households can be seen as constituting an informal economy in its own right. Yet as educational and occupational opportunities increased in the twentieth century, more and more working-class families strove to escape from such environs. Both Ross and Stack show how this kind of informal economy makes any accumulation of wealth or goods, any improvement in standard of living, almost impossible given the assumption that resources must be shared between households and neighbouring kin. Chaytor (1980) shows how essentially the same economy operated in pre-industrial England. The lateral bonds of neighbourhood also threatened the vertical, hierarchical bonds of marriage. When men became able to command a family wage, they were usually anxious to sever ties from the informal economy (which had given their wives considerable power within the household) and to establish their wives and children as dependants in more isolated, private surroundings which gave husbands much greater power within the household.

Arthur Harding relates how, after the First World War, when he was able to secure reasonable employment, he was anxious to move with his wife and children away from the neighbourhood in which he had grown up: 'we moved away to Leyton but my brother's family stayed put. My children didn't mix with 'em, from the time when we moved away to Leyton . . . (one cousin is) still a bit of a villain. I've often thought to myself, sooner or later, that's how my children would have gone, if we hadn't got away from Bethnal Green' (Samuel, 1981a, p. 247). Thus in times of relative prosperity, those groups who are able to improve their economic situation through the formal economy tend to sever ties with the informal economy – and also often with kin – thereby privatising their households and making housework and childcare exclusively the wife's responsibility, and wage earning the husband's. Such changes obviously also have dramatic effects on the power relationship between husband and wife. A higher standard of living via a husband's more secure employment is often achieved at the expense of the wife's relative independence within the household and community.

An informal economy tends to exist wherever there is poverty, just as it has for centuries. On the whole, it is a woman's economy and one operating between households. The exchange involved may be in the form of work, cash, goods or sometimes children. That it is an informal organisation and thus relatively 'invisible' should not disguise the fact that housework of all sorts has an exchange value, and that, moreover, housework is not always specific either to one individual woman or to an individual household. But it does remain specific to women.

The fact that many men still did not – and do not – earn a family wage, that many women of all classes were not married or were widowed or separated, and that government legislation and trade union policy have made it increasingly difficult for women to earn a living in the formal economy, often meant finding ways of survival outside it. For many women the strength of patriarchal ideology caused them to find some kind of employment within the home. They worked either in their own homes or in others as childminders, charwomen, laundresses, doing outwork, or as prostitutes. While in the nineteenth century many women eked out an existence doing straw-plaiting, lace making, or making matchboxes at home, so in modern industrial society women often work in similar circumstances for low wages – sewing up dresses in isolated cottages in Wales, soldering components at home for multinationals, or selling kitchenware to friends and neighbours.

One of the most common means by which women have combined their domestic role with that of earning a living has been through taking in lodgers. As the practice of residential apprenticeship declined, and as urbanisation and geographical mobility increased, there was a real need for accommodation for people of all walks of life who were relatively rootless. Many, as Anderson (1971) has shown, relied on kin for lodging and support, but this was not always available or desired. Taking in lodgers provided a valuable source of income for many women: 'An activity such as the housing and feeding of lodgers can be understood as a kind of subsistence employment, one of a variety of forms of labour existing side by side or even carried on by the same people: a way of life, as much as making a living' (Davidoff, 1979, p. 67).

Taking in lodgers, however, was regarded by the Victorian middle classes as a travesty of the notion of privacy and the sanctity of the family. It was also seen as sexually dangerous, particularly for women lodgers. The Common Lodging Houses Act of the 1850s was an attempt ostensibly to control overcrowding, but was more concerned with the problem of 'morality' and, in particular, what was seen as a threat to that most sacred of Victorian institutions, the family. Such legislation put increasing pressure on both landladies and lodgers to conform to the middle-class ideal of a nuclear family, even if this was seldom in fact possible.

Although the number of lodging houses declined, taking in lodgers into private households continued. Landladies almost always lived in the premises themselves, and an essential part of their work was the servicing of their lodgers – cleaning, providing meals, doing their laundry. It was, essentially, a relationship that duplicated most of the notions of a patriarchal household, except that the sexual aspect was missing, the head was usually a woman, and, more important, it involved a cash relationship and created exchange value. It both replicated and transgressed the ideology of a patriarchal household. While providing an important means of economic survival for many women, it was essentially a part of the informal economy. Its decline was partly a result of the growth of building societies and owner-occupation, housing policies which designed houses which were only suitable for nuclear families (even now most mortgage contracts stipulate that no lodgers should be taken in), and the increasingly prevalent notion that just as all individuals should marry, so all families should be nuclear and private.

In both urban areas and tourist areas today, taking in lodgers and providing bed and breakfast still provides both a useful service to transients and travellers, and an important source of income to many families and women alone who cannot support themselves adequately through the formal economy. Lodging is, above all, a good example of the way in which the economy does permeate the household and housework and how the latter does, or can, constitute an economic relationship and produce exchange value.

While many thus, through necessity, implicitly and informally challenged and defied the middle-class notion of the privacy of the home and the non-economic nature of housework, others challenged these assumptions in a more explicitly political and formal way. Two pioneers in the idea that women's inequality could only be eradicated through the socialisation of housework and childcare were Robert Owen and Charles Fourier. As Hayden (1982, p. 33) relates: 'their campaigns against the isolated household were only part of their larger social and economic goals . . . their conviction that the built environment must be transformed to reflect more egalitarian systems of production and consumption persuaded them of the importance of making a full critique of conventional housing and domestic life.' Both advocated collective housework and childcare, and in 1813 Owen published designs for socialist communities with collective kitchens, nurseries and dining rooms.

The writings and plans of Owen and Fourier and later generations of feminists resulted in a number of experimental communities being established from the 1820s, most of which were in the USA. They differed in organisation and structure in a variety of ways. The Shaker communities in the USA, for instance, formed celibate communities and adopted orphan children. The Oneida communities established by John Noyes, on the other hand, believed in and practised free love. They all opposed nuclear families and private housework and childcare, seeing these as obstacles to their goal of equality for all and the collective well-being of the community. Nevertheless, while domestic labour in these experimental communities was indeed socialised, it still remained women's work. The same applies to the collective domestic work of Israeli kibbutzim.

From the 1860s a number of American feminists began agitating for, and planning, what they called 'co-operative housekeeping', by which a group of housewives would perform all domestic work collectively and then charge their husbands for their services. They then hoped to be able to buy communal buildings where baking, laundry, sewing, and so on, could be carried out collectively. Husbands, unfortunately, were generally unwilling to co-operate, and property developers were even less interested in the schemes. Other feminists, such as Charlotte Perkins Gilman, argued along similar lines. There were a number of disagreements, in particular as to whether marriage should be retained in a new form or whether there should be free love, while others argued for celibacy. Financing co-operative housework projects was extremely difficult, particularly as husbands and fathers regarded them usually as either crazy or threatening – or both. This is hardly surprising, given that the women were directly challenging patriarchal authority as well as many of the tenets of capitalism. Few of the schemes ever got off the ground, and those that did soon ran into overwhelming difficulties.

These challenges to patriarchy and capitalism were important in the emphasis they put on the need to abolish private domestic labour if true equality were ever to be attained. They also demonstrated that there were alternatives to the sacrosanct ideal of the middle-class nuclear family. Perhaps most important, they drew attention to the fact that housework, even if unpaid, was – and still is – work, and as such deserves proper recognition and remuneration.

The demise of these ideas and communities after the early years of this century – not to emerge again until the 1960s – can be seen as a result of various forces. As a direct challenge to patriarchy, male hostility from all classes was inevitable. There was also hostility from many women who fully accepted the patriarchal ideal. As a challenge to the capitalist economy, no matter how eccentric the notions may have seemed, they would and did inevitably incur the wrath of industrialists, entrepreneurs and politicians. Few working-class men or trade unionists sympathised with the ideas, for they not only threatened their male authority, but also ran counter to their desire for a family wage.

Since the middle of the nineteenth century the works of Marx had become far more influential in radical politics than those of Fourier or Owen, and Marx's theory of labour paid scant attention to the realm of unpaid domestic labour. His work was addressed primarily to the inequalities existing between classes rather than to those between the sexes. The family, for Marx, was but another bourgeois institution which would – or could – vanish with the overthrow of the bourgeoisie. Once the family had disappeared, so too, he argued, would sexual inequality. He never bothered to question seriously who, in a communist society, would carry out the domestic tasks. Like many subsequent theorists, such questions were regarded as largely peripheral or irrelevant to the more central – male – issues of class and paid work within the formal economy.

Understanding why 'a woman's work is never done' means first of all accepting the dual nature of the 'work' for women. For a very long time the idea of womanhood – and increasingly wifehood – has been synonymous with a woman's 'natural' responsibility for childcare and domestic work. However a society or household is organised, there has always been the assumption that a certain core of domestic work is by definition woman's work. This regardless of whether she engages in paid work, whether she is totally or partly dependent on a husband or father, regardless of whether she is single, married, widowed or divorced, young or old. There is no equivalent assumption for men. A man *may* empty the rubbish, bath the baby, wash the dishes or sweep the floor, but if he elects not to do so – as many have and do – he is in no way socially or economically ostracised or penalised. His domestic participation is totally and always voluntary.

If a woman chooses not to keep the house clean, not to supervise the children adequately, she is in danger of being labelled as a 'bad' mother or a bad wife – she can be divorced, she can have her children taken away from her by the State. Housework and childcare are not voluntary for married women in contemporary society, unless their class position is such that they have the financial resources to pay others to carry out their responsibilities. But they remain their responsibilities.

Domestic labour does have more than just a use value. It can be bought, exchanged and sold, and frequently is. Although domestic labour is an integral and implicit part of the marriage contract, it is not specific to married women only – single mothers are equally held responsible for carrying out domestic work for their children. Adult daughters are seen as having special responsibility for caring

7

The State: creator or destroyer of family solidarity?

There is an on-going debate about the relationship between the State and the family. Theorists from Left and Right, feminist and anti-feminist, have been arguing often seemingly confusing and contradictory viewpoints. Essentially the controversy amounts to disagreement as to whether the growth of the State, and the Welfare State in particular, has actually enhanced the position of families and family 'solidarity', or whether it has exacerbated a decline and erosion of what is seen as previously greater family solidarity and support. Both sides tend to suffer equally from a rather monolithic interpretation of both 'the State' and 'the family'.

Since at least the eighteenth century there have been recurring outbursts of fear that the family is in a state of crisis or decline. Indeed, the debate really began parallel with the establishment of the bourgeois notion of 'the family'. Concern about families has also tended to occur most noticeably during times of economic and political crisis. Industrialisation, urbanisation, socialism, and the growth of the State have all at times been cited as reasons for the alleged decline of families. In the 1930s, while Hitler was exhorting Aryan women to return to their 'natural' tasks of bearing future warriors and extolling the virtues of women's place in the home, Left-wing critical sociologists such as Adorno and Horkheimer were arguing that the increasing 'rationalisation' of modern industrial society, the growth of fascism, and of the State in particular, were all eroding the primary ties of families.

Functionalist sociologists like Parsons and Murdock in the 1940s and 1950s maintained that earlier 'functions' of the family, notably production and education, had been taken over by the State with the result that families had become much more specialised institutions, catering primarily for socialisation, emotional needs and mutual support. Inherent in these theories was the notion of a male breadwinner supporting a dependent wife and children, with the onus of emotional support on the wife/mother. From the 1960s some feminists in Britain and the USA argued that families were a source of women's inequality in society and the workplace. Others, however, argued that the home was woman's natural sphere and needed greater recognition as such by society and by the State.

Christopher Lasch argues from a Marxist standpoint in *Haven in a Heartless World* (1977), that the growth of the capitalist State, the increase of 'scientific management' and the growth of professional medical and welfare experts has virtually destroyed the private security and closeness of families. A not dissimilar view is taken, but from a Right-wing stance, by Ferdinand Mount in *The Subversive Family* (1982), where he sees the private world of the family as a last bastion against State interference, a realm for individual development and expansion which is constantly resisting the meddling policies of the State. Both Lasch and Mount, with some validity, stress that the family must be seen as a product of human agency rather than as a totally passive recipient of abstract social and economic forces, and State interference in particular. Families, for them, are the last defence of the individual against an increasingly tyrannical and interfering social and political system.

A more elaborate, though not wholly dissimilar, stance is taken by Jacques Donzelot in *The Policing of Families*. Donzelot argues that just as families were in various ways influenced by socio-economic and political factors, so society was influenced and affected by families. His definition of 'the family' is a much more flexible one than that of most earlier theorists, claiming that it needs to be seen 'not as a point of departure, as a manifest reality, but as a moving resultant, an uncertain form whose intelligibility can only come from studying the system of relations it maintains with the sociopolitical level' (1979, p. xxv). His argument is that while the development of capitalist industrial society, hygiene technicians and medical technology, and so on, have weakened families in various ways, at the same time society has become increasingly influenced by the ideal of 'the family', and that consequently society has become increasingly 'familialised'. This is a forceful and in many ways a cogent argument, although it is necessary to examine it in more detail against historical evidence.

Despite some of the many cogent and stimulating ideas that Donzelot puts forth (as well as some unnecessarily obscure arguments), there is a body of functionalist assumptions underlying most of his theory. In particular, he frequently refers to the *needs* of society in much the same way as functionalists do. What are these needs? Can a society really be understood in this way at all? Moreover, he seldom differentiates between the different effects of legislation and policies on men and women, adults and children, the married and non-married. In short, although he tries to deconstruct the idea of the family in a number of important ways, most of his arguments are based on an assumed monolithic type family, which he sees varying only by social class.

There is also an inherent assumption, as in the works of Mount, Lasch, and others, that once upon a time there was a 'real family' that has subsequently been lost to us through the forces of modern industrial society, and this is treated as a cause for despair. This recurrent theme of a 'lost family' bears many similarities to the frequent mourning over the loss of a 'real community' since the nineteenth century. The problem of defining either, much less finding either, is so difficult as to render the concepts of both family and community questionable; perhaps what is being talked about is more a sense of change and loss as symbolised by family and community.

All these theorists have largely ignored the question of gender as crucial in understanding the relationships between families and the State. Feminists, however, have concentrated on this problem. Theorists like Heidi Hartmann (1979), Ehrenreich and English (1979), and Hilary Land (1976) have argued that the Welfare State is largely premised on the assumption that women and children are – or should be – dependent on a man, and that therefore legislation relating to families has promoted the nuclear family both as an ideal, and as an increasing necessity for survival. Hartmann points out that protective legislation for women and children depended on prior agreements between capitalists and working-class men, whose interests converged in keeping women out of well-paid, skilled work, and who both benefited from women's service and dependence as wives and mothers. In other words, they argue that patriarchy is just as important a factor to consider as class. Yet much legislation relating to families and to protection was in fact demanded by women – often feminists – themselves. The contemporary women's movement has pressed for *increased* State involvement by demanding free contraception, abortion on demand and State nurseries. The idea of wages for housework also demands greater State involvement in family matters. What exactly is the relationship between families and the State? This is a highly complex question which cannot be answered in full. An examination of certain pieces of legislation may, however, shed more light on the problem.

It is important to reiterate and remember the enormous variety of family structures that existed and exist in society. It cannot be assumed that a law supposedly directed at 'the family' will affect all families identically or, indeed, all individuals within a family. What may enhance security and solidarity for one family may also undermine it in another. In fact, very little legislation has been addressed at families as such, but rather relates to different categories of individuals within families – for example, children, married women, divorced women, and so on. In many cases whole families are affected by it, but, again, not necessarily in equal ways.

It is also important to be cautious about thinking of 'the State' as a monolithic, single-minded entity. Agitation for reform may originate from very radical groups proposing radical changes, but as it progresses (if it progresses) through civil service reports and enquiries, parliamentary debate and actual implementation at a local level, may end up as having quite a different form and effect at the end of the process than that originally intended. What a national government intends as policy may be implemented at a local level quite differently, perhaps not implemented at all. Some legislation may be carried through with the intent of making concessions to certain groups, yet may end up as a means of oppressing these, or other, groups. Moreover, it cannot be assumed that the State always acts in the interests of one class,[1] or, indeed, of one sex. It will be useful, then, to consider briefly the growth of the State and State agencies before examining specific issues affecting individuals within and outside families.

The weakening power of the feudal lords which resulted from the Wars of the Roses in the fifteenth century and the growth of mercantile capitalism made it possible for the Tudor monarchs of the sixteenth century to take over at a national level many of the areas previously controlled by individual lords. The dissolution of the monasteries increased the wealth of the State as well as decreasing the wealth and power of the Church. Defence and justice

became more centralised nationally, although resting also on implementation at a local level. The Church was nationalised. Social
and political order were seen more and more as matters of national
rather than local concern and policy.

The most pressing problems facing the sixteenth-century State
were ones with which we remain familiar – poverty and unemployment. Enclosures, the growth of wage labour and the demise of
feudal and Catholic charity all exacerbated these twin problems.
Rapid economic changes in some areas resulted in changing employment opportunities and a growth in geographical mobility ('vagrancy'). Access to land was becoming more difficult and a greater
proportion of the population was becoming landless. Wages were
low and erratic. Widows, deserted wives and single women, once
able to survive in smallholdings with access to the resources of
common lands, were increasingly deprived of these rights and
became one of the most impoverished groups in society. Church
refuge and charity no longer existed and, as we have seen, community notions of mutual assistance were changing. Women who bore
illegitimate children were in a particularly precarious position
economically.

The Tudor Poor Laws tried to solve some of these problems by
differentiating between those who could work, but would not, and
thus deserved harsh punishment, and those who would work, but
could not, and were therefore deemed worthy of parish relief. Then,
as now, work was seen as the solution to poverty, although unlike
today the Tudor laws made the parish responsible for finding or
creating work for those with no employment. Orphaned children
were to be made apprentices in other people's households where
they could learn skills and earn their board and lodging, so that they
could eventually become economically independent. This practice
survived in some areas – notably Devonshire – until well into the
nineteenth century. The infirm and elderly who were too old to
work were to be cared for by their kin, and only if they had no kin
were they eligible for parish relief. Single women who were pre-
gnant had to name and enforce marriage or maintenance on the
man responsible. The relief of poverty, in other words, was to be
achieved first and foremost through kinship responsibility, and only
when that was non-existent, through community and State responsibility.

By making kin responsible for dependants the Tudor Poor Laws reiterated and reinforced patriarchal notions of service, dependence and family responsibility. All the legislation was buttressed by a firm work ethic. Whenever and wherever possible, those who were in dire circumstances and lived outside patriarchal households were forced to live within others' households, whether kin or non-kin. The concept of a household was broadly equated with economic independence through access to work and the parallel obligation to maintain and/or train dependants within it. By emphasising the responsibility of kin and households to care for dependants, considerable financial savings were accrued for the rest of the parish. It was therefore in the community's economic interests to ensure that all individuals lived within independent households. This obligation, an economic one, was usually expressed in religious or moral terms.

These broad principles, which continue to influence contemporary policies, were inextricably linked to the perceived governmental problem of social and political order. Individuals with no responsibilities for others were – and are – seen as more likely to cause disturbances and to rebel than those who knew that if they did not work and obey orders a houseful of hungry dependants might starve. Debates about family allowances and unemployment pay in twentieth-century Britain, for example, have been characterised by groups who argue that 'giving' assistance for dependants will result in those theoretically held responsible no longer feeling obliged to work for their provision. Work and responsibility for others, but particularly one's kin, have for centuries been seen by those in political power as the essential ingredients for maintaining a docile workforce and social and political order.

It has also been believed for a long time that by ensuring as many individuals as possible lived within a patriarchal household, such individuals would also learn therein the importance of deference to patriarchal authority and service. Acknowledging and accepting authority and hierarchy have been regarded as essential to the maintenance of the authority of the State at both a local and a national level. Those who did not live in patriarchal households were therefore feared and regarded with suspicion. Whenever possible they were forced to live in patriarchal households, and if this was not possible they were frequently ostracised or punished, as was the case with 'witches'. Since at least Tudor times, therefore, people who live outside a household environment have been seen, and treated, as a financial, political and social threat to both the local community and the State. These fears and assumptions have continued to influence State policies and their implementation.

These principles have also all along been imbued with concepts of, and assumptions about, gender. Although until the nineteenth century it was always assumed that women and older children should work, they were expected to do so as dependants within a patriarchal household. Dependence and working were not, and are not, mutually exclusive. As discussed earlier, women and children were always paid less because it was assumed they would form part of a patriarchal household. Their contributions were vitally important, but their work was seen as of necessity being located within this framework of overall dependence and service.

Thus, when from the eighteenth century there was a growing move to establish separate institutions for the destitute, dependent and disorderly who could not be cared for within individual households, the structure of orphanages, reformatories, workhouses, prisons and hospitals was informed by the concept of both patriarchal authority and a patriarchal household. They were equally strongly imbued with the importance of work and the work ethic. Obedience and deference were deemed crucial, and any challenge to authority was punished severely. Nobody suggested setting up groups of orphans or prisoners or destitute widows on their own without a formal and rigid hierarchical organisation.

For those who really had no household in which to live and work, the State established surrogate institutions modelled on their ideal of what a patriarchal household should be. The growth of institutions from the eighteenth century can be seen as one way in which the concept of patriarchy and family influenced legislation. Even in contemporary society institutions retain these ideals and structures. Hospitals, for example, are characterised by a rigid schedule, on obedience to rules and regulations (regardless of whether or not they relate to one's physical or mental well-being), strict segregation by sex, and deference and obedience to the orders of the paternalistic doctor, as well as to the demands and services of the maternalistic nursing staff.

Both in the past and in the present, individuals are only institutionalised if and when it is deemed impossible for them to be cared for within family households. If they are put into institutions, these are closely modelled on the ideal of a patriarchal household.

In this way, as Donzelot and Barret and Mackintosh have pointed out, social institutions have been 'familialised', although arguably it is more useful to consider families and institutions as all being imbued with the concept of patriarchal authority as symbolised by 'the family'.

The rapid changes brought by population growth, industrialisation, urbanisation and the political upheavals of the French Revolution made governments more than ever concerned with the maintenance of political and social order as well as with the problems of poverty. A new concern, however, was that of population which, for the first time, became perceived as a public and political issue: 'One of the great innovations in the techniques of power in the 18th century was the emergence of "population" as an economic and political problem: population as wealth, population as manpower or labor capacity, population balanced between its own growth and the resources it commanded' (Foucault, 1979, p. 25).

In late eighteenth- and early nineteenth-century France, population was perceived as a problem because the fertility rate was declining and it was feared this would result in a shortage of labour and recruits for the armed services. In Britain, on the other hand, population was seen as a problem because fertility was increasing so rapidly it was feared this would result in growing poverty, a shortage of resources (as Malthus argued), and, by implication, political unrest and increased economic demands on the State to alleviate it.

Yet the issue was not straightforward. Industrial capitalists welcomed a surplus of cheap labour. The growth of illegitimacy, mobility and poverty, however, meant that a greater number of people – but particularly women and children – were living outside an 'acceptable' household arrangement and posed a financial threat to the government at both a national and local level. A massive pool of cheap and destitute labour also posed a threat to skilled craftsmen, whose relatively privileged economic positions were being threatened by mechanisation (which generally meant the use of cheap unskilled labour). For the poorer sectors, the more members of the household available for work, the greater their chances of survival. On the other hand, as we have seen, the growth of the middle classes (not all of whom, of course, were industrial capitalists – many were doctors, clerks, or administrators) was accompanied by a strong domestic ideology preaching the virtues of middle-class family life as 'natural' and 'moral'. There were, in other words, a number of competing and conflicting views both between social classes and within social classes.

Largely because of these conflicts no 'population policy' or 'family policy' as such emerged. Rather, a number of separate pieces of legislation were enacted to deal with different aspects of the problem, often in different and contradictory ways. While landowners and the newly enfranchised middle classes obviously had the parliamentary power to legislate, other groups were not entirely without means of exerting pressure politically through petitions, strikes, acts of violence and boycotts.[2] The New Poor Law of 1834 attempted to make poverty as unappealing as possible, thereby encouraging more people to 'want' to work. By introducing the principle of less eligibility, it curtailed governmental expense and also widened State powers by making the workhouse a compulsory institution for the entire country, and centrally controlled by the government. It also tried to enforce the notion of dependency, both through the Poor Law and through the Poor Law Bastardy Act. In some areas, however, the New Poor Law was resisted and it took some two decades for it to be thoroughly implemented on a national scale. Even then, the ways in which it was actually implemented at a local level varied. The Bastardy Act was amended and eventually revoked as a result of pressure and protest from a variety of groups.

Early legislation on women's and children's labour was erratic and sporadic. The 1842 Mines Act really paid lip-service to the pressures from middle-class moral reformers by forbidding women and children to work underground. Most of them continued to work at the mines doing surface work, and in some areas the act was totally defied. In some parts of the country women continued working at the surface of mines until into the twentieth century.[3]

Similarly, legislation restricting the hours women and children could work in factories (which did not apply to many industries, and certainly not to women in outwork or domestic service), meant more a reshuffle of hours, shifts and wages on the part of factory owners than any dramatic shift in work patterns. Such legislation tended to pacify the pressures of reformers while not adversely affecting the labour supply or general economic interests of industrialists. The curtailment of hours, and thus wages, however, did mean that the financial situation of women, particularly the single, separated or widowed, was adversely affected. This, perhaps inadvertently, put pressure on women living alone to seek marriage, remarriage or co-residence with other kin as a buffer against increasingly difficult economic circumstances. Indirectly, protective legislation thus reinforced the notion, and importance attached to, marriage and living in patriarchal households.

Yet lack of employment opportunities and the effects of male out-migration in many areas meant that marriage or cohabitation was simply not possible for many working women. When necessary many moved in either with kin or with friends. In the Devon textile town studied, there was a marked decrease during the period of proletarianisation and male out-migration of widows living alone, and an increase in women – young and old, single and separated – who lived together or in lodgings. There was an increase in female-headed households and a decrease in the proportion of women who lived in patriarchal-type households (Gittins, 1983).

Economic changes and government legislation were unable directly to force people into living in a patriarchal household – indeed, their measures often undermined the possibility – but they did result in a reduction in the proportions living alone and a proliferation of people banding together to form households of all sorts, whether made up of kin or non-kin. Proletarianisation, which frequently meant feminisation, of the workforce, often actually discouraged marriage, both by driving skilled men out of their occupations and into other geographical areas altogether, and by putting a premium on the economic advantages to parents of unmarried daughters' labour power. For some, then, government policies which sought to encourage marriage and residence in patriarchal households actually had the reverse effect. Nevertheless, so long as people did not become either a financial liability to the State or a threat to social and political order, despite the plethora of middle-class moralising, governments cared (and care) very little as to the actual living arrangements people entered into in order to survive.

Demands for labour slackened from the middle of the nineteenth century as industry became more capital intensive. As the growing strength of the unions pressed increasingly for protective legislation and a family wage, government concern focused more and more on the problem of children and youth. Then, as now, the relative freedom from responsibility and the energy of youth were seen as potentially disruptive forces in society. More specifically, middle-class perception of working-class families and childrearing patterns as immoral, lacking in discipline and control aroused much fear over their future as disciplined and docile workers. As countries like Germany and America became more of a threat to British industry, and could also boast a more advanced education system for training skilled workers, so it was progressively felt by middle-class reformers and parliamentarians that compulsory education was essential for the well-being of society. More organised sectors of the working class also campaigned for better educational opportunities for their children. Disagreement over how religion should be taught in schools, however, delayed a national system for some decades.

Forster's Education Act of 1870, and subsequent legislation making primary schooling compulsory and free, resulted in the almost total exclusion of one age group from the labour market. It also meant that from then on all children under the age of 10 were by law economically wholly dependent on their parent(s). Although many evaded the law, and truancy was common among the poorer sectors well into the twentieth century (and was usually condoned in the case of younger girls whose domestic labour was needed at home), it resulted in many families being deprived of a valuable source of income. It put added pressure on many mothers to seek paid work in the labour market or to take in outwork. It thus also added fuel to trade union pressure for men to earn a family wage so as to be able to support their dependants.

Enforced dependency had substantial effects on working-class family structure. For the skilled sectors it helped develop or reinforce a patriarchal type household with the male as chief breadwinner. It provided the children of such families with a slightly greater chance of social mobility. For the poorest sectors, however, particularly households headed by women, it resulted in an exacerbation of poverty and a greater necessity for the woman to take a full double burden of both wage labour and domestic work.

The State education system, as distinct from the separate and private education system for the middle classes and aristocracy, was never originally intended to give working-class children opportunities for academic excellence or even of social mobility. It was intended first and foremost as a system where working-class children would learn to be obedient, punctual, clean and deferential to authority. It was proposed to a large extent to substitute for what were seen as the deficiencies of working-class families. While the rudiments of reading, writing and arithmetic were taught, the main emphasis was on moral education and discipline.

Boys were taught basic skills of carpentry and gardening, while girls were taught needlework, cooking and other domestic skills. The idea was to provide a more skilled and docile male workforce as well as a more domesticated group of future mothers, wives and domestic servants. The ways in which schools were organised were very much along the lines of the middle-class notion of a patriarchal household. As well as an institution designed to instil deference to authority, it was also organised so as to teach deference and respect along class lines. Class, gender and the importance of patriarchal authority were all deeply imbued in the curriculum and organisation of the State education system – and still are.

As S. Humphries has shown, these quite overt and blatant power relations within the education system were often challenged and resisted by working-class parents and children alike. Parents resented and resisted the often brutal ways in which their children were beaten by teachers. There were occasions when school children came out on strike, often supported by their parents, in protest against unfair treatment and brutality.

As discussed earlier, much of nineteenth-century legislation was concerned with the general middle-class desire to reorganise, categorise and separate groups. Legislation on education achieved a more rigid and separate definition and concept of childhood and children's dependency. Categories and definitions of gender were also changed. The growing emphasis placed on the importance of childhood led to a similar emphasis on the importance of motherhood. This was linked with an anxiety about the quantity and quality of the population from the 1870s, particularly as it affected the armed services, the empire, a declining birth rate, a high rate of infant mortality, the persistence of poverty, and general unease over the quality of future generations of workers and soldiers.

Despite the surveys of Booth and Rowntree in the late nineteenth century which drew attention to the economic origins of poverty and poor health, many – and especially middle-class women – saw the problem in terms of working-class ignorance of 'proper family life', domestic routine and careful childrearing. As Davin (1978, p. 12) explains: 'Middle class convention of the time took for granted that the proper context of childhood was the family, and the person most responsible the mother. So if the survival of infants and the health of children was in question, it must be the fault of the mothers . . . Thus the solution to a national problem of public health and of politics was looked for in terms of individuals, of a particular role – the mother, and a social institution – the family.'

Motherhood came to be seen by middle-class reformers, male and female alike, as more important than wifehood, although of course the one was premised on the other. Mothering was stressed more and more as a national, patriotic duty. The impetus of these ideas and early movements to 'educate' working-class women came from middle-class voluntary organisations, run almost entirely by women. They emphasised philanthropy – teaching women to be good mothers and wives, how to manage on scarce resources – rather than charity, which was seen as simply reinforcing bad habits of bad household management, ignorance, and profligate spending on non-essentials.

Influenced by evolutionary theory, eugenics and the disaster of finding an appallingly high rate of disease and poor health among working-class soldiers in the Boer War, the government took a greater interest in passing legislation which would promote the health of working-class children. The importance of good mothering of future soldiers and workers as a crucial lynchpin to national prosperity, and defence was used 'to justify not only contemporary measures such as the power given to the Poor Law guardians to remove children from unsuitable parents (Poor Law Act 1899) or the provisions of school meals, but also the campaigns for maternity insurance . . . and for the "endowment of motherhood", the forerunner of family allowances' (ibid., p. 13).

Such legislation made 'bad' mothering a travesty and grounds for State removal of children from their families. As such it was a real form of blackmail to working-class families, but to working-class women in particular. It undermined and penalised traditional working-class ways of childcare and supervision, especially the ways in which girls and women, kin or non-kin, took mutual responsibility for one another's children. It eroded traditional forms of women's support networks based on neighbourhood. Working-class women who had to work outside the home and left children to be looked after by older sisters or neighbours became particularly vulnerable – as they are now. The legislation was both class-specific (middle-class women never had their children removed from the family; whatever horrors of incest or brutality might occur, middle-class families and mothers were by definition *good* families and mothers) and sex-specific – although it was considered irresponsible if working-class men failed to provide adequately for their children financially, they were seldom penalised in the ways mothers were if they were deemed to be bad mothers.

Subsequent legislation aimed at working-class mothers, such as the 1918 Maternity and Child Welfare Act which resulted in the provisions of infant, and later ante-natal, clinics was never aimed at helping the mothers themselves, their health or diet, but at ensuring they did their proper job bearing and raising healthy children 'correctly'. Thus children increasingly received aid and protection from state legislation. Union pressure and negotiation gave men more protection and security in times of illness or unemployment. Mothers received virtually no protection – married women were not covered by the National Insurance Act of 1911 (nor were domestic servants or agricultural labourers). All they got was a barrage of exhortations to be better mothers to the future generation.

Married women who worked were frequently condemned as by definition bad mothers, even if – as was often the case – their children's meals and shelter depended on their work. They were blamed if they failed to breastfeed their babies, even if they were physically unable to do so. Government legislation thus made it very difficult for poor women to raise children alone. By condemning married women for working, the government made it in effect more important for working-class women to 'make' a 'good' marriage – one where the husband alone could support the family. Yet for the unskilled and semi-skilled sectors of the working class, whose work was frequently erratic and almost always poorly paid, this was simply not possible and many families continued to have to rely on a wife's, and often the children's (illegal) work. Both put the family in danger of having the children removed from the household altogether.

State legislation was effectively trying to undermine many of the ways in which the poorer sectors had coped, while at the same time reinforcing the middle-class ideology of a patriarchal household with a dependent wife and children supported by a male breadwinner. 'Deviant' (i.e. poor) families were more and more subject to surveillance and interference by State agencies. Yet these policies failed to take account of the very real economic bases and determinants of different family structures and survival strategies. The result was a general condemnation and penalisation of the poor, but particularly of poor mothers. Many of these assumptions and policies were reinforced in the post-war welfare state legislation – especially the ideal of dependent wife and children and the importance of good mothering. The economic prosperity of the 1950s and 1960s made it possible for more families to approximate to such ideals. With the current recession it is possible to see many of these old problems reappearing on a wide scale with the blame being put, as before, primarily on the shoulders of poor women rather than on poverty itself and the economic conditions that cause and exacerbate it.

Legislation was not limited to defining and delimiting motherhood and childhood. Various attempts were also made to define, categorise and control sexuality. This was to a large extent linked with Victorian concern abour purity and pollution. Overall, the essence of legislation regarding sexuality since the nineteenth century has been concerned with trying to enforce heterosexuality as the only acceptable, 'normal' and 'natural' form. Directly related to concern for the race, motherhood and population generally, the two main targets for attack from legislators were homosexuality and prostitution – the two often conflated in middle-class eyes.

While a homosexual act – sodomy – has always been condemned by the Church and severely punished as a sin, the growth of science and medicine in the nineteenth century condemned it further as 'unnatural', 'pathological' and a direct threat to the family. The term 'homosexuality' was not even coined until 1869 and did not become current in the English language until the 1890s. From then, homosexuality became seen and defined more and more as a type, a social role, rather than an individual act: 'The late nineteenth century sees a deepening hostility towards homosexuality, alongside the emergence of new definitions of homosexuality and the homosexual' (Weeks, 1977, p. 2). Sodomy had been legislated against in the sixteenth century, but the law related to the act of sodomy and included acts between men, between men and women, men and animals – and the penalty was death. The law was tightened up in 1826, and although the death penalty for it was abolished in 1861, the Criminal Law Amendment Act of 1885 made all homosexual acts illegal, whether committed in public or private.

Because women in the nineteenth century were defined as by nature asexual, debates about homosexuality related overwhelmingly to men. Concern about it was an inherent part of the general disquiet about the race, the perceived need to reproduce a strong and healthy new generation, and fears about the declining birth rate. Homosexuality was seen as a direct threat to the purity of children and, above all, to families and family life, which were seen as by definition heterosexual. It was feared that if homosexuality were to spread, it would not only threaten the future of society by adversely affecting the birth rate, but would also undermine patriarchal authority as epitomised in families and thus, by implication, authority and order generally. It was, in effect, a renewed fear about the problem of equality versus hierarchy, of lateral bonding and allegiance versus vertical bonding. By not involving procreation it threatened the survival of society itself.

The trials of Oscar Wilde in 1895 'created a public image for the homosexual, and a terrifying tale of the dangers that trailed closely behind deviant behaviour' (ibid., p. 21). Henceforth 'the' homosexual became a social role and character type, and this stereotype remains with us. By making male friendships suspect as all being potentially homosexual, it put increasing pressures on men to be seen in the company of women, to be seen as heterosexual, and thus further pressurised men to marry and have children. The same sort of process occurred when lesbianism was perceived in the 1920s as a danger, a type, a role. Male and female homosexuals in contemporary society are seen both as types to be feared and as objects of derision. The 'queer' is always portrayed as effeminate, the 'dyke' is always masculine. These types represent a reversal of acceptable male and female heterosexual roles, and as such are seen as dangerous to 'ordinary' men and women and the heterosexual families in which they are alleged to live.

In Britain, pressure from gay reform groups resulted in an apparent liberalisation of the laws on homosexuality in 1967, when 'the state partially removed itself from direct intervention in personal lives, and a free space was created for men in England and Wales, as long as they were aged over 21, acted in private and worked outside the merchant navy and armed services. But it is also true that since 1967 the number of convictions for homosexual offences has actually *increased*' (ibid., p. 11).

While in the past five decades it has been further recognised – largely as a result of the emphasis put on the importance of motherhood – that women should have custody of their children in divorce cases, and while a wife's adultery no longer counts against her in custody cases, if she is a lesbian then the courts usually rule against her having custody. No matter how good or careful a mother, the assumption is that by being lesbian a woman is by definition incapable of providing a 'natural' family environment for children. The so-called 'sexual revolution' of the 1960s has been quite explicitly a heterosexual revolution. Tolerance for homosexuality, despite the law of 1967, has decreased in modern industrial society. Increasingly rigid norms and definitions of heterosexuality have undoubtedly contributed to pressures on both men and women to be seen as 'normal' (i.e. heterosexual) by marrying and having children. Living outside families has thus arguably become more, rather than less, difficult for both men and women.

One of the most blatant and brutal ways in which the State attempted to control, redefine and categorise sexuality was in the nineteenth-century legislation on prostitution. The specific and immediate reasons for the legislation resulted from general anxiety over the spread of venereal disease among troops stationed in garrison towns. There was also fear of homosexuality among the troops (venereal disease is also spread between men), although this was kept as quiet as possible. While the civilian population was encouraged and pressurised in a number of ways to marry, the military population was required to be *un*married. The reason for this was that it was feared marriage and family ties would create conflicting allegiances for military men. Soldiers and sailors needed to be rootless so that their only responsibility and loyalty would be to the institution they served and the demands it made upon them – there are obvious similarities here with monasteries, public schools and universities.[4]

The need for men in the services to be unmarried, however, created problems of sexual outlets. Homosexuality was seen as thoroughly immoral and debilitating and likely to lead to degeneracy within the troops. Denied both marriage and homosexuality (in theory), their principal outlet was therefore either through some form of common law marriage or through using prostitutes. As we have seen, it was believed that men *had* to have regular sexual release for 'natural' reasons. The spread of venereal disease, however, threatened the health of the troops and thus implicitly the strength of the military and of the empire itself.

The resolution of the conflict between the men's 'needs' and the threat of disease was achieved through the Contagious Diseases Acts of 1864, 1866 and 1869, which by 1869 were in force in eighteen 'subjected districts'. The laws put the entire onus of blame and responsibility for veneral disease on to the woman: 'Under the acts, a woman could be identified as a "common prostitute" by a special plainclothes policeman and then subjected to a fortnightly internal examination. If found suffering from gonorrhea or syphilis, she would be interned in a certified lock hospital . . . for a period not to exceed nine months' (Walkowitz, 1980, pp. 1–2). Earlier there had been attempts to subject the men themselves to genital inspection, but they had objected and this had been discontinued. By not inspecting the men, of course, they completely destroyed any actual medical benefits the acts might have occasioned. In fact, venereal disease *increased* in the subjected districts between 1876 and 1882, and this was a weapon used by those agitating for their repeal, notably Josephine Butler who led the Ladies' National Association.

The operation of the laws meant that any working-class woman was liable to police suspicion and subjection to an internal examination whether or not she worked as a prostitute and whether or not she carried veneral disease. As Walkowitz shows clearly, prostitution was essentially a transitory occupation for many poor working-class girls and young women who were unemployed or underemployed. Many were orphans, deserted wives or young widows who, having little or no kin support, were entirely reliant on their own labour power to survive. When and where employment was scarce (as it was in garrison towns like Plymouth and Southampton), and traditional occupations such as millinery and dressmaking were unable to provide a living wage for single or deserted women, no matter how hard they worked, many had to supplement their earnings through occasional prostitution.

These young women

were not social outcasts but poor working women trying to survive in towns that offered them few employment opportunities and that were hostile to young women living alone. Their move into prostitution was not pathological; it was in many ways a rational choice, given the limited alternatives open to them. Moreover, their 'sexually deviant' behaviour must be measured against the standards of their own social class, whose norms were often distinct, if not fully autonomous, from the values of the dominant culture. (Ibid., p. 9)

Because the laws were from the beginning medically useless, by excluding men, their enactment and enforcement can be seen as a blatant attempt to penalise one class and one sex under the guise of 'national interest' – that is, the sexual gratification of male servicemen. Working-class women who were forced, or chose, to live alone or with other women, rather than in families, were put in a constantly dangerous position of possible harassment, examination and incarceration in lock hospitals. Even working-class women who were married or cohabited were not above suspicion or police harassment, although they were relatively more secure. Many women moved away from garrison towns altogether, leaving only the most desperate and most committed to prostitution. Prostitution thus increasingly became a 'type' and a role rather than an individual act or temporary phase.

Single working-class women must have felt under greater pressure than ever to marry simply as a means of self-protection from police harassment. The lock hospitals themselves were run in a strict way and organised along the lines of a patriarchal household. There was more emphasis on inculcating morals and the importance of family life than there was on actual medical treatment: 'Most lock hospitals felt obliged to compensate for the checkered reputation of their female patients by stressing efforts at their moral reclamation. As a result, lock hospitals subjected female inmates to a repressive moral regime, further discouraging their main source of female patients – prostitutes – from applying for admission' (ibid., p. 61).

Whereas previously women who worked occasionally as prostitutes had been tolerated by the working-class communities in which they lived (often bringing valuable trade and money to the community), and while their necessity to work was more or less accepted by neighbours and, in some cases, kin, the enforcement of the Contagious Diseases Acts put all local poor women at risk. Not surprisingly, this caused rifts between working-class women themselves. Once identified, casual prostitutes became both a liability to their community, and to its women in particular, and, having been labelled, became endangered themselves of never being able to get out of prostitution. Another crucial means of support for poor single and separated women was thus removed. Being seen as 'respectable' became more important than ever, and now the only viable way of doing so was by trying to live within a family-type household.

By the end of the nineteenth century living alone had become a very dangerous position for working-class women. The persecution of these women in garrison towns was not dissimilar to the persecution of witches in the seventeenth century. If, however, a woman had independent financial means then living alone was much more acceptable, if not desirable. Single middle-class women were never harassed. The Contagious Diseases Acts, initially proposed as a means of solving a medical problem, in their implementation had nothing to do with eradicating that problem. In their exercise they were blatantly class-specific and sex-specific and had important repercussions on attitudes to women's sexuality, to marriage, and to women who for one reason or another had to work and live outside a patriarchal type of household. It is ironic that one law made it illegal for one group to marry, and that as a result other laws were passed which made it difficult for another group *not* to marry. No doubt there is 'one law for the rich and one law for the poor', but there is also one law for men and another for women.

The growth of the State in modern industrial society has resulted in an ever-growing body of legislation which, in different ways, affects families and the individuals who live in them. How such legislation affects individuals depends very much on both their sex and on their social class; one law may act to the detriment of one member in a family while another law may benefit another member of the same family. Legislation on sexuality, marriage, divorce, childcare, abortion, birth control, mothering all have crucial effects on families in different ways.

Much of this legislation has been concerned with the overall problem of population – the quality and quantity of a nation's populace, an issue directly related to a nation's wealth and resources, but also to its political and social stability. At an individual level such laws affect individuals within families. In many modern industrial societies family allowances, while often demanded initially by feminist and radical pressure groups, have usually been awarded by governments when they have sought to encourage people to have more children. Legislation directed at the health and welfare of children was carried out with the specific purpose of improving the quality of the country's future labour force and military strength.

Tax awards made to the married and to those with children, are not specifically to encourage marriage as such, but to assist parents – and men particularly – to take full financial responsibility for their families, rather than rendering the State liable. Much legislation has been directed specifically at women. To a great extent this has been because, while men were regarded by the State as capable of protecting themselves by organising independently within unions, women were neither especially welcomed by the unions nor deemed capable of independent organisation on their own behalf. As 'naturally' dependent and weak, middle-class legislators and many working-class men alike saw them as needing special protective legislation. In fact, very little legislation is particularly protective towards women, but acts rather to ensure that they fulfil their appointed roles as wives and mothers 'properly'.

Broadly speaking, the State's overriding concern has been with its resources: economic and demographic. Very little legislation exists regarding what should go on *inside* families, or what precise form families should take. Domestic violence was not considered an appropriate political issue until the 1970s, when the Domestic Violence and Matrimonial Proceedings Act was passed in 1976 (O'Donovan, 1979). Only very recently has marital rape begun to be taken seriously. The police still remain reluctant to interfere with domestic disputes and this issue has gained prominence since the Cleveland Crisis and the opening of the debate about child sexual abuse. Unless seriously mentally ill people cause a public nuisance, social workers and police are very unwilling to remove them from their families and put them into hospital, regardless of the suffering they may be causing others – and themselves – in the family. Those who are, and have been, most susceptible to state legislation and interference are the poor. For it is the poor who pose a serious financial risk to the government.

At the same time, legislation has developed in such a way that it has become more difficult for individuals to live alone or with members of the same sex. Social disapproval, financial discrimination and fear of interference by social workers and police in non-heterosexual or otherwise atypical households – particularly those where children are involved – put very strong pressures on both men and women – especially women – to live in some sort of family.

Thus State legislation over the past 200 years has reinforced the

8

Is the family in a state of crisis?

Concern that 'the family' is in a state of crisis is not a new phenomenon. It was of grave concern to many middle-class legislators and reformers of various political hues in the nineteenth century; it was a concern during the inter-war period, and in the past decade has re-emerged as a contentious political issue. It causes most concern during periods of economic recession, when there is a change in the rate of population growth, and/or during times when fear of political unrest and upheaval is acute. The three, of course, often go together, and all provide an insight into why 'the family' becomes a political issue during such periods.

As we have seen, there is no clear, unambiguous definition of what a family is – indeed, it has been argued that the family is little more than an ideology that influences and informs the ways in which people interact and co-reside with one another. Yet if we take it as an ideology, it is one that permeates virtually every social institution in modern industrial society. Organisations are said to be 'run like a family', the highest compliment a man can receive is that he is 'a good family man' (women are never accrued the compliment of being a 'good family woman', as by definition they are assumed to be just that). The notion of family informs the education system, the business world, asylums, the media and the political system itself (Mrs Thatcher was labelled as 'the mother' of the Conservative Party). So when concern about the 'crisis in the family' becomes a recurrent theme, what is more probably being expressed is a fear that *society itself* is in a state of crisis. How has this come about? If the concept of family is so broad, is it then a useless concept for understanding how people live and work together? Do we need new concepts?

155

Deconstructing the concept of family shows that inherent in it are a number of quite distinct ideas and phenomena. Co-residence; marriage; power relations between men and women; power relations between adults and children; domestic labour; sexuality and sexual relations; procreation; motherhood and mothering; fatherhood; sibling relationships; definitions of kinship, gender, authority, dependence, service; economic relations – all these can be seen as important and implicit and explicit in definitions of the family. These are also a lot of subcategories to fit into one concept. It is hardly surprising, therefore, that people have disagreed so radically in their interpretations of whether or not families are in a state of crisis, whether they are a 'good' or a 'bad' thing, whether or not they are a constant attribute of modern industrial society. The interpretations and definitions that can be made of the family are so wide and all-encompassing that as such the concept is of very limited analytical value indeed.

Any study of, or reference to, the family needs to differentiate clearly between the *ideology* and the actual ways in which individuals interact, co-reside, have sexual relations, have babies, marry, divorce, work, rear children, move away, and so on. Obviously an ideology influences the ways people interpret their lives, though there has never been a clear way of showing just how influential ideologies are on patterns of behaviour. Ideology cannot exist in limbo; it must have some relation to people's material existence or at least be perceived as having such a relation, otherwise it would be irrelevant. Separating ideology from patterns of behaviour is thus arguably a hypothetical exercise, because the two must always be related in some way or other. Nevertheless, analysing them as logically distinct is a useful way of disentangling some of the complexities inherent in the concept of family, and enables us to see more clearly whether the alleged crisis in the family is more of a belief that an ideology is under threat than an accurate reflection of dramatic changes in people's behaviour patterns.

The ideology of the family, as we have seen, is an historical creation. The very concept of family was not used in the way it is today until the late eighteenth century. Its development as a concept and an ideology was an inherent part of the development of the industrial bourgeoisie during the later stages of capitalist development. It is possible to see its growing influence in the way in which society was conceptualised as a fusion between earlier religious patriarchal ideology and the secularisation of society with the growth of scientific rationalism. The western form of patriarchy, a direct legacy of Judaeo-Christian theology, has been formed on the concept of a single male god, the source of all authority, and also justice, righteousness and charity. Salvation is attainable through a combination of strict obedience to God's will and through love of, and faith in, the redeeming nature of his son.

Women in western patriarchy have always been a lesser form of being, the originator of man's fall from divine grace, temptresses, sinners, more subject to lust, and only capable of salvation through deference, obedience to male authority, and motherhood. When people interpreted their lives in religious terms, any threat to authority was a threat to God and to the whole social order. Perceived crises, at that time, were therefore religious crises. Rebellion, riots, sodomy, illegitimacy, women alone, any form of deviance, were interpreted as a weakness in society's religious institutions, and above all, in the faith of the individual.

From the seventeenth century onwards, the development of science and scientific paradigms for interpreting the world perpetuated fundamental beliefs about authority and gender, except that they increasingly became expressed in terms of 'nature' rather than through direct reference to God. Men were seen as 'naturally' authoritative, stronger, more intelligent, and women were 'naturally' deferential, weak, passive and intuitive. Men, therefore, were suited to govern, to make decisions, to direct women and children, and these patriarchal assumptions became an integral part of science, of the ways in which governments and government policies were perceived and formulated. Acts of deviation became labelled as unnatural or pathological rather than sinful.

As earlier religious patriarchal ideology had been symbolised as, and enshrined in, the Church, so secular scientific ideology became symbolised as, and enshrined in, the family. The growing affluence of the bourgeoisie from the eighteenth century, and their decreasing need for family labour in the production process, made it relatively easy to adapt and modify scientific (and religious) notions of masculinity, femininity, adulthood and childhood so as to present the husband/father as the 'natural' head of the unit, the breadwinner, with wife and children as both his economic and political dependants. The ideal of the middle-class family household extended to include not only earlier notions of the 'Englishman's castle', but also of a temple, a church, a locus of sanctity, purity and harmony. The development of middle-class ideology, focusing on the family in this way, was a means of demarcating the middle classes as unique and distinct from the perceived extravagant and debauched excesses of the aristocracy, and from the perceived immorality and promiscuity of the working classes.

Thus middle-class family ideology was informed and influenced by patriarchal discourses from both religion and science. Inherent in it were most of the pre-existing patriarchal concepts of authority, dependence and service, but all fused into the idea of a monolithic family, to which ideal and practice all members of society should aspire. Thus the ideas as such were not new, but the rubric by which they were presented, was. Henceforth any form of deviation became labelled as both unnatural and as a direct threat to The Family. As the middle classes gained political power so family ideology became further enshrined into state policies.

The family was a historical, class-specific ideology premised on earlier patriarchal religious ideals and beliefs. Its particular strength as an ideology has lain in its presentation as a tangible reality to which all can – and should – aspire, and which every individual should and does experience. Individuals' concrete experiences and interpretations of 'family' may relate to kin, household, friends or neighbours – indeed to an institution in which they were brought up. But the all-encompassing and yet elusive concept of family makes it appear both as a universally shared experience and a goal which all can, and should, achieve – regardless of economic circumstances – even if its realisation remains obscure.

Its strength and endurance as an ideology lies in its appearance as a universal experience not specific to a particular class. In this way it comes to have what amounts to a religious character: it is (in theory) open to all and, through 'good works', that is a well-ordered family life, salvation can be achieved by all. Yet its premises are conservative because they are based on notions of authority, service, dependence and deference, in short, it is founded on inequality. From the Victorian era onwards, perceived social threats and radical movements have been seen as both a threat *to* the family, and *a result of* a crisis in the family.

Since Victorian times, of course, some of the specific content of family ideology has changed. Ideas and ideals about sexuality have altered; women are now expected to enjoy (hetero)sexual relationships, men are encouraged to 'help' in the home and take an active interest in their children – though are stigmatised if they want to take *full* responsibility. Children are allowed more freedom of expression, and while married women working is not actively encouraged (except when there is a labour shortage, as in the Second World War), it is not seen as so serious a threat as it was during Victorian times. Among women married for the first time, 48 per cent had cohabited previously in 1987, compared with only 7 per cent in the 1970s. It is estimated that some 70 per cent of second marriages are now preceded by a period of cohabitation.[1] The basic ideals, however, remain the same: the husband/father should be the head of the household and the principal breadwinner; the women should be responsible for domestic work and childcare, while children are defined as dependants within families for a longer period than ever before.

Family ideology has increasingly purported to be egalitarian, yet it remains based on notions of gender, age and authority that are by definition unequal. The ideal that families are egalitarian, like the ideal that class no longer divides society, has enjoyed considerable support, even if it seldom tallies with reality. Is the problem perhaps that patterns of behaviour have altered and that it is these that are in a state of crisis because they no longer relate in any important way to the ideology?

Many of the ideals imbued in family ideology are now well written into the legal system as a direct result of the political power of the middle classes. Definitions of dependency and responsibility are not just ideals but are laws, transgression of which is penalised. While some laws have become liberalised – for instance, those relating to married women's property and to divorce – others have become stricter – notably those relating to children. Thus while it has become easier for women to retain access to their own property after marriage and to get out of unhappy marriages, the onus on women in terms of childcare and good mothering has increased.

The areas where families are most often seen as both villains and victims of alleged crisis relate to divorce, child abuse and delinquency. Above all else, rising rates of divorce have been used to 'show' that marriages are less stable and thus families are less secure and united. Yet we have seen how, if anything, families were just as unstable in the past – death broke up *both* good *and* bad marriages in a totally arbitrary way. The consequence was high rates of widowhood, orphanage, remarriage, and single-parent families.

Families were also broken by separation in the past, except that because divorce was impossible for all except the very wealthy, those left behind had no rights to protection or maintenance. The rise in divorce rates in modern·society reflects first and foremost a legal change in the accessibility of the population to formal separation and divorce. It means that wives and children have somewhat better guarantees of economic support than they once had – though recent legislation is eroding this.

Moreover, the dramatic increase in the duration of people's life expectancy has meant that marriages that remain intact last on average for much longer periods of time than in the past. Age at marriage has fluctuated, but has not changed very dramatically. A couple marrying at 22 or 23 nowadays is likely to be together for forty or fifty years, while in the past this was more likely to have been fifteen or twenty years. The meaning of the phrase 'till death do us part' has radically different implications for couples now than previously; the marriage contract is a much longer one. Perhaps it is more surprising, considering these factors, that two-thirds of marriages do *not* end in divorce.

More is expected of, and from, marriage than in the past. Family ideology over the past 150 years has laid greater emphasis on the romantic and companionate ideal of marriage while disguising its fundamental economic and inegalitarian aspects. Where not long ago marriage was presented as a working partnership with the husband the acknowledged head, the primary purpose of which was to produce children, it has been presented increasingly as a loving relationship between two equal partners whose aim is to create domestic harmony through co-operation, mutual sexual gratification, and the careful and loving rearing of two or three children. It has been further defined as a private and exclusive relationship; others – kin or non-kin – who previously formed an essential supportive network to one another in times of crisis, have become seen as intrusive and disruptive. As an ideal, and one which has to survive a long test of time, this is a tall order and one that is unlikely to survive in reality for long.

Success or failure undoubtedly rests on many contingencies; the degree to which each partner is willing to both compromise his or her ideal of the marriage and of the other partner, the ways in which each is able to find other strategies of survival and support, as well as more elusive but important ingredients relating to economic circumstances, personalities and past histories. Divorce, though more accessible, remains a painful and difficult experience, and contrary to certain stereotypes of 'Hollywood' type marriages, divorces and remarriages, it is seldom a tactic people adapt lightly. It remains much easier to get into marriage than it is to get out of it.

Broken marriages are frequently cited as a principal cause of children's emotional disturbances and juvenile delinquency. Undoubtedly divorce is a source of upset and disruption for children, yet it can also be a great source of relief and release from a previously painful and intolerable situation. Arguments about the deleterious effects of broken homes on children's behaviour, however, tend to focus on the working classes. Divorce is, in fact, class-specific; the divorce rate per 10 000 married women in 1961 stood at 22 in Social Class I, 32 in Social Class III, and 51 in Social Class V.[2]

While age at marriage varies somewhat by class, it is difficult to ascribe the high divorce rate among the unskilled to this alone. Rather, remembering how research such as Stack's showed the ways in which severe poverty undermined the durability of marital ties, it is more cogent to see this as a result of poverty and economic insecurity. Family ideology implicitly presupposes a relatively secure economic base: the husband should be *able* to support the family by his income alone, the household income should *provide* adequate shelter, food, comfort, space, and consumer durables, the wife should be *able* to cease paid work when she has small children. In other words, the poorer a family–household's resources, the wider the gap will be between the ideal of what a family should be and what it has to be in reality. Moreover, as we have seen, legislation relating to families has been quite consistently class-specific and sex-specific. Everyone is supposed to aspire to a certain kind of family life, while the realities of economic inequality make it virtually impossible for the poor to achieve the ideal.

By insisting that happy marriages and happy families are made by individuals through love, devotion and hard work, the reality of the economic and patriarchal bases of marriage and family life are disguised and ignored. Thus crises of family violence, sexual abuse and delinquency are not attributed to poverty or unequal relations between men and women and parents and children, but to individuals' – and most frequently, women's – failings *within* their families. Just as nineteenth-century social reformers advocated teaching working-class wives the importance of thrift and good housekeeping as a 'solution' to their poverty, so contemporary social reformers advocate individual solutions like marriage therapy and child guidance rather than seeing the political and economic origins of such problems.

Poverty in modern industrial society has changed in important ways. Couples with poor economic resources and dependent children remain, as in the past, one of the prime groups experiencing poverty, as do single-parent households. But the past few decades have witnessed an enormous growth in the number of elderly people experiencing poverty. Greater longevity has meant that modern industrial society is an increasingly old society, and this trend will continue. Differential rates of mortality between men and women mean that the very elderly, and also the very poor, are overwhelmingly women. Their poverty is a reflection of their age, their previous occupational experience, and their previous marital history. The problem of the ever-growing rates of the elderly in society is often attributed to a decline in 'family solidarity', and is seen as yet another indicator of a 'crisis in the family'. Families, it is argued, are neglecting and rejecting their elderly more and more.

Yet care of the elderly in contemporary society is carried out more by families than it was in the past; labels such as 'community care' are only a thin disguise for the reality of care by female kin. The stresses and strains of caring for an elderly parent put tremendous pressure on a daughter's own family household, and thus multiply her own problems. An ageing society is one of the biggest problems facing contemporary society, and trying to shift the burden of care on to kin, rather than providing adequate state-financed and state-run care, is apt to create new crises for families, to make new problems for married couples and family households. An ageing society is a social problem, not a family problem.

The twentieth century has also witnessed a marked decrease in the proportion of the young, and couples seldom have more than two or three children. This is in marked contrast with earlier times, when a woman might expect to bear children at fairly regular intervals of two or three years between the ages of 25 and 40. As we have seen, however, fewer survived. Consequently, women's childbearing takes up a relatively small period of their lives now, and this has resulted in a general improvement in women's health. Yet far more is expected of women in terms of rearing their children than in the past. Children almost never leave home before the age of 16.

While the physical strain of childbearing has decreased, the emotional and caring strains have increased. Thus even though married women are 'free' once their children go to school, their freedom is strictly limited between certain hours of the day and certain times of the year, which sharply curtails the possible occupations they can enter. Their 'freedom' to enter the labour market is not only restricted by time, but by social expectations and assumptions by husbands and children that they must also continue to put their family first and foremost, caring and servicing all physical, mental and emotional needs of all household members. While women now enjoy greater physical health than in the past, married women with children are arguably under greater emotional and mental strain than before, witness the higher proportion of women in mental hospitals and on tranquillizers.

Delinquency and adolescent 'disrespect for authority' are cited as strong proof that families no longer socialise children properly and that families are in a state of crisis. Adolescence has always been a difficult period and has always incurred adult suspicion and hostility – apprentices in pre-industrial society who got drunk and mis- behaved were seen as just as problematic as adolescents are today. What has changed is that where once the majority of adolescents would go to live and work in households other than those of their parent(s), now they do not. From the fifteenth to the nineteenth centuries sending adolescents elsewhere to work was a very com- mon practice. While no doubt an important means of creating space in households and giving children training and a chance to accrue savings, it was also an important way of simply removing the stress and strain of adolescent problems and rebellions from the family household.

Now family ideology preaches instead the importance of parents trying to understand and communicate with teen-age children, of giving them love, warmth and security. Yet arguably adolescents want and need to test their independence, to rebel against parental values, to live a separate life from them. Middle-class children are more able to do this in fairly non-disruptive ways. Their parents' economic resources make it easier for them to attend boarding school, to travel abroad, to go on exchange visits, and so on. Working-class adolescents, more confined economically and spa- tially, have to test their independence and rebel on the streets and in school, where their rebellions are more visible to authorities. Hence the problem becomes perceived as a working-class problem specific to working-class families, and thus implicitly working-class mothers. It is seldom seen as a problem relating to adolescence generally, or to the real economic problems facing working-class family households.

Youth culture – or sub-culture – is not new; from pre-industrial charivaris to gangs of youths roaming and terrorising the streets of Victorian and Edwardian England, adolescents have always had ways of showing their independence. Rebellion in public, however, has mostly been specific to boys. Girls, more confined spatially within the home, have had fewer outlets for adolescent rebellion. Their main way of rebelling has been through premarital sex and early marriage against their parents' wishes.

Considering questions which relate to an alleged crisis in the family historically shows that while certain things have changed, there is very little evidence that families are any 'better' or 'worse' than in the past. Yet the belief that families were once more solidaristic, more caring, remains strong. How many times do we hear older persons from many walks of life insisting that 'it wasn't like that then' or 'in our family we all used to care for each other, not like kids today'. Much of this is arguably just a tendency for people to select happy memories from their past. Remembering the good times is a much pleasanter pastime than dwelling on the bad times.

For most people early childhood is a time of receiving a great deal of care and attention and as such is looked back upon with nostalgia. It may be this personal nostalgia which is then translated into a more general perception of one's family – and thus families generally – as more solidaristic and loving than contemporary families. If people are actually questioned in depth about early recollections, however, blacker ones begin to emerge of drunken fathers, violence, poverty, and sexual abuse. Growing-up is a process that invariably brings with it a sense of loss and sense of change for the worse. This sense of personal loss translated into a notion of general loss of family and community gives much support to the idea that families are in a state of crisis, and these beliefs reinforce the nebulous but all-pervasive appeal of 'the family' as an ideology.

This 'pool' of a sense of loss and change for the worse among the adult population can easily be manipulated into the belief that 'the family' has changed and that this is the real source of most social problems – of broken homes, battered children, delinquency, vandalism and a high crime rate. Similarly, it can be translated into a belief that women's liberation has exacerbated all these problems by undermining the family through encouraging women to work and, it is suggested by some, thereby neglecting their families. Yet just as none of these problems is new, so few of them relate directly to families or women as in any way a *cause* of social crisis. They are overwhelmingly social, economic and ideological problems, manifestations of inequality, growing poverty, patriarchal assumptions and the effects of these on people's behaviour patterns. Perceiving them as family problems disguises their economic origin and nature, and presents a general social crisis as an individual/family crisis, just as in earlier times similar problems were treated as individual religious failings.

While ideology undoubtedly affects the ways in which people think and act, it also masks reality and diverts attention away from any attempt to tackle the real cause of social problems. Patriarchal family ideology, like religious ideology, also effectively translates social and political problems into personal and individual ones and thus changes potential political anger into individual guilt and malaise.

Family ideology does not represent the reality of how individuals interact together. Yet it manifests just enough similarity to people's life situations to make it seem tangible and real to most. Thus the never-married, the divorced, and the childless can at least identify part of the 'ideal family' with a past childhood or family distorted in memory, and feel that their own 'failure' has been an individual failing rather than an unrealistic ideal.

The distribution of guilt, however, is unequal. Because it is predominantly women who are identified with the family, who are allocated primary responsibility for its well-being, unity and happiness, failure to achieve such goals is overwhelmingly seen as a woman's problem and failure – her guilt. Men's responsibilty for the family now, as in the past, is seen as solely a financial one. While many men undoubtedly feel guilty if they fail to provide for their families as a result of unemployment or disability, they can and do perceive that failing more as a socio-economic failure than as a fault of their own. In this sense, socialism has been a crucial factor in 'lifting' guilt from men. But because of the close identity between the family and women, a perceived crisis in the family tends also to be seen as women's fault both as individuals and collectively. The idea of a 'crisis in the family' is thus both class-specific and sex-specific.

Perhaps the biggest change in families and family ideology is that now more is expected from marriage, childrearing and sexuality than in the past. Moreover, as family ideology has become stronger over time, by definition the reality and the ideal become further and further apart. Most important, as Lasch points out, is that there is a serious anomaly in family ideology. On the one hand, families are presented as the most fundamental and basic social institution. Yet, on the other hand, they have been idealised since the nineteenth century as a crucial *refuge from* society and all its ills and injustices. An institution that is the pillar of society obviously cannot at the same time be a refuge from it. In fact, the notion of its being a refuge only applies to men.

The family household is the place where men are supposed to be able to escape from the realities of their work-world, where they can expect comfort, service, care and loving attention from a wife, daughters or sisters. It is presented as the opposite to the world of work. But as we have seen, the family household is a large part of the world of work for women. Whether or not they enter the formal labour market, women are always the providers of the essential components of men's refuge from society. For women, therefore, the family household never can be a refuge from the demands of work and society. Arguably, a women's only 'refuge' in contemporary society is escaping domestic drudgery by entering the labour market – but that is only an escape from one set of demands to another. The real point is that because family households are always social institutions and form an integral part of society, it is completely spurious to argue that they are either private or a sort of a-social oasis in the middle of a desert of work, competition and malaise. Indeed, the way in which the concepts of 'work' and 'family' are treated as totally separate categories and spheres is fallacious.

Market relations and labour contracts are as much a part of family households as they are of the formal economy, and are implicit in the marriage contract and legislation affecting families. Work is just as much an integral part of families as it is of formal organisations, with the crucial difference that it is neither formally paid nor formally acknowledged as work. This consequently reinforces patriarchal ideas of women's lower social status and importance in the 'real' world of formal paid work. Divisions between public and private, work and family, are artificial *ideological* divisions which serve to reinforce patriarchal concepts of men's greater social, economic and political worth. If we break down these artificial divisions we see how work and interpersonal relations permeate all society and social institutions. The family can never be treated in isolation from the rest of society, and thus to argue that there is a crisis in the family is merely a way of saying that there is a crisis in society.

There is a crisis in society. More than ever society is faced with numerous serious crises – increasing poverty and unemployment, homelessness, AIDS, ecological disasters, widespread child abuse, the ever growing numbers of the elderly, and so on. To treat these as family problems, however, is to treat effects as causes. Everybody lives in some form of family household; everybody has some form of problem. Attributing problems of delinquency or incest or emotional problems to the individual's family – though these problems become *manifest* there – is obviating the social nature of most problems and results in blaming individuals for social crises.

For if one thing should have become obvious by now, it is that to speak in terms of 'the' family is totally misleading. There is no such thing. While everybody at some point will share space, time, skills, sexuality, affection and love with others, the ways in which individuals live, struggle and interact together are too varied to be able to encase these activities into a term such as 'the family'. The organisation and structure of family households are bound to be variable because of the different access of individuals to economic resources, labour, skills, time and space. Moreover, because individuals themselves are constantly changing through the ageing process, family households are in a constant state of flux and change.

Yet the ideology of the family would have us believe that there is one type of family, one correct way in which indivuals should live and interact together, just as Christian theology insists that there is one god, one saviour, one path to salvation. An ideology that claims there is only one type of family can never be matched in reality, for it presents an ideal to which only some can approximate, and others not at all. It is this attribute of family ideology which makes people believe there is a crisis in the family while the real problem is the gap between the ideology and reality.

Discarding family ideology would abolish the idea that there is a crisis in the family and reveal the realities of social problems and crises. Without such an ideology people would expect less from marriage and childrearing and would be less likely to become disillusioned – which is not to say that everyone would consequently become 'happier'. But they would be less likely to expect an unrealistic degree of bliss and contentment from a mythical marriage and family; they could begin to think of new and different ways of coping and co-operating with others in a variety of ways. It would mean, however, that people began to see the real nature of social and economic problems and not perceive them as individual/family failings and guilt. It might well mean that people started challenging social, economic and political injustice more directly – rather than blaming themselves or their spouse or children. It would mean challenging patriarchal ideology and thus challenging the inequalities between men, women and children.

Family ideology has been a vital means – the vital means – of holding together and legitimising the existing social, economic, political and gender systems. Challenging the ideology thus means challenging the whole social system, but it would not mean that as a result people ceased living and interacting together in some form of family household. It would mean a radical reappraising of such arrangements. Family households are a vital and integral part of any society in some shape or form. Family ideology is not. There is no ideal family. When politicians articulate a fear that there is a crisis in the family, they are not worried about divorce or rape or incest as such, but rather that the *ideology* is being challenged, and that were this to gain momentum people might start to question the legitimacy of the existing socio-economic, political and patriarchal systems. Without family ideology modern industrial society and its political system might be very different indeed. Without family ideology it would be possible to reconsider and reconstruct the realities of relationships between men, women and children and to work towards more equal and more caring ways of living and working together.

9

Why do men abuse children sexually?

The recent moral panic about child sexual abuse has been treated as though it were something unique to the 1980s and 1990s. Historical evidence shows clearly that child abuse – physical, emotional, and sexual – has been endemic to western culture for centuries. The scale and nature of child abuse has undoubtedly varied and changed, but it is certainly not something new. What has happened is that a long-existing phenomenon has been rediscovered by professionals and the media and dealt with, in many cases, as evidence for a 'crisis in the family'. 'Child abuse' is a very broad category that includes a wide spectrum of cruelty and violence that cannot be covered in its entirety here. I intend instead to focus on the sexual abuse of children by their kin – incest – as this has been the most recent and most controversial issue and the one that relates most obviously to the perspective of this book.

The sexual abuse of children, most of whom are girls, by adult relatives, most of whom are men, has caused considerable confusion about boundaries between children, parents and state agencies. It is taken by some as evidence of the breakdown of 'traditional' family values where instant gratification (for men) is valued more highly than the traditional patriarchal tenets of protection and responsibility for those defined as weak and vulnerable. But what is seldom articulated yet certainly most threatening about incest is that it throws open important questions about patriarchy generally. Protection of wife and children is the positive side of a patriarchal continuum – with male violence at the other side of the continuum. Patriarchal definitions of masculinity, therefore, assume that all 'normal' men, as fathers and husbands, will protect their families from rapists, abusers and murders – that is, from other men.

The fact that children, but especially girls, are being raped and abused within their own families by those who are supposed to protect them should have shaken patriarchal assumptions. But what has in fact happened is that the media have generally twisted the situation so as to focus public attention and sympathy not on the children who have suffered often horrendous abuse, but on the 'poor' parents whose rights have been infringed by 'interfering' social workers.

Undoubtedly mistakes were made by social-work agencies in some of the cases. But to focus on this aspect predominantly has deflected attention from the core issue: that in possibly as many as a quarter of all families, fathers, stepfathers and grandfathers are sexually abusing their own young female kin, at great emotional and physical cost. Surveys show that in the United States between 17 per cent and 28 per cent of women were sexually abused by men prior to puberty (Herman, 1981, p. 13). Blaming social workers and doctors is a desperate ploy to sweep the real issue back under the carpet – where it had festered for a very long time already.

Media confusion has been characteristic of the crisis generally, with initially no clear perspective on who was innocent and who was to blame. In the end, the issue was to some extent 'resolved' by placing the onus of guilt on the professionals who tried to rescue the children in the first place. Increasingly, parents came to be seen as 'the good guys'. Relatively little attention was paid to the children themselves, except in considering whether or not they were capable of telling the truth. But least attention of all was focused on those who actually perpetrate sexual abuse – overwhelmingly men and, in an estimated half of all cases, the fathers of the victims (Campbell, 1988). The use of the term 'parents' throughout not only disguised the responsibility of fathers, but implicated mothers in a way that is often not justified. It is more than ironic that the huge moral panic that has surrounded this issue over the past few years has bypassed the central moral issue of why men in general, and fathers in particular, sexually abuse girls and daughters.

In the 1960s there was widespread concern and panic about the physical abuse of children – baby-battering – as 'discovered' and discussed by the Kempes in particular (Kempe and Kempe, 1983). The Kempes explained the phenomenon in medical terms, saw it as evidence for 'pathological' or 'dysfunctional' families. Later investigation found that baby-battering and family violence generally correlated strongly with families living in poverty (Parton, 1985; Gordon, 1989). Where sexual abuse has differed significantly from physical abuse is that it is patently *not* related to social class, but is as endemic in 'respectable' middle-class families as it is among working-class families. Scandals over individual cases such as the death of Maria Colwell in 1973 and of Jasmine Beckford in 1984 could be seen as problems 'out there', among the poor, the deranged, the desperate. Child sexual abuse, however, was (and is) going on right in the heart of those families who claim to be responsible, respectable and 'moral'. Neither social class nor age nor ethnicity can explain why men from right across the social spectrum, many of whom are regarded as upstanding citizens in their communities, nonetheless sexually abuse their own, and other people's, daughters.

Why child sexual abuse is widespread is so uncomfortable a question that it is rarely asked. It was never addressed in the Butler-Sloss report on the Cleveland Crisis. But it nevertheless needs to be asked. It is a huge and complex issue that can only be tackled here in a very general way. I suggest, however, that several interrelated issues need to be considered. First, it is necessary to understand how children have been regarded as their parents', but especially their fathers', property for centuries. Second, this needs to be analysed in the context of wider patterns of inequalities within families, an issue that has already been discussed at some length in this book. Third, child abuse generally, but incest in particular, needs to be understood as one aspect of a broader pattern of male violence. Finally, it is worth considering how power and power relations have become increasingly eroticised over time.

It is only since the late nineteenth century that there has been any acknowledgement of such a thing as 'childrens' rights'. Under Roman law, children below the age of majority had no legal rights at all: 'the concept of *patria potestas* subordinated them entirely to the control of the father' (Thane, 1981, p. 12). Children could not own property or marry without their father's permission, and could only live where their father directed. For many centuries fathers were allowed to sell a child under the age of seven. Up until the nineteenth century it was understood that the father owned his children's labour-power, and children were expected to work from an early age. Their earnings belonged to their father. In a like manner, their bodies also belonged to him; the mother had no legal rights over her own children because she, too, was regarded as part of the father's household and property. Of course the father, the head of the household, was also responsible for those who belonged to him – for their upkeep, their behaviour – and was expected to protect them. As mentioned earlier, the Latin word *famulus*, from which our word 'family' derives, means slave. And our legal system is based on the precepts of Roman law.

It was John Stuart Mill who commented that 'one would almost think that a man's children were supposed to be literally, and not metaphorically, a part of himself, so jealous is (public) opinion of the smallest interference of law with his absolute and exclusive control of them' (*On Liberty*, quoted in Behlmer, 1982, p. 2). This precept, that a man can own his children, still runs deep in our culture – witness the horrified reactions of both middle-class parents and the media when state agencies dared to intervene into the hallowed privacy of middle-class families and remove children to be protected from sexual abuse. It went to the heart of a century's uneasy debate as to who has ultimate responsibility – who 'owns' – children: parents or state.

A study of sexual assault in eighteenth-century England by Anna Clark found that sexual assault was only taken seriously by the law if it involved a man's property – that is, a virginal daughter or a wife. Rape was then punishable by death because it was defined as akin to murder: 'a woman's chastity defined her worth as a person, so without it, she herself was worthless. . . This posed a paradox for legal practice. On the one hand, the rapist deserved to be punished because he had attacked female chastity, a valuable possession. On the other hand, the violated woman had lost her credibility as a prosecutrix along with her chastity. It is this paradox which accounts for the low conviction rate for rape' (Clark, 1987, p. 47). In the case of incest, however, the girl was *already* the father's property. So, although incest was prohibited by ecclesiastical law until the nineteenth century, because there was no crime against property in the eyes of either the perpetrator or of the law, incest was rarely reported or condemned. As Herman points out: 'though the incest taboo forbids him to make sexual use of his daughter, no particular man's rights are offended, should the father choose to disregard this rule' (Herman, 1981, p. 60).

The assault of children by men outside the family, however, was generally taken seriously by the courts in the late eighteenth and early nineteenth centuries. Clark suggests that women may have taken sexual abuse of children much more seriously than men. She describes how a Mrs Poultney, the wife of a powder-flask maker, found that a coachman had assaulted her four-year-old daughter. She went to her husband and said: "'What does the fellow mean by playing tricks with my child. I'll go and kick up a dust with him"; he said, "pho, pho, the coachman is always playing with children"' (Clark, 1987, p. 49). Her evidence shows sexual violence both to women and children was extremely common during that time, particularly in the new industrial areas.

Historical evidence for incest, however, is almost impossible to come by in England, largely because it was not declared a crime until 1908. Forms of ecclesiastical punishment existed in pre-industrial society where under canon law the guilty party convicted of incest had to do solemn penance at church or in the marketplace, bare-legged, bare-headed, and wrapped in a white sheet for two or three years (Wohl, 1978, p. 209). When the church courts were abolished in 1857, however, incest remained legal during the next 51 years. Victorian pornography, a boom industry, was full of representations of incest, where it was portrayed as 'great fun' (S. Marcus quoted in Wohl, 1978). It is possible to argue that an indulgent attitude towards incest was therefore implicit in the (recently much-celebrated) 'Victorian values' of the family.

The issue of incest first became defined as a social problem towards the end of the nineteenth century as part of increasingly widespread middle-class concern over the social, economic and health conditions of the working classes. This can be seen very much as integral to wider middle-class concern to impose their own family ideology on to society overall, for the family was a central core to middle-class ideology and thus also intrinsic to their political and economic power.

The subject of working-class incest was brought up in 1882 by the House of Lords Select Committee on the Protection of Young Girls, and again in 1884–5 in the Royal Commission on the Housing of the Working Classes. The Offences Against the Person Act of 1861 had made it a felony to have intercourse with a girl under ten, but since then the social purity movement had been agitating to raise the age of consent. In 1875 it was raised to 13. The notion of children as property continued to run through legislation. If, for instance, a girl under 16 had sexual intercourse with a man and entered into a relationship with him, her parents could charge him as an abductor who deprived them of the services of their daughter (Gorham, 1978, p. 363).

The moral panic over the publication of Stead's 'The Maiden Tribute of Modern Babylon' in the *Pall Mall Gazette* in 1885 brought issues surrounding children and sexuality to the fore. The article was an impassioned exposé of the prevalence of child prostitution among working-class girls. Stead exposed the widespread belief that a man could be cured of syphilis by having intercourse with a virgin. The article led to a public outcry and the raising of the age of consent to 16, where it stands today (Gorham, 1978). Beatrice Webb's research on sweat-shops uncovered prevalent incest among the working classes where 'young girls. . . could chaff each other about having babies by their fathers and brothers' (Wohl, 1978). Webb, however, gave little prominence to her findings until much later.

Throughout the nineteenth century there was a conflict between two powerful discourses on childhood. On the one hand was the tradition stemming largely from Rousseau that saw the child as essentially innocent. On the other hand was the older view of Original Sin, promulgated by St Augustine and taken up by Calvinists, that saw a child as naturally evil and in need of firm guidance and discipline. It is arguable that these two discourses were implicitly gendered: girls, and especially working-class girls, tended to be regarded as sexually precocious, wicked and capable of corrupting others, especially if they had been 'corrupted' by rape or incest themselves. Boys were more apt to be seen as initially innocent.

The focus on sexual exploitation of working-class girls at this time diverted middle-class attention from issues of wider exploitation of working-class girls and women, but also from exploitation of *all* girls and women in family situations where incest remained an unspoken secret. It can reasonably be assumed, however, that incest did go on in some, possibly many, middle-class families at the time. It has long been known, for instance, that Virginia Woolf was sexually abused by her brother as a child; De Salvo exposes the whole Woolf family as widely abusive beneath their correct middle-class veneer (De Salvo, 1989).

Given the prevalent late age at marriage for middle-class men during the nineteenth century and the belief that children and women must defer to and obey fathers' and brothers' wishes, it is probable that incest may have been widespread. But because middle-class family ideology was the dominant discourse and working-class immorality, symbolised by incest, was poised in opposition to this, to admit that incest existed among middle-class families would transgress class boundaries as well as moral codes. To admit its existence would be tantamount to challenging middle-class family ideology which, as we

have seen, was intricately bound up with middle-class political hege-
mony.

It is well-known that Freud encountered widespread accounts of
incest from his middle-class women clients in Vienna at the end of the
century. Initially he believed them. Soon, however, and probably for
the reasons just mentioned, he changed his opinion and, tragically for
thousands of women then and subsequently, declared memories of
incest among women to be fantasies. He probably saved his career by
so doing, of course. In his *Introductory Lectures on Psychoanalysis*
Freud states:

> Almost all of my women patients told me that they had been
> seduced by their fathers. I was driven to recognize in the end that
> these reports were untrue and so came to understand that the
> hysterical symptoms are derived from phantasies and not from real
> occurrences. . . it was only later that I was able to recognize in this
> phantasy of being seduced by the father the expression of the typical
> Oedipus complex in women. (Freud, quoted in Herman, 1981, p. 7)

No wonder Freud felt puzzled by not knowing what women want in
the context of his disbelief. His denial of the existence of incest in
contemporary society was later reinforced by Lévi-Strauss who argued
that the incest taboo was about men being able to give their mothers,
sisters or daughters to other men, an exchange which was the basis of
society itself. Neither Lévi-Strauss nor Freud believed incest to be a
feature of western society, except in the rarest of cases (Herman,
1981, p. 50).

Linda Gordon's research on social welfare agencies in Boston
between 1870 and 1980 (Gordon, 1989) shows, however, that social
workers throughout that time were well aware of the existence of
incest as one form of prevalent family violence. Her data, unfortunately, are confined to the working classes and this seemed to confirm
the assumption that incest did exist, but only among the most
'depraved' sectors of society. The cover-up of its existence in other
social classes continued unchallenged until Florence Rush's publication of *The Best Kept Secret* in 1980. If ever it were suggested that
incest existed within a middle-class family, the Freudian explanation
of fantasy was ready and waiting to dismiss it. It is interesting to note,
therefore, that in a summary of several studies in the USA, 52.5 per

cent of the families of incest victims were middle-class; 65.5 per cent of their parents had had some higher education; 77.5 per cent of their mothers did *not* work (Herman, 1981).

The question remains, however, as to why men did, and do, abuse children as frequently as seems to be the case, and why they have been able to get away with it for so long. An obvious reason is simply that inequalities within families are such, and patriarchal ideology operates in such a way, that it is extremely easy for men both to do it and to get away with it. Central to Judaeo-Christian ideology, after all, is the injunction to honour your parents, especially father. Inherent in that precept are trust and unquestioning obedience. If a young child is taught, and believes, that parents are always right and must always be obeyed, and this is endorsed by all the major institutions in society, how is she to realise that Daddy's behaviour is wrong, even if it is so painful? And even at the point where she does feel this, to whom can she turn in a culture that has so much invested in disbelieving her betrayal?

Patriarchal family ideology holds mothers responsible for all the nurturing and protection of their children. So perhaps it is not so surprising that when children do seek help in cases of incest, it is frequently the mother who gets blamed. It has often been argued that mothers 'collude' in their husbands' behaviour, and undoubtedly some do know what goes on and, for various reasons, feel forced to keep the secret. One of the prime reasons, of course, is economic. If a woman's husband is convicted of incest, her economic support-system is, in many cases, destroyed.

But victims of incest also frequently blame their mothers. Janet Jacobs considered this issue and concluded that in the family division of labour under patriarchy, mothers are assigned sole responsibility for childcare and this leads their daughters to imagine them as omnipotent (Jacobs, 1990). Fellman suggested that western ideology of the family produces the fantasy of a perfect mother and when that ideal is not met, it is mothers who get blamed. Mothers thus get blamed both by their own daughters and by a plethora of social agencies for crimes they never committed and may never have known went on (Fellman, 1990). Men thus remain protected from blame.

It is arguable that child sexual abuse is not something pathological or symptomatic of 'sick' families, but rather a logical result of a family ideology based on patriarchal values and inequality that is constantly informing, and played out in, a number of social and political institutions. Inherent in these is a body of assumptions about masculinity and sexuality. Again and again arguments have been made that men's sexual 'needs' are something innate, natural and uncontrollable which, if not met, must seek out alternatives as quickly as possible. Such a biological determinist account of male sexuality lies behind the arguments frequently made that child sexual abuse is really the *mother's* fault – for not adequately meeting her husband's 'needs'. So the mother becomes labelled first by the husband, and then subsequently by doctors, social workers, psychiatrists and judges as 'frigid' or sexually inadequate. Mothers are scapegoated for their daughters' sexual abuse, as Macleod and Saraga point out:

> Once the family system is analysed in detail to see why it has broken down, then in almost every case it is the mother who is seen as ultimately responsible. There is an unwritten assumption that families are functional when men's needs are met. (Macleod and Saraga, 1988, p. 33)

It is a good example of how patriarchy acts along both age and gender axes, where abuse of a young female by an older male is blamed on an older female.

Male sexuality, defined as biological need, is central to definitions of marriage and family ideology. Definitions of women's or children's needs are conspicuous by their absence. To see men's sexuality as 'natural' is to deny its variability and its existence as a social construct. It is an inherent part of patriarchal ideology and is linked with notions of ownership. Even if now written out of the legal system, the assumption remains common that marriage entitles a man to own both his wife and their children. Ownership confers all rights, including sexual access. Looked at this way, there is an implicit affirmation of men's right to use *their own* (but not others') children sexually. In a system where virginity is essential, then such acts would be seen as foolish – they would spoil the 'goods' which could be used to great advantage politically and in acquiring wealth through marriages. As the importance of virginity declines, so the reasons for men not using their daughters sexually decline.

While it is still generally assumed that women should be accessible for men's sexual 'needs', in the case of children there is a contradiction. Childhood has, since at least the eighteenth century, been defined as a time of innocence and, in particular, sexual innocence.

Arguably this has become *the* feature distinguishing adults from children.   At the same time, however, girls as 'little women' are encouraged, particularly by fathers, to be 'feminine', defined as flirtatious, seductive, cute. This discourse conflicts with that of childhood innocence, and there is only a very thin line between 'innocent' sexuality in girls and 'corruption' which could then lead to them ceasing to be defined as children and becoming labelled instead as deviant/pathological. Once again, women take the blame for their own betrayal.

Linked to this is what could be described as an increased eroticisation of power since the early nineteenth century. Consider, for instance, that between the years 1863 and 1887 there were 5314 cases of homicide in England and Wales. Of these, 3355, or 63 per cent involved infants. In 1977, however, only 6.1 per cent of all English murder victims were children under one year of age (Behlmer, 1982). The number of child sexual abuse cases reported, however, has sky-rocketed. So, contrary to popular arguments, society may have become less violent since the nineteenth century in certain ways, although arguably violence and power have become sexualised.

Foucault argued that power relations have become increasingly based on, and organised through, sexuality. Power is articulated through bodies and control of bodies. Sexual acts have in this sense become less actions related to desire and more related to power – or rather power and desire have merged. Much of this is reinforced by advertising, where women are represented as sexual and childlike simultaneously, while girls are represented as both innocent and sexually seductive. As other forms of control over children have been eroded, particularly since education became compulsory and child labour was outlawed, fathers' control over their childrens' labour power and training has diminished, but their easy access to their children's bodies remains intact. Arguably sexuality is one of the few remaining areas where a father can exercise direct and total power over his children's bodies.

Once supervised and taught by parents, siblings, kin and neighbours, children now live in a narrower world of parental supervision until school age, followed by intensive surveillance and monitoring through the education system. For the State has taken on an overall and ultimate responsibility for the physical and moral welfare of children – though the precise nature and form of this responsibility remains blurred. Parents, however, can interfere with a child's body in many ways: they may touch, hold, hit, lock up, withold food from children, choose their clothing, their friends, when they can play, go to bed, bath, and so on. Parents still have almost total control over their children's bodies. The State's claims to ultimate authority over children are very recent and not always clear. As Ennew points out, the child today is 'the State's hostage in the centre of the family' (Ennew, 1986).

Middle-class notions of purity, morality and sexuality were imposed, through the State and charity organisations on to working-class families. While many of these were designed to protect children from cruelty, violence and exploitation – which in many cases they did – they also disempowered working-class families, and children in particular, as well as strengthening the central State itself. The State, despite ideals of *laissez-faire*, increasingly encroached on the privacy of working-class families, paradoxically arguing that if they weren't already private, then they should be. Powers once accorded to fathers were, if not exactly taken over, at least increasingly supervised by state agencies. For many working-class families, of course, fathers were either simply not there or were unemployed/underemployed, and this in itself was seen as deviant. To be a 'natural' family it was essential to have a father/husband to provide for his dependants. Class power, in other words, was articulated and exercised in conjunction with control of gender and age groups through the ideology of the middle-class family.

The State, however, is not monolithic, and different agencies, such as the civil service, local government, central government, social services, the police, all developed their own structures, codes and modes of practice. Sometimes these came, and come, into conflict. This was the case with the moral panic over child sexual abuse that erupted in Cleveland in 1987. Connell referred to the State as the 'institutionalisation of hegemonic masculinity' (Connell, 1987), but it might be more useful to think of it as an institutionalisation of family ideology within which are conflicting discourses of masculinity and femininity. On the one hand, the police and armed forces could be seen to epitomise traditional discourses of masculinity: strong, active, ready to fight for a wider 'good'. Other state agencies such as social services and the NHS could be seen to represent the more caring 'feminine' side of family ideology, with concern about individual nurturance uppermost. Arguably much of the conflict witnessed during the Cleveland Crisis was influenced by the conflict between these discourses.

The Cleveland Crisis erupted when the police took the law into their own hands and decided not to act on the uncorroborated evidence of the doctors: 'They not only refused to seek corroboration but they rejected the diagnosis itself, after it had been repudiated by the constabulary's police surgeon, Dr. Alistair Irvine. This was at odds with police surgeons' forensic literature, as well as the advice of Dr. Irvine's own professional association (that). . . recommended. . . that anal dilatation should arouse "strong suspicions of sexual abuse".' (Campbell, 1988, p. 7)

Why did the police refuse to examine the doctors' evidence in an objective and scientific way, as they were supposed to? What did they find so threatening that they were prepared to abandon their statutory duties and commitment to scientific and rational investigation? First, they simply refused to believe that sexual abuse on such a scale was possible: 'and it was that belief that underwrote their readiness to break off diplomatic relations with social services and hospital doctors' (Campbell, 1988, p. 11). There are distinct echoes here of Freud in the strength of their disbelief and willingness to go against their scientific training and judgement to support patriarchy.

Implicit in patriarchal ideology are definitions of masculinities. The 'real' man, the 'natural' man is supposed to be tall, strong and 100 per cent heterosexual. Homosexual masculinities are a threat to this ideal because homosexuality is seen as being too feminine, too much like women – passive, emotional, receiving instead of giving – and homosexuality blurs the boundary between ideals of femininity and masculinity, threatens the division between men and women. And if this boundary becomes blurred, how then can patriarchy be legitimised, how can it be justified?

The sexual abuse uncovered at Cleveland was largely in the form of buggery. It was the bottoms of abused children that the police refused to photograph. The problem was that these children had allegedly been buggered not by 'perves' and deviants, but by their own fathers, stepfathers, uncles and grandfathers. Buggery was apparently being carried out on young children, mostly but not exclusively girls, by apparently heterosexual, often middle-class, 'normal' men who were seen as pillars of their communities. Indeed, police surgeon Dr Irvine said he had seen anal dilatation in his own practice but knew it could not be a reliable indicator of buggery, because he knew the family concerned personally and found the possibility 'unthinkable'. Yet of 608 referrals confirmed recently in Leeds, 337, i.e. over 50 per cent, showed signs of anal abuse (Campbell, 1988, p. 133). Indeed, 'forensic scientist Michael Green urged Dr. Wynne to look at bottoms on grounds that at least 10% of heterosexual adults practised anal intercourse' (ibid, p. 23). Wynne and Hobbs found in 1986 that 'more children were being buggered than battered' (ibid, p. 25).

Such discoveries raised issues about the boundaries between masculine and feminine, the boundaries between adults and children and thus challenged the very premises of the family ideology of a patriarchal State. Child sexual abuse has the potential to undermine some of the most cherished notions of manhood, fatherhood, childhood and the family. Looked at in this way the attitude of the police in Cleveland becomes rather clearer. The police, as bastions of a patriarchal State, and as a state agency made up of 90 per cent men, would certainly have a vested interest in refusing to acknowledge the evidence for child sexual abuse. But if the State is patriarchal, then arguably social services were acting against the interests of the State.

Social services are there to protect individuals' needs and rights (although the police could make a similar claim, to a great extent rightly, they are arguably more concerned with protecting property) and in recent years social services have dealt increasingly with the protection of children. Originating from middle-class women's involvement in charity organisations, social services have long emphasised the salience of families as the locus for childrens' security and well-being. With sexual abuse, however, if social workers choose to protect the child, then it is often in direct conflict with the parents and the family overall. This has raised the dilemma as to whether social services are there primarily to protect children or to protect the unity of families when the two aims conflict. In Cleveland social services opted for the children, much to the anger of the Reverend Michael Wright and Labour MP Stuart Bell, among others, who saw it as a threat to families and a 'feminist plot'. Both social workers and doctors were pilloried by the tabloid press and the conflict was firmly drawn along gender lines, with the women doctor and social workers portrayed as the villains.

Focus on this issue has not been on children themselves nor on the abusers. The debate, at least the debate that the media allowed us to see, raged between different state agencies drawn up along gender

Notes

Chapter 1: How have families changed?

1. This argument has been typical of the functionalist school of family sociology, and notably of Talcott Parsons, Robert Merton and Neil Smelser.
2. Particularly the work done by Peter Laslett, E. A. Wrigley and other demographers at the Cambridge Group for the History of Population and Social Structure.
3. J.-L. Flandrin (1979), p. 68.
4. *Social Trends*, HMSO (1983) London.
5. *The Guardian*, 31 January 1983.
6. *Social Trends*, 21, HMSO (1991) London.
7. *Social Trends*.
8. Leonore Davidoff pointed out how the importance of access to common land was crucial for women to be able to collect herbs.
9. From an interview in the Essex Oral History Archives.

Chapter 2: Is patriarchy relevant in understanding families?

1. *Oxford English Dictionary*
2. See, for instance, the classic discussion of this in M. Weber (1967) *The Protestant Ethic and the Spirit of Capitalism*, Allen & Unwin, London.
3. See K. Thomas (1978) *Religion and the Decline of Magic*, Penguin, Harmondsworth, and C. Larner (1983) *Enemies of God: Witch Hunt in Scotland*, Blackwell, Oxford, for further discussion of witchcraft.
4. *Census for England and Wales* (1881) HMSO, London.
5. Coward (1983) p. 205. Although Freud's ideas on women's sexuality are also notoriously ambiguous, notably in relation to 'Dora' – see T. Moi, 'Representation of Patriarchy: Sexuality and Epistemology in Freud's Dora', *Feminist Review*, Autumn 1981, for a useful synopsis and discussion

of the debate. Mitchell (1975), in *Psychoanalysis and Feminism*, posits a feminist defence of Freud.

    6. See T. Mason (1976) 'Women in Nazi Germany', *History Workshop Journal* for an excellent background to this.

Chapter 3: What is the family? Is it universal?

    1. Murdock quoted in Morgan (1975), p. 20.
    2. Notably C. C. Harris, J. Goody, W. Goode.
    3. For a full discussion of power relationships between men and women with regard to contraceptive practice see Gittins (1982).

Chapter 4: Why do people marry?

    1. E. Shorter (1975) posits this argument.
    2. Among others, P. Stearns.
    3. P. Wilmott and M. Young (1973) *The Symmetrical Family*, Routledge & Kegan Paul, London.
    4. Blackstone quoted in O'Donovan, 'The Male Appendage' in Burman (1979), p. 136.
    5. Especially the 'modernisation' theorists such as Shorter and Stearns.
    6. See Davidoff and Hall, *Family Fortunes* for a comprehensive analysis and discussion of marriage and courtship in the eighteenth and nineteenth centuries; also John Gillis, *For Better, For Worse: British Marriages, 1600 to the Present*.
    7. *Social Trends* (1983) HMSO, p. 31.
    8. Ibid.
    9. *Social Trends*, p. 31.

Chapter 5: Why do people have children?

    1. For a full discussion of the decline of family size see J. Banks (1954) *Prosperity and Parenthood*; D. Gittins (1982) *Fair Sex: Family Size and Structure 1900–1939*.
    2. *Social Trends*.

Chapter 6: Why is a woman's work never done?

    1. Interview from the Essex Oral History Archives.
    2. See C. Cockburn (1983) *Brothers*, Pluto Press, London, for a discussion of this in the newspaper industry.

Chapter 7: The State: creator or destroyer of family solidarity?

1. See K. Marx, *The 18th Brumaire of Louis Bonaparte* for a classic discussion of the relation between the State and social class.
2. There is an excellent analysis of these sorts of pressures in J. Foster (1974) *Class Struggle and the Industrial Revolution*, Methuen, London.
3. See A. John (1984) *By the Sweat of Their Brow* for a discussion of women's work in mining.
4. For a discussion of 'total institutions' see Coser (1974) *Greedy Institutions*, Free Press, New York, and Goffman *Asylums*, Penguin, Harmondsworth.

Chapter 8: Is the family in a state of crisis?

1. *Population Trends*, HMSO (1990) London.
2. Gibson in I. Reid (1981) *Social Class Differences in Britain*, Grant MacIntyre, London.

Bibliography

P. Abrams and E. A. Wrigley (eds) (1978) *Towns in Society*, Cambridge University Press, Cambridge.

G. Allan and G. Crow (1989) *Home & Family: Creating the Domestic Sphere*, Macmillan, London.

M. Anderson (1980) *Approaches to the History of the Western Family, 1500–1914*, Macmillan, London.

M. Anderson (1971) *Family Structure in Nineteenth Century Lancashire*, Cambridge University Press, Cambridge.

R. Anker, M. Buvinic and N. Youssef (eds) (1982) *Women's Roles and Population Trends in the Third World*, Croom Helm, London.

B. Antonis (1981) 'Motherhood and Mothering', in Cambridge Women's Study Group, *Women in Society*, Virago, London.

S. Ardener (ed.) (1981) *Women and Space: Ground Rules and Social Maps*, Croom Helm, London.

P. Ariès (1973) *Centuries of Childhood*, trans. R. Baldick, Peregrine, London.

M. Arthur (1977) 'Liberated Women: The Classical Era', in Bridenthal and Koonz, *Becoming Visible*, Houghton Mifflin, Boston.

J. Banks (1954) *Prosperity and Parenthood*, Routledge & Kegan Paul, London.

D. Barker and S. Allen (eds) (1976a) *Sexual Divisions and Society: Process and Change*, Tavistock, London.

D. Barker and S. Allen (eds) (1976b) *Dependence and Exploitation in Work and Marriage*, Longman, London.

M. Barrett (1980) *Women's Oppression Today: Problems in Marxist–Feminist Analysis*, Verso, London.

M. Barrett and M. McIntosh (1991, second edition) *The Anti-Social Family*, Verso, London.

N. Bashar (1983) 'Rape in England between 1550 and 1700', in London Feminist History Group, *The Sexual Dynamics of History*, Pluto Press, London.

R. Baxandall (1976) 'Women in American Trade Unions: An Historical Analysis', in Mitchell and Oakley, *The Rights and Wrong of Women*, Penguin, Harmondsworth.

V. Beechey (1973) 'On Patriarchy', *Feminist Review*, no. 3.

G. K. Behlmer (1982) *Child Abuse and Moral Reform in England 1870–1908*, Stanford University Press, Stanford, California.

D. R. Bender (1979) 'A Refinement of the Concept of Household: Families, Co-residence and Domestic Functions', *American Anthropologist*, vol, 69.

J. Benjamin (1983) 'Master and Slave: The Fantasy of Erotic Domination', in Snitow *et al*, *Powers of Desire*, Monthly Review Press, New York.

H. S. Bennett (1979) *The Pastons and their England*, Cambridge University Press, Cambridge.

V. Bennholdt-Thomsen (1981) 'Subsistence Production and Extended Reproduction', in Young *et al. Of Marriage and the Market*, CSE Books, London.

L. K. Berkner (1972) 'The Stem Family and the Development Cycle of the Peasant Household: An 18th Century Austrian Example', in *American Historical Review*, vol.77, no. 2.

L. K. Berkner (1976) 'Inheritance, Land Tenure and Peasant Family Structure: A German Regional Comparison', in Goody, Thirsk, Thompson, *Family and Inheritance: Rural Society in Western Europe, 1200–1800*, Cambridge University Press, Cambridge.

L. K. Berkner and F. Mendels (1978) 'Inheritance Systems, Family Structure, and Demographic Patterns in Western Europe, 1700–1900', in Tilly (ed.) *The Historical Study of Changing Fertility*, Princeton University Press, Princeton.

J. Bernard (1973) *The Future of Marriage*, Souvenir Press, London.

R. Bloch (1978) 'Untangling the Roots of Modern Sex Roles: A Survey of Four Centuries of Change', *Signs*, vol. 4, 2.

L. Bonfield (1981) 'Marriage Settlements, 1660–1749: The Adoption of the Strict Settlement in Kent and Northamptonshire', in Outhwaite, *Marriage and Society*, Europa, London.

J. Bornat (1981) *An Examination of the General Union of Textile Workers: 1883–1922*, Ph. D Thesis, University of Essex.

R. Braun (1978) 'Protoindustrialization and Demographic Changes in the Canton of Zurich', in Tilly (ed.) *The Historical Study of Changing Fertility*, Princeton University Press, Princeton.

R. Bridenthal (1982) 'The Family: The View from a Room of Her Own', in Thorne and Yalom (eds) *Rethinking the Family*, Longman, New York.

R. Bridenthal and C. Koonz (1977) *Becoming Visible: Women in European History*, Houghton Mifflin, Boston.

V. Brodsky Elliott (1981) 'Single Women in the London Marriage Market: Age, Status and Mobility, 1598–1619', in Outhwaite, *Marrige and Society*, Europa, London.

C. Brooke (1981) 'Marriage and Society in the Central Middle Ages', in Outhwaite, *Marriage and Society*, Europa, London.

J. Brophy and C. Smart (1981) 'From Disregard to Disrepute: The Position of Women in Family Law', *Feminist Review*, Autumn.

C. Brown (1982) 'Home Production for Use in a Market Economy', in Thorne and Yalom, *Rethinking the Family*, Longman, New York.

P. Brown, M. MacIntyre, R. Morpeth, S. Prendergast (1981) 'A Daughter: A Thing to be Given Away', in Cambridge Women's Study Group, *Women in Society*, Virago, London.

R. L. Brown (1981) 'The Rise and Fall of the Fleet Marriages', in Outhwaite, *Marriage and Society*, Europa, London.

S. Burman (ed.) (1979) *Fit Work for Women*, Croom Helm, London.

R. Burr Litchfield (1978) 'The Family and the Mill: Cotton Mill Work, Family Work Patterns, and Fertility in Mid-Victorian Stockport', in A. Wohl, *The Victorian Family*, Croom Helm, London.

B. Bush (1990) *Slave Women in Caribbean Society 1650–1838*, Heinemann, London.

D. Bythell (1969) *The Handloom Weavers*, Cambridge University Press, Cambridge.

J. Caird (1852) *English Agriculture in 1850–51*, Longman, Brown & Longmans, London.

Cambridge Women's Study Group (1981) *Women in Society: Interdisciplinary Essays*, Virago, London.

B. Campbell (1988) *Unofficial Secrets – Child Sexual Abuse: The Cleveland Case*, Virago, London.

M. Cantor and B. Laurie (eds) (1977) *Class, Sex and the Woman Worker*, Greenwood Press, Westport, Connecticut.

H. Carby (1982) "Schooling in Babylon", in Centre for Contemporary Cultural Studies, *The Empire Strikes Back: Race and Racism in 70s Britain*, Hutchinson, London.

Census for England and Wales, *Occupational Tables, 1881*, HMSO; London.

J. Chambers (1972) *Population, Economy and Society in Pre-Industrial England*, Oxford University Press, London.

M. Chaytor (1980) 'Household and Kinship: Ryton in the late Sixteenth and early Seventeenth Centuries' *History Workshop Journal*, Issue 10.

N. Chodorow (1978) *The Reproduction of Mothering: Psychoanalysis and the Sociology of Gender*, University of California Press, Berkeley.

N. Chodorow (1979) 'Mothering, Male Dominance and Capitalism', in Eisenstein (ed.) *Capitalist Patriarchy and the Case for Socialist Feminism*, Monthly Review Press, London.

H. Chudacoff (1978) 'Newlyweds and Family Formation: The First Stage of The Family Cycle in Providence, Rhode Island, 1864–65 and 1879–80', in Hareven and Vinovskis (eds) *Family and Population in Nineteenth Century America*, Princeton University Press, Princeton.

A. Clark (1968) *Working Life of Women in the Seventeenth Century*, Frank Cass, London.

A. Clark (1983) 'Rape or Seduction? A Controversy over Sexual Violence in the Nineteenth Century', in London Feminist History Group, *The Sexual Dynamics of History*, Pluto Press, London.

A. Clark (1987) *Women's Silence, Men's Violence: Sexual Assault in England 1770–1845*, Pandora Press, London.

L. Clarkson (1981) 'Marriage and Fertility in Nineteenth Century Ireland', in Outhwaite, *Marriage and Society*, Europa, London.

C. Cockburn (1983) *Brothers: Male Dominance and Technological Change*, Pluto Press, London.

M. Cohen (1976) *House United, House Divided: The Chinese Family in Taiwan*, Columbia University Press, New York.

J. Collier, M. Rosaldo, S. Yanagisako (1982) 'Is There a Family? New Anthropological Views', in Thorne and Yalom, *Rethinking the Family*, Longman, New York.

L. Comer (1982) 'Monogamy, Marriage and Economic Dependence', in Whitelegg *et. al.*, *The Changing Experience of Women*, Martin Robertson, Oxford.

P. Cominos (1963) 'Late Victorian Sexuality and the Social System', *International Review of Social History* vol. III.

R. W. Connell (1987) *Gender and Power*, Polity, Oxford.

D. Cooper (1971) *The Death of the Family*, Penguin, Harmondsworth.

L. A. Coser (1974) *Greedy Institutions*, The Free Press, New York.

N. Cott (1977) *The Bonds of Womanhood: 'Woman's Sphere' in New England 1780–1835*, Yale University Press, New Haven.

M. Coulson, B. Magas, H. Wainwright (1980) 'The Housewife and Her Labour under Capitalism – A Critique', in Malos, *The Politics of Housework*, Allison & Busby, London.

R. Coward (1983) *Patriarchal Precedents: Sexuality and Social Relations* Routledge & Kegan Paul, London.

L. Davidoff (1976b) 'The Rationalization of Housework', in Barker and Allen (eds) *Dependence and Exploitation in Work and Marriage*, Longman, London.

L. Davidoff (1979) 'The Separation of Home and Work? Landladies and Lodgers in Nineteenth and Twentieth Century England', in Burman, *Fit Work for Women*, Croom Helm, London.

L. Davidoff and C. Hall (1981) 'The Petite-Bourgeoisie and the Sexual Division of Labour in England, 1780–1850: Countryside and Town', Paper given at Petite-Bourgeoisie Round Table, December 1981.

L. Davidoff and C. Hall (1982). 'Marriage as an Enterprise: Middle Class in Town and Countryside, 1780–1850', American Historical Society Meeting, Washington, DC.

L. Davidoff and C. Hall (1987) *Family Fortunes: Men and Women of the English Middle Class 1780–1850*, Hutchinson, London.

R. Davies (1975) *Women and Work*, Arrow, London.

N. Z. Davis (1976) 'Women's History in Transition: The European Case', *Feminist Studies*, Spring.

N. Z. Davis (1977) 'Ghosts, Kin and Pregeny: Some Features of Family

Life in Early Modern France', *Daedalus*, Spring.

A. Davin (1978) 'Imperialism and Motherhood', *History Workshop Journal*, Issue 5.

C. Delphy (1977) *The Main Enemy: A Materialist Analysis of Women's Oppression*, Women's Research and Resources Centre Publications. London.

J. Demos (1970) *A Little Commonwealth: Family Life in Plymouth Colony*, London, Oxford University Press.

J. Demos and S. Boocock (1978) 'Turning Points: Historical and Sociological Essays of the Family', *American Journal of Sociology* (Supplement), vol. 84.

L. De Salvo (1989) *Virginia Woolf: The Impact of Childhood Sexual Abuse on Her Life and Work*, Beacon Press, Boston.

S. Dietrich (1980) 'An Introduction to Women in Anglo-Saxon Society, (c. 600–966)', in Kanner, *The Women of England*, Mansell, London.

S. M. Dombusch and M. H. Strober (1988) *Feminism, Children and the New Families*, Guilford Press, London.

J. Donzelot (1979) *The Policing of Families*, Hutchinson, London.

M. Douglas (1966) *Purity and Danger*, Routledge & Kegan Paul, London.

S. Dowrick and S. Grundberg (eds) (1980) *Why Children?*, The Women's Press, London.

E. Durkheim (1933) *The Division of Labour in Society*, Collier-Macmillan, London.

C. Dyhouse (1981) *Girls Growing Up in Late Victorian and Edwardian England*, Routledge & Kegan Paul, London.

B. Easlea (1981) *Science and Sexual Oppression: Patriarchy's Confrontation with Woman and Nature*, Weidenfeld & Nicolson, London.

S. Edgell (1980) *Middle Class Couples: A Study of Segregation, Domination and Inequality in Marriage*, Allen & Unwin, London.

F. Edholm (1982) 'The Unnatural Family', in Whitelegg *et al.*, *The Changing Experience of Women*, Martin Robertson, Oxford.

B. Ehrenreich and D. English (1979) *For Her Own Good: 150 Years of the Experts' Advice to Women*, Pluto Press, London.

M. Eichler (1981) 'The Inadequacy of the Monolithic Model of the Family', *Canadian Journal of Sociology* 6(3).

Z. R. Eisenstein (ed.) (1979) *Capitalist Patriarchy and the Case for Socialist Feminism*, Monthly Review Press, London.

Z. R. Eisenstein (1979) 'Some Notes on the Relations of Capitalist Patriarchy', in Eisenstein (ed.) *Capitalist Patriarchy and the Case for Socialist Feminism*.

G. H. Elder (1978) 'Family History and the Life Course', in Hareven, *Transitions*, Academic Press, New York.

D. Elson and R. Pearson (1981) 'The Subordination of Women and the Internationalization of Factory Production', in Young *et al.*, *Of Marriage and the Market*, CSE Books, London.

(1968) *Employment of Women and Children in Agriculture, 1843*, vol. XII British Parliamentary Papers, Irish University Press, Shannon.

F. Engels (1972) *The Origin of the Family, Private Property and the State*, Lawrence & Wishart, London.

J. Ennew (1986) *The Sexual Exploitation of Children*, Polity, London.

J. K. Evans (1991) *War, Women and Children in Ancient Rome*, Routledge, London.

M. Evans and C. Ungerson (eds) (1983) *Sexual Divisions: Patterns and Processes*, Tavistock, London.

C. Fairchilds (1978) 'Female Sexual Attitudes and the Rise of Illegitimacy: A Case Study', *Journal of Interdisciplinary History*, VIII: 4, Spring.

A. Fauve-Chamoux (1983) 'The Importance of Women in an Urban Environment: The Example of the Rheims Household at the Beginning of the Industrial Revolution', in Wall, Robin and Laslett, *Family Forms in Historic Europe*, Cambridge University Press, Cambridge.

A. C. Fellman (1990) 'Laura Ingalls Wilder and Rose Wilder Lane: The Politics of a Mother-Daughter Relationship', *Signs*, vol. 15, no. 3, Spring.

J. Finch (1989) *Family Obligations and Social Change*, Polity, London.

J.-L. Flandrin (1979) *Families in Former Times*, Cambridge University Press, Cambridge.

S. Forward and C. Buck (1981) *Betrayal of Innocence: Incest and its Devastation*, Penguin, Harmondsworth.

J. Foster (1974) *Class Struggle and the Industrial Revolution*, Methuen, London.

M. Foucault (1979) *The History of Sexuality*, Allen Lane, London.

R. Fox (1967) *Kinship and Marriage*, Penguin, Harmondsworth.

E. Gamarnikow, D. Morgan, J. Purvis, D. Taylorson (eds) (1983a) *Gender, Class and Work*, Heinemann, London.

E. Gamarnikow, D. Morgan, J. Purvis, D. Taylorson (eds) (1983b) *The Public and the Private*, Heinemann, London.

J. Gillis (1979) 'Servants, Sexual Relations and the Risks of Illegitimacy in London, 1801–1900', *Feminist Studies*, 5, no 1, Spring.

J. Gillis (1981) *Youth and History*, Academic Press, New York.

J. R. Gillis (1988) *For Better, For Worse: British Marriages 1600 to the Present*, Oxford University Press, London.

D. Gittins (1982) *Fair Sex: Family Size and Structure 1900–1939*, Hutchinson, London.

D. Gittins (1983) 'Inside and Outside Marriage: A Nineteenth Century Case Study', *Feminist Review*, Summer.

L. Glasco (1978) 'Migration and Adjustment in the Nineteenth Century City: Occupation, Property and Household Structure of Native-born Whites, Buffalo, New York, 1855', in Hareven and Vinovskis (eds) *Family and Population in Nineteenth Century America*, Princeton University Press, Princeton.

J. Goodale (1980) 'Gender, Sexuality and Marriage: A Kaulong Model of Nature and Culture', in MacCormack and Strathern, *Nature, Culture and Gender*, Cambridge University Press, Cambridge.

W. J. Goode (1975) 'Force and Violence in the Family', in Steinmetz and Straus, *Violence in the Family*, Harper & Row, New York.

J. Goody (1972) 'The Evolution of the Family', in Laslett and Wall (eds) *Household and Family in Past Time*, Cambridge University Press, Cambridge.

J. Goody (1976) 'Inheritance, Property and Women: Some Comparative Considerations', in Goody, Thirsk and Thompson (eds) *Family and Inheritance: Rural Society in Western Europe, 1200–1800*, Cambridge University Press, Cambridge.

J. Goody, J. Thirsk, E. P. Thompson (eds) (1976) *Family and Inheritance: Rural Society in Western Europe, 1200–1800*, Cambridge University Press, Cambridge.

L. Gordon (1989) *Heroes of their own Lives: The Politics and History of Family Violence*, Virago, London.

D. Gorham (1978) '"The Maiden Tribute of Modern Babylon" Re-examined: Child Prostitutes and the Idea of Childhood in Late Victorian England', *Victorian Studies*, vol 21, part 3.

D. Gorham (1982) *The Victorian Girl and the Feminine Ideal*, Croom Helm, London.

R. Gough (1981) *The History of Myddle* (ed. by David Hey) Penguin, Harmondsworth.

P. Greven (1970) *Four Generations: Population, Land and Family in Colonial Andover, Massachusetts*, Cornell University Press, Ithaca.

S. Griffen and C. Griffen (1977) 'Family and Business in a Small City: Poughkeepsie, New York, 1850–1950', in Hareven, *Family and Kin in Urban Communities*, New Viewpoints, London.

H. Gutman (1976) *The Black Family in Slavery and Freedom, 1750–1925*, Basil Blackwell, Oxford.

C. Hall (1979) 'The Early Formation of Victorian Domestic Ideology', in Burman, *Fit Work for Women*, Croom Helm, London.

C. Hall (1980) 'The History of the Housewife', in Malos, *The Politics of Housework*, Allison & Busby, London.

C. Hall (1981) 'Gender Divisions and Class Formation in the Birmingham Middle Class 1780–1850', in Samuel (ed.) *People's History and Socialist Theory*, Routledge & Kegan Paul, London.

P. Hall (1977) 'Family Structure and Economic Organization: Massachusetts Merchants 1700–1850', in Hareven, *Family and Kin in Urban Communities*, New Viewpoints, London.

C. Hamilton (1981) *Marriage as a Trade*, The Women's Press, London.

E. Hammel (1972) 'The Zadruga as Process', in Laslett and Wall (eds) *Family and Household in Past Time*, Cambridge University Press, Cambridge.

C. Hammer (1983) 'Family and *Familia* in Early Medieval Bavaria', in Wall, Robin, Laslett (eds) *Family Forms in Historic Europe*, Cambridge University Press, Cambridge.

T. Hareven (1976) 'Modernization and Family History: Perspectives on Social Change', *Signs*, vol. 2,1, Autumn.

T. Hareven (ed.) (1977) *Family and Kin in Urban Communities 1700–1930*, New Viewpoints, London.

T. Hareven (1978) *Transitions: The Family and the Life Course in Historical Perspective,* Academic Press, New York.

T. Hareven (1982) *Family Time and Industrial Time,* Cambridge University Press, New York.

T. Hareven and M. Vinovskis (eds) (1978) *Family and Population in Nineteenth Century America,* Princeton University Press, Princeton.

T. Hareven and M. Vinovskis (1978) 'Patterns of Childbearing in Late Nineteenth Century America: The Determinants of Marital Fertility in South Massachusetts Towns in 1880', in Hareven and Vinovskis (eds) *Family and Population in Nineteenth Cenhury America,* Princeton University Press, Princeton.

B. Harris (1976) 'Recent Work on the History of the Family: A Review Article', *Feminist Studies,* Spring.

O. Harris (1981) 'Households as Natural Units', in Young *et al, Of Marriage and the Market,* CSE Books, London.

O. Harris (1982) 'Households and their Boundaries', *History Workshop Journal,* Issue 13.

N. Hart (1976) *When Marriage Ends: A Study in Status Passage,* Tavistock, London

H. Hartmann (1979) 'Capitalism, Patriarchy and Job Segregation by Sex', in Eisenstein (ed.) *Capitalist Patriarchy and the Case for Socialist Feminism,* Monthly Review Press, London.

D. Hayden (1982) *The Grand Domestic Revolution: A History of Feminist Designs for American Homes, Neighbourhoods and Cities,* MIT Press, Cambridge.

H. Heaton (1965) *The Yorkshire Woollen and Worsted Industries,* Oxford University Press, Oxford.

E. Hellerstein, L. Hume, K. Offen (eds) (1981) *Victorian Women: A Documentary Account of Women's Lives in Nineteenth Century England, France, and the United States,* Harvester, Brighton.

U. Henriques (1967) 'Bastardy and the New Poor Law', *Past and Present,* no. 37, July.

J. Herman (1981) *Father–Daughter Incest,* Harvard University Press, Cambridge, Massachussetts.

A. Hewins (ed.) (1981) *The Dillen: Memories of a Man of Stratford-upon-Avon,* Elm Tree Books, London.

N. Himes (1931) *A Medical History of Contraception,* Williams & Wilkins, Baltimore.

E. Hobsbawm and G. Rudé (1973) *Captain Swing,* Penguin, Harmondsworth.

L. Holcombe (1977) 'Victorian Wives and Property – Reform of the Married Women's Property Law, 1857–1882', in Vicinus, *A Widening Sphere,* Indiana University Press, Bloomington.

R. Houston and R. Smith (1982) 'A New Approach to Family History?', *History Workshop Journal,* Issue 14.

C. Howell (1976) 'Peasant Inheritance Customs in the Midlands 1280–1700', in Goody, Thirsk and Thompson, *Family and Inheritance* Cambridge University Press, Cambridge.

O. Hufton (1981) 'Women, Work and Marriage in Eighteenth Century France', in Outhwaite, *Marriage and Society,* Europa, London.

J. Humphries (1981) 'Protective Legislation, the Capitalist State and Working Class Men: The Case of the 1842 Mines Regulation Act', *Feminist Review,* no. 7, Spring.

S. Humphries (1981) *Hooligans or Rebels? An Oral History of Working-Class Childhood and Youth 1889–1939,* Basil Blackwell, Oxford.

M. Ingram (1981) 'Spousal Litigation in the English Ecclesiastical Courts *c.* 1350–1640', in Outhwaite, *Marriage and Society,* Europa, London.

J. Jacobs (1990) 'Reassessing Mother Blame in Incest", in *Signs,* vol. 15, no. 3, Spring.

R. Jacoby (1977) 'The Women's Trade Union League and American Feminism', in Cantor and Laurie, *Class Sex and the Woman Worker,* Greenwood Press, Westport.

A. John (1984) *By the Sweat of Their Brow: Women Workers at Victorian Coal Mines,* Routledge & Kegan Paul, London.

L. Jordanova (1981) 'The History of the Family', in Cambridge Women's Study Group, *Women in Society,* Virago, London.

J. Kagan (1977) 'The Child in the Family', *Daedalus,* Spring.

B. Kanner (ed.) (1980) *The Women of England: From Anglo-Saxon Times to the Present,* Mansell, London.

L. Kelly (1988) *Surviving Sexual Violence,* Polity, London.

R. and C. Kempe (1983) *Child Abuse,* Fontana/Open Books, Suffolk.

J. Kelly-Gadol (1977) 'Did Women Have a Renaissance?', in Bridenthal and Koonz, *Becoming Visible,* Houghton Mifflin, Boston.

A. Kessler-Harris (1982) *Out to Work: A History of Wage-Earning Women in the United States,* Oxford University Press, New York.

J. Khatib-Chahidi (1981) 'Sexual Prohibitions, Shared Space and Fictive Marriages in Shi'Ite Iran', in Ardener, *Women and Space,* Croom Helm, London.

R. Kittel (1980) 'Women Under the Law in Medieval England, 1066–1485', in Kanner, *The Women of England,* Mansell, London.

A. Kleinbaum (1977) 'Women in the Age of Light', in Bridenthal and Koonz, *Becoming Visible,* Houghton Mifflin, Boston.

C. Koonz (1988) *Mothers in the Fatherland: Women, the Family and Nazi Politics,* Methuen, London.

A. Kussmaul (1981) *Servants in Husbandry in Early Modern England,* Cambridge University Press, Cambridge.

R. D. Laing (1960) *The Divided Self,* Penguin, Harmondsworth.

R. D. Laing (1971) *The Politics of the Family and other Essays,* Tavistock, London.

H. Land (1976a) 'Women: Supporters or Supported?', in Barker and Allen, *Sexual Divisions and Society: Process and Change,* Tavistock, London.

C. Lasch (1977) *Haven in a Heartless World: The Family Besieged,* Basic Books, New York.

P. Laslett (1972) 'The History of the Family', in Laslett and Wall (eds)

Household and Family in Past Time, Cambridge University Press, Cambridge.
P. Laslett (1983) 'Family and Household as Work Group and Kin Group: Areas of Traditional Europe Compared', in Wall, Robin and Laslett, *Family Forms in Historic Europe,* Cambridge University Press, Cambridge.
P. Laslett and R. Wall (eds) (1972) *Household and Family in Past Time,* Cambridge University Press, Cambridge.
P. Laslett, K. Oosterveen and R. Smith (eds) (1980) *Bastardy and Its Comparative History,* Edward Arnold, London.
E. Leacock (1977) 'Women in Egalitarian Societies', in Bridenthal and Koonz, *Becoming Visible,* Houghton Mifflin, Boston.
D. Leonard (1980) *Sex and Generation: A Study of Courtship and Weddings,* Tavistock, London.
D. Leonard and J. Hood-Williams (1988) *Families,* Macmillan, London.
D. Levine (1977) *Family Formation in an Age of Nascent Capitalism,* Academic Press, New York.
D. Levine and K. Wrightson (1980) 'The Social Context of Illegitimacy in Early Modern England', in Laslett, Oosterveen and Smith, *Bastardy and its Comparative History,* Edward Arnold, London.
S. Lewenhak (1980) *Women and Work,* Fontana, Glasgow.
J. Lewis (1980) *The Politics of Motherhood,* Croom Helm, London.
E. Lipson (1921) *The History of the Woollen and Worsted Industries,* A. & C. Black, London.
O. Löfgren (1974) 'Family and Household among Scandinavian Peasants', *Ethnologia Scandinavka.*
London Feminist History Group (1983) *The Sexual Dynamics of History: Men's Power, Women's Resistance,* Pluto Press, London.
J. Lown (1983a) 'Not So Much a Factory, More a Form of Patriarchy: Gender and Class during Industrialisation', in Gamarnikow *et al.* (eds) *Gender, Class and Work,* Heinemann, London.
S. Lukes (1974) *Power: A Radical View,* Macmillan, London.
C. MacCormack (1980) 'Nature, Culture and Gender: A Critique', in MacCormack and Strathern, *Nature, Culture and Gender,* Cambridge University Press, Cambridge.
A. MacFarlane (1970) *The Family Life of Ralph Josselin: A Seventeenth Century Clergyman,* W. W. Norton, New York.
A. MacFarlane (1978) *The Origins of English Individualism: The Family, Property and Social Transition,* Basil Blackwell, Oxford.
A. MacFarlane (1980) 'Illegitimacy and Illegitimates in English History', in Laslett, Oosterveen and Smith (eds) *Bastardy and its Comparative History,* Edward Arnold, London.
M. Macleod and E. Saraga (1988) 'Challenging the Orthodoxy: Towards a Feminist Theory and Practice', in *Feminist Review,* No. 28, Spring.
L. Mackie and P. Pattullo (1977) *Women at Work,* Tavistock, London.
M. MacKintosh (1979) 'Domestic Labour and the Household', in Burman, *Fit Work for Women,* Croom Helm, London.

M. MacKintosh (1981) 'Sexual Division of Labour and the Subordination of Women', in Young *et al.*, *Of Marriage and the Market*, CSE, London.

V. Maher (1981) 'Work, Consumption and Authority within the Household: A Moroccan Case', in Young *et al*, *Of Marriage and the Market*, CSE, London.

E. Malos (1980) *The Politics of Housework*, Allison & Busby, London.

T. Malthus (1966) *First Essay on Population*, Macmillan, London (first published 1798).

S. Marshall Wyntjes (1977) 'Women in the Reformation Era', in Bridenthal and Koonz, *Becoming Visible*, Houghton Mifflin, Boston.

K. Marx (1973) *The Eighteenth Brumaire of Louis Bonaparte*, in Fernbach (ed.) *Surveys from Exile*, Penguin, Harmondsworth.

K. Marx and F. Engels (1977) *The German Ideology*, Lawrence & Wishart, London.

T. Mason (1976) 'Women in Nazi Germany', *History Workshop Journal*, Issues 1 and 2.

O. R. McGregor (1957) *Divorce in England*, Heinemann, London.

M. McIntosh (1979) 'The Welfare State and the Needs of the Dependent Family', in Burman, *Fit Work for Women*, Croom Helm, London.

A. McLaren (1977) 'Women's Work and the Regulation of Family Size', *History Workshop Journal*, Issue 4.

M. McNamara and S. Wemple (1977) 'Sanctity and Power: The Dual Pursuit of Medieval Women', in Bridenthal and Koonz (eds) *Becoming Visible: Women in European History*, Houghton Mifflin, Boston.

M. Mead (1971) *Male and Female*, Penguin, Harmondsworth.

H. Medick (1976) 'The Protoindustrial Family Economy', *Social History*, no. 3.

S. Menefee (1981) *Wives for Sale*, Basil Blackwell, Oxford.

Alice Miller (1985) *Thou Shalt Not Be Aware: Society's Betrayal of the Child*, Pluto, London.

K. Millett (1970) *Sexual Politics*, Ballantine, New York.

J. Mitchell (1975) *Psychoanalysis and Feminism*, Penguin, Harmondsworth.

J. Mitchell and A. Oakley (eds) (1976) *The Rights and Wrongs of Women*, Penguin, Harmondsworth.

M. Mitterauer and R. Sieder (1982) *The European Family: Patriarchy to Partnership from the Middle Ages to the Present*, trans. K. Oosterveen and M. Horzivger, Basil Blackwell, Oxford.

J. Modell and F. Furstenberg (1978) 'The Timing of Marriage in the Transition to Adulthood: Continuity and Change, 1860–1975', in Demos and Boocock, *Turning Points*, AJS Supplement.

T. Moi (1981) 'Representation of Patriarchy: Sexuality and Epistemology in Freud's Dora', *Feminist Review*, Autumn.

D. H. J. Morgan (1975) *Social Theory and the Family*, Routledge & Kegan Paul, London.

M. Morokvasic (1981) 'Sexuality and the Control of Procreation', in Young *et al.*, *Of Marriage and the Market*, CSE, London.

F. Mount (1982) *The Subversive Family*, Jonathan Cape, London.
G. Murdock (1949) *Social Structure*, Macmillan, New York.
M. Nava (1988) 'Cleveland and the Press: Outrage and Anxiety in the Reporting of Child Sexual Abuse', *Feminist Review*, No. 28, Spring.
K. O'Donovan (1979) 'The Male Appendage – Legal Definitions of Women', in Burman, *Fit Work for Women*, Croom Helm, London.
N. Osterud and J. Fulton (1978) 'Family Limitation and Age at Marriage: Fertility Decline in Sturbridge, Massachusetts, 1730–1850', *Population Studies*, vol. 30.
R. Outhwaite (1981) (ed.) *Marriage and Society: Studies in the Social History of Marriage*, Europa Publications, London.
D. Owen Hughes (1978) 'Urban Growth and Family Structure in Medieval Genoa', in Abrams and Wrigley, (eds) *Towns in Society*, Cambridge University Press, Cambridge.
T. Parsons (1964) *The Social System*, Routledge & Kegan Paul, London.
N. Parton (1985) *The Politics of Child Abuse*, Macmillan, London.
A. Phoenix (1990) 'Theories of Gender and Black Families', in T. Lovell (ed.), *British Feminist Thought*, Blackwell, Oxford.
R. Phillips (1976) 'Women and Family Breakdown in Eighteenth Century France: Rouen 1780–1800', *Social History*, 2, May.
I. Pinchbeck (1981) *Women Workers and the Industrial Revolution 1750–1850*, Virago, London.
I. Pinchbeck and M. Hewitt (1973) *Children in English Society*, vol. 2, Routledge & Kegan Paul, London.
A. Pollert (1983a) 'Women, Gender Relations and Wage Labour', in Gamarnikow *et al.*, *Gender, Class and Work*, Heinemann, London.
L. Pollock (1983) *Forgotten Children-Parent-Child Relations from 1500 to 1800*, Cambridge University Press, Cambridge.
L. Pollock (1983) *Forgotten Children: Parent–Child Relations from 1500 to 1900*, Cambridge University Press, Cambridge.
G. Quaife (1979) *Wanton Wenches and Wayward Wives: Peasants and Illicit Sex in Early Seventeenth Century England*, Croom Helm, London.
R. Rapp (1980) 'Family and Class in Contemporary America: Notes Towards an Understanding of Ideology', *Science and Society*, vol. 42.
R. Rapp, E. Ross and R. Bridenthal (1979) 'Examining Family History', *Feminist Studies*, Spring.
I. Reid (1981) *Social Class Differences in Britain*, Grant McIntyre, London.
J. Renvoize (1982) *Incest: A Family History*, Routledge & Kegan Paul, London.
A. Rich (1977) *Of Woman Born: Motherhood as Experience and Institution*, Virago, London.
A. Rich (1983) 'Compulsory Heterosexuality and Lesbian Experience', in Snitow *et al.*, *Powers of Desire: The Politics of Sexuality*, Monthly Review Press, New York.
D. Riley (1981) 'Left Critiques of the Family', in Cambridge Women's Study Group, *Women in Society*, Virago, London.

H. Roberts (ed.) (1981) *Women, Health and Reproduction*, Routledge & Kegan Paul, London.

A. F. Robertson (1991) *Beyond the Family: The Social Organisation of Human Reproduction*, Polity, London.

R. Rohrlich-Leavitt (1977) 'Women in Transition: Crete and Sumer', in Bridenthal and Koonz, *Becoming Visible*, Houghton Mifflin, Boston.

M. Rosaldo (1980) 'The Use and Abuse of Anthropology: Reflections on Feminism and Cross-Cultural Understanding', *Signs*, vol. 5, no. 3.

E. Ross (1983) 'Survival Networks: Women's Neighbourhood Sharing in London', *History Workshop Journal*, Issue 15.

E. Ross and R. Rapp (1983) 'Sex and Society: A Research Note from Social History and Anthropology', in Snitow *et al*, *Powers of Desire*, Monthly Review Press, New York.

S. Rowbotham (1981b) 'The Trouble with Patriarchy', in Samuel, *People's History and Socialist Theory*, Routledge & Kegan Paul, London.

L. Rubin (1976) *Worlds of Pain*, Basic Books, New York.

F. Rush (1980) *The Best Kept Secret: Sexual Abuse of Children*, McGraw-Hill, New York.

M. Ryan (1979) 'Femininity and Capitalism in Antebellum America', in Eisenstein (ed.) *Capitalist Patriarchy and the Case for Socialist Feminism*, Monthly Review Press, New York.

M. Ryan(1981) *Cradle of the Middle Class: The Family in Oneida County New York, 1790–1865*, Cambridge University Press, Cambridge.

L. Salzman (1926) *English Life in the Middle Ages*, Oxford University Press, London.

R. Samuel (1981a) *East End Underworld: Chapters in the Life of Arthur Harding*, Routledge & Kegan Paul, London.

R. Samuel (ed.) (1981b) *People's History and Socialist Theory*, Routledge & Kegan Paul, London.

L. Scharf (1980) *To Work and to Wed: Female Employment, Feminism and the Great Depression*, Greenwood Press, Westport, Connecticut.

R. Schlesinger (1949) *The Family in the USSR*, Routledge & Kegan Paul, London.

L. Segal (ed.) (1983) *What Is To Be Done About the Family?*, Penguin, Harmondsworth.

A. Serrano and D. Gunzburger (1983) 'An Historical Perspective of Incest', in *International Journal of Family Therapy* 5 (2), Summer.

M. Shanley (1979) 'The History of the Family in Modern England', *Signs*, vol. 4, Summer.

E. Shorter (1975) *The Making of the Modern Family*, Fontana/Collins, London.

C. Smart (1983) 'Patriarchal Relations and Law: An Examination of Family Law and Sexual Equality in the 1950s', in Evans and Ungerson, *Sexual Divisions*, Tavistock, London.

R. T. Smith (1978) 'The Family and the Modern World System: Some Observations from the Caribbean', *Journal of Family History*, vol. 3 .

C. Smith-Rosenberg (1978) 'Sex as Symbol in Victorian Purity: An Ethnohistorical Analysis of Jacksonian America', in Demos and Boocock, 'Turning Points', *American Journal of Sociology* (Supplement).

T. C. Smout (1981) 'Scottish Marriage, Regular and Irregular 1500–1940', in Outhwaite, *Marriage and Society*, Europa, London.

A. Snitow, C. Stansell, S. Thompson (eds) (1983) *Power of Desire: The Politics of Sexuality*, Monthly Review Press, New York.

N. J. Sokoloff (1980) *Between Money and Love*, Praeger, New York.

N. Soliende de Gonzalez (1965) 'The Consanguineal Household and Matrifacality', *American Anthropologist*, vol. 67.

M. Spufford (1974) *Contrasting Communities: English Villages in the Sixteenth and Seventeenth Centuries*, Cambridge University Press, Cambridge.

M. Stacey and M. Price (1981) *Women, Power and Politics*, Tavistock, London.

M. Stacey (1982) 'Social Sciences and the State: Fighting Like a Woman', *Sociology*, vol. 16, no. 3.

C. Stack (1974) *All our Kin: Strategies for Survival in a Black Community*, Harper & Row, New York.

P. Stearns (1975) *European Society in Upheaval*, Collier Macmillan, London.

P. Stearns (1977) *Old Age in European Society: The Case of France*, Croom Helm, London.

J. Stevenson (1979) *Popular Disturbance in England 1700–1870*, Longman, New York.

S. Stienmetz and M. Straus (eds) (1975) *Violence in the Family*, Harper & Row, New York.

M. Stivens (1981) 'Women, Kinship and Capitalist Development', in Young *et al.*, *Of Marriage and the Market*, CSE Books, London.

V. Stolcke (1981) 'The Naturalisation of Social Inequality and Women's Subordination', in Young *et al.*, *Of Marriage and the Market*, CSE Books, London.

L. Stone (1977) *The Family, Sex and Marriage in England 1500–1800*, Weidenfeld & Nicolson, London.

A. Swerdlow, R. Bridenthal, J. Kelly, P. Vine (1981) *Household and Kin*, The Feminist Press, New York.

B. Taylor (1981b) 'Socialist Feminism: Utopian or Scientific?', in Samuel, *People's History and Socialist Theory*, Routledge & Kegan Paul, London.

P. Thane (1981) 'Childhood and History', in Michael King (ed.), *Childhood Welfare and Justice*, Batsford, London.

J. Thirsk (1976) 'The European Debate on Customs of Inheritance, 1500–1700' in Goody, Thirsk and Thompson, *Family and Inheritance*, Cambridge University Press, Cambridge.

K. Thomas (1978) *Religion and the Decline of Magic*, Penguin, Harmondsworth.

T. Thompson (1981) *Edwardian Childhoods*, Routledge & Kegan Paul,

London.
B. Thorne and M. Yalom (1982) (eds) *Rethinking the Family: Some Feminist Questions*, Longman, New York.
C. Tilly (ed.) (1978) *Historical Studies of Changing Fertility*, Princeton University Press, Princeton.
C. Tilly (1978) 'The Historical Study of Vital Processes' in Tilly (ed.) *Historical Studies of Changing Fertility*, Princeton University Press, Princeton.
L. Tilly and J. Scott (1978) *Women, Work and Family*, Rinehart & Winston, New York.
A. Tolson (1977) *The Limits of Masculinity*, Tavistock, London.
P. Uhlenberg (1978) 'Changing Configurations of the Life Course', in Hareven, *Transitions*, Academic Press, New York.
C. Ungerson (ed.) (1985) *Women and Social Policy: A Reader*, Macmillan, London.
R. Vann (1977) 'Toward a New Lifestyle: Women in Preindustrial Capitalism', in Bridenthal and Koonz, *Becoming Visible*, Houghton Mifflin, Boston.
M. Versluysen (1981) 'Midwives, Medical Men and "Poor Women Labouring of Child": Lying in Hospitals in Eighteenth Century London', in H. Roberts (ed.) *Women, Health and Reproduction*, Routledge & Kegan Paul, London.
M. Vicinus (ed.) (1974) *Suffer and Be Still: Women in the Victorian Age*, Indiana University Press, Bloomington.
M. Vicinus (ed.) (1977) *A Widening Sphere: Changing Roles of Victorian Women*, Indiana University Press, Bloomington.
J. Wajcman (1981) 'Work and the Family: Who "Gets the Best of Both Worlds"?', in Cambridge Women's Studies Group, *Women in Society*, Virago, London.
S. Walby (1986) *Patriarchy at Work*, Polity, London.
J. Walkowitz (1980) *Prostitution and Victorian Society: Women, Class and the State*, Cambridge University Press, Cambridge.
R. Wall (1981) 'Women Alone in English Society', *Annales de Démographie Historique*.
R. Wall, J. Robin, P. Laslett (eds) (1983) *Family Forms in Historic Europe*, Cambridge University Press, Cambridge.
M. Walzer (1976) *The Revolution of the Saints: A Study in the Origins of Radical Politics*, Atheneum, New York.
E. Ward (1984) *Father Daughter Rape*, The Women's Press, London.
M. Weber (1967) *The Protestant Ethic and the Spirit of Capitalism*, Allen & Unwin, London.
J. Weeks (1977) *Coming Out: Homosexual Politics in Britain from the Nineteenth Century to the Present*, Quartet, London.
A. Whitehead (1981) '"I'm Hungry Mum": The Politics of Domestic Budgeting', in Young *et al*, *Of Marriage and the Market*, CSE, London.
E. Whitelegg, M. Arnot, E. Bartels, V. Beechey, L. Birke, S. Himmelweit, D. Leonard, S. Ruehl and M. Spearman (eds) (1982) *The*

Changing Experience of Women, Open University/Martin Robertson, Oxford.
M. Wicks (1990) 'The Battle for the Family', in *Marxism Today*, August.
E. William Monter (1977) 'The Pedestal and the Stake: Courtly Love and Witchcraft', in Bridenthal and Koonz, *Becoming Visible*, Houghton Mifflin, Boston.
P. Wilmott (1979) *Growing Up in a London Village: Family Life Between the Wars*, Peter Owen, London.
P. Wilmott and M. Young (1962) *Family and Kinship in East London*, Penguin, Harmondsworth.
P. Wilmott and M. Young (1973) *The Symmetrical Family*, Routledge & Kegan Paul, London.
E. Wilson (1980) *Only Halfway to Paradise: Women in Postwar Britain, 1945–1968*, Tavistock, London.
E. Wilson (1983) *What Is To Be Done About Violence Against Women?*, Penguin, Harmondsworth.
A. S. Wohl (ed.) (1978) *The Victorian Family: Structure and Stresses* Croom Helm, London.
E. A. Wrigley (1966) 'Family Limitation in Preindustrial England', *Economic History Review*, no. 19.
E. A. Wrigley (1969) *Population and History*, Weidenfeld & Nicolson, London.
E. A. Wrigley (ed.) (1972) *Nineteenth Century Society; Essays in the Use of Quantitative Methods for the Study of Social Data*, Cambridge University Press, Cambridge.
E. A. Wrigley (1981) 'Marriage, Fertility and Population Growth in Eighteenth Century England', in Outhwaite, *Marriage and Society*, Europa, London.
K. Wrightson (1981) 'Critique: Household and Kinship in Sixteenth Century England', *History Workshop Journal*, Issue 12.
K. Wrightson (1982) *English Society 1580–1680*, Hutchinson, London.
S. J. Yanagisako (1977) 'Women-Centered Kin Networks in Urban Bilateral Kinship', *American Ethnologist*, vol. 4.
S. J. Yanagisako (1977) 'Family and Household: The Analysis of Domestic Groups', *Annual Review of Anthropology*, vol. 8.
K. Young, C. Wolkowitz, R. McCullagh (eds) (1981) *Of Marriage and the Market: Women's Subordination in International Perspectrve*, CSE Books, London.
E. Zaretsky (1976) *Capitalism, the Family and Personal Life*, Pluto Press, London.
E. Zaretsky (1982) 'The Place of the Family in the Origins of the Welfare State', in Thorne and Yalom (eds) *Rethinking the Family*, Longman, New York.

Index